S
AMERICAN
MW01147334

ADVANCE PRAISE FOR *Speaking American*

"*Speaking American* speaks well, speaks vigorously, speaks
with the kind of passion and clarity missing from the Democrats
Mr. Kusnet seeks to advise."

–Norman Lear

"David Kusnet's fresh ideas and candid prose are true to his
book's title. *Speaking American* is about reconnecting politics to
the concerns and values of ordinary citizens and why that's
necessary to make America extraordinarily successful again."

–Albert Shanker, President,
American Federation of Teachers

"A revealing analysis by a campaign insider....Richly rewarding
for those who care about the future of politics in the U.S."

–Kathleen Hall Jamieson, Dean,
The Annenberg School for Communication, University of Pennsylvania

"Anyone who wants to understand how to make progressive
politics make sense to Main Street America ought to begin with
Speaking American."

–Geoffrey Garin, President,
Garin-Hart Strategic Research Group

"Progressives have been asking how to build a national electoral
majority for more than a decade. This book answers that question
with provocative insight and practical advice."

–Heather Booth, Executive Director,
Coalition for Democratic Values; former president, Citizen Action

Speaking
A·M·E·R·I·C·A·N

HOW THE DEMOCRATS
CAN WIN IN
THE NINETIES

David Kusnet

THUNDER'S
MOUTH PRESS
NEW YORK

First edition

First printing 1992

Published by

THUNDER'S MOUTH PRESS

54 Greene Street, Suite 4S

New York, NY 10013

Page 55, "Fortunate Son," words and music by John C. Fogarty of
Creedence Clearwater Revival. Copyright © 1969 Jondora Music,
courtesy of Fantasy, Inc. All rights reserved. Used by permission.

Library of Congress Cataloging-in-Publication Data

Kusnet, David, 1951-

  Speaking American : how the Democrats can win in the nineties / by
David Kusnet. — 1st ed.

    p. cm.

    Included bibliographical references (p.   ).

    ISBN 1-56025-027-5

    1. Democratic Party (U.S.) 2. Communication in politics — United States.
3. United States — Politics and government — 1989-
I. Title.

JK2317 1992b

324.7'0973 — dc20   91-45307

                                                   CIP

Text design by Loretta Li

Printed in the United States of America

Distributed by

Publishers Group West

4065 Hollis Street

Emeryville, CA 94608

(800) 788-3123

For my parents,
and for Ruth

CONTENTS

Acknowledgments

■■■

I owe the idea for this book to my friend, the religion writer Jim Castelli. Long after the 1988 campaign was an unpleasant memory, I mentioned to Jim that I had the dubious distinction of having helped draft the concession speeches of Michael Dukakis and Walter Mondale before him.

Something clicked in Jim's mind, and he told me he didn't think anyone had written a decent Democratic party campaign book since *Right from the Start,* Gary Hart's memoir of the McGovern campaign. Jim suggested the idea to a literary agent, Jeff Herman, who kept pestering me to put together a book proposal. Over time the idea evolved into a book about how to improve the political language of the Democratic party. Jeff's entrepreneurial energy helped make the idea a reality.

The title for this book was suggested to me in a conversation with Page Gardner, a political consultant and former co-worker. Page didn't know she was naming a book when she used the phrase "speaking American," but the phrase came to mind when I was casting about for a new title in a conversation with Neil Ortenberg of Thunder's Mouth Press.

I am grateful to Neil and the folks at Thunder's Mouth, and I am also indebted to Joan Fucillo, for her skills not only as an editor but as a social worker and sounding board.

Researching this book was a reminder that there are many people in and around the Democratic party who think and care about what's happening to our country. Among those who shared their ideas and findings with me were: Richard Trumka, the president of the United Mine Workers; public opinion pollsters Victor Fingerhut, Geoff Garin, Stanley Greenberg, Peter Hart, Tom Kiley, Celinda Lake, John Marttila, and Michael McKeon; political consultants David Axelrod, Peter Harris, Tony Podesta, and David Wilhelm; and political and social analysts Ethel Klein, Fred Siegel, Ralph Whitehead, and Linda Williams.

During a research trip to Illinois, and in my preparation for that visit, Henry Bayer, Heather Booth, Michael Calabrese, Bob Creamer, Joseph Gardner, Christine George, Gary LaPaille, Marge Laurino, Roberta Lynch, Jim McPike, Barbara Pape, Patrick Quinn, and Nancy Shier were particularly helpful.

Members of what the news media portray as "rival" wings of the Democratic party, helped me with information and analysis. I extend my thanks to Heather Booth of the Coalition for Democratic Values, and Bill Galston of the Progressive Policy Institute. I also want to thank Jeff Faux and Roger Hickey of the Economic Policy Institute; Ira Arlook, Bob Brandon, Lorraine Driscoll, Cathy Hurwitt and Mike Podhorzer of Citizen Action; Jim Grossfeld of the United Mine Workers; Guy Molyneux of the Commonwealth Institute; Phil Sparks of the Communications Consortium; and the folks at Citizens for Tax Justice.

I am grateful to the people who took the time to read some or all of this book at its different stages: Susan Anderson, Edith Bond, Heather Booth, Jim Castelli, Peter Edelman, Jim Sleeper, Helen Toth, and Ben Wattenberg. Victoria VanSon helped me find information I couldn't have located otherwise.

While many of my friends have influenced my thinking, two who have been particularly influential (and original in their thinking), in addition to those I've already named, are Bob Cottrol and Steve Silbiger.

The ritual disclaimer is really true: None of these good people is to blame for the eclectic mixture of views propounded here.

I owe an intellectual debt to Robert Kuttner, whose *The Life of the Party* propounds the economic populism for which I try to find a political language in this book, and to the authors of some of the leading books of the 1992 political pre-season. These include *Why Americans Hate Politics* by E.J. Dionne, Jr., *Chain Reaction* by Thomas and Mary Edsall, *The Politics of Rich and Poor* by Kevin Phillips, and *Reinventing Government* by David Osborne and Ted Gaebler, which hadn't appeared when I wrote this book but whose ideas were already influencing public debate.

And I owe an even greater debt to two activist intellectuals who understood that politics should be a mechanism for improving people's lives: Jerry Wurf, who tried to speak American without losing his gift for outrage, and Michael Harrington, who tried to seek "the Left wing of the possible." This book is a modest contribution to that search.

Ruth Wattenberg endured the challenge not only of living with me but marrying me while I staggered towards the deadline. She has my enduring gratitude.

Speaking
A·M·E·R·I·C·A·N

Introduction:
■ The Lost Language of
Democrats

It was the third week in September, just six weeks before the end of the 1988 presidential campaign, when Michael Dukakis told me that country clubs were less exclusive than they used to be.

We were at the hotel across the street from Dukakis's campaign headquarters in downtown Boston. A preparation session for the first debate with George Bush was about to begin, and Dukakis was mingling with some of his staff. When he got to me—a speechwriter who'd joined his campaign a month earlier— he told me to stop attacking country clubs in the drafts I was preparing. Some of his friends in the suburbs belonged to country clubs now, Dukakis said. In fact, country clubs were letting in lots of people who would have been turned away in the past.

Dukakis's discussion of changing admissions policies at country clubs seemed, at least to me, as one more sign that he didn't want to sound like a Democrat—at least not like other Democrats I'd worked for.

For generations, Democratic orators have used symbols like country clubs to represent the primal passion of our party's politics: the conflict between honest working people and the idle rich. Dukakis's reluctance to attack the symbols of wealth and privilege was just one of the many signs suggesting that the kind of rhetoric that once elected Democratic presidents was in danger of becoming a lost language. But it's not just the loss of a style of rhetoric that we're looking at, it's the loss of what political types call a party's "message," which is not only what the voters are told but how it's said to them.

Dukakis's refusal to use the kind of language traditionally used by Democrats trailing in the polls (embracing their fellow under-dogs and flailing at the fat cats) reflected a Democratic party in deep trouble. Having lost five of the last six presidential elections, the Democrats' disfunctioning threatens the health of our political system because a two-party system needs two national parties. And this system needs at least one party whose purpose is to speak for people who aren't wealthy, who need some protection from the ups and downs of the economy, and who need an organized voice in government. Representing those in the middle has always been the purpose of the Democratic party. But Democrats have also represented those at the bottom of the economic ladder, those who have been the victims of discrimination of all kinds, and those who seek social and economic reform.

In recent years, however, Democrats have become more and more associated with those on the bottom and they seem to have lost the support of those in the middle, without whom no political party can prevail. When asked about politics, most middle-class voters say that Democrats "used to" or are "supposed to" represent everyday working people, not that the Democratic party actually does represent them. This seems to indicate just how tenuous the Democratic party's link is to those who used to be its strongest supporters. The middle class's disillusionment with Democrats doesn't seem to be the result of any new-found faith in Republi-cans either. The same people, if they vote at all, may vote Repub-lican at the national level and Democratic at the state level, while badmouthing both parties. And a political system where most people agree that "nobody speaks for me" is a system in deep trouble.

Part of the Democrats' trouble stems from the growing divi-siveness among people who, for all their differences, used to be-lieve that Democrats represented their common concerns. The Democratic party has always been the party of inclusion—

embracing cultural outsiders as well as economic underdogs—but now it seems powerless to ease growing racial tensions or answer racially tinged attacks. Instead, it finds itself both caught in, and contributing to, a political dynamic that emphasizes racial divisions. Here, too, not only the Democratic party but the entire political system suffers, because, if Democrats seem unable to ease racial divisions, Republicans seem eager to exploit them.

The Democrats' political language demands our attention because it's a significant part of the Democrats' dilemma. The elements of political language—words, symbols, and the ideas behind them—are the currency of political debate and, on the national level, Democrats have been losing political debates for the last decade or more. And the failure of their language not only signifies larger problems, but contributes to them as well. As George Orwell wrote in his classic essay on political language: "Now, it is clear that the decline of a language must ultimately have political and economic causes. . . . But an effect can become a cause, reinforcing the original cause and producing the same effect in an intensified form, and so on indefinitely. It [political language] becomes ugly and inaccurate because our thoughts are foolish, but the slovenliness of our language makes it easier for us to have foolish thoughts."

A classic example of the Democrats' inability to communicate occurred during the battle over the nomination of Clarence Thomas to the Supreme Court. In the first round of hearings, Thomas's supporters presented him as the embodiment of the classic American success story: the conscientious young man who worked his way up from poverty. For their part, Thomas's adversaries played the White House-assigned role of the heavies: the special-interest groups trying to crush this independent-minded individual.

Democrats did no better in the second round, which covered charges of sexual harassment against Thomas. Republicans were masterful as defense attorneys for Thomas, but the Democrats seemed unsure of what role they should play, so they ended up playing no recognizable role at all. Republicans presented a cohesive message to the television audience, who were the real jury in this case. The Democrats displayed a series of contradictory shortcomings, appearing wimpy and malicious, clumsy and elitist.

The result was a replay of the Dukakis campaign—only worse. Judge Thomas won the support of an overwhelming majority of Americans, including constituencies Democrats used to claim as their own: women, blacks, and people of moderate incomes. A party that knew what it wanted to say—and how to say it—wouldn't have found itself in such a fix.

Unfortunately, their failure here was not unique. During the first three years of the Bush presidency, Democrats on the national stage have been gripped by failures of analysis, articulation, and action. Indeed, the Democratic party has suffered from the atrophy of its "presidential wing," that part of a party whose purpose is winning the White House and leading the nation. Yet, there have been plenty of opportunities to make a start.

Why didn't Democrats make more of the scandals in the Department of Housing and Urban Development and the savings-and-loans? Why didn't Democrats act on Sen. Daniel Patrick Moynihan's proposal to cut the social security payroll tax that hits hardest at ordinary working people, and whose proceeds have been hijacked to finance the federal deficit? Why didn't Democrats offer an economic recovery program earlier in the recession? Why didn't Democrats dramatize the country's losses in cutting-edge industries—from computer chips to consumer electronics—that would produce the jobs of the twenty-first century? And why did it take so long for Democrats to champion middle-class tax relief, propose a national health insurance program, or develop a way to help jobless workers who were being denied unemployment benefits?

Truly, it is the absence of an agenda that appeals to most Americans, one that can be seen as relevant to their lives, that has jeopardized the Democratic party. And the loss of its middle-class voting base has diminished the party's ability to protect civil rights and civil liberties. In the past, Democrats enjoyed the credibility that came from producing programs like Medicare, and they spent that coin to promote less popular causes like fair housing. However, Democrats became vulnerable to the charge that they wanted to force quotas down working people's throats because they were no longer seen as championing the issues that benefitted the middle class.

Unfortunately, while the results of recent presidential campaigns suggest that Democrats could attract a majority by being populist on economics and mainstream on cultural questions, just the opposite seems to have occurred. Democratic congressional campaigns are heavily funded by corporate political action committees, which hardly inspire economic populism, and by wealthy individual donors, whose liberalism is cultural, not economic.

Increasingly, the Democratic party has been defined by its "interest groups"—those institutions and individuals whose common denominator is the fact that they don't need the approval of a majority of the national electorate. Often these organizations, including advocates of good causes such as civil liberties and environmentalism, promote their agendas by mobilizing their own members rather than by persuading the public at large. Particularly when they recruit members and raise funds through direct mail solicitation, the temptation is to frame an issue in the most confrontational way in order to make headlines and develop persuasive fundraising appeals. Of the various institutional influences on congressional Democrats, the most culturally mainstream and economically populist is still the party's old standby —the union movement. Recently, however, the unions have found themselves focused on issues involving their very survival (such as preventing permanent replacements of strikers), making them less effective at setting a larger agenda for the Democratic party.

Furthermore, the liberals who should be the Democrats' shock-troops have increasingly relied on an institution that's only marginally accountable to voters: the courts. To most people, liberalism has been defined by court decisions on controversial issues like affirmative action, school busing, and criminal defendants' rights. Victorious in the courts, liberals have rarely had to make a public case for these positions or try to assemble majorities in their behalf. They've ended up speaking "legalese," not plain English.

But this form of redress may no longer be so readily available. When President Bush named two new members to the Supreme Court, he locked in a conservative majority, ensuring that liberals could no longer win in federal courts what they could not win in the court of public opinion. So now, it's more important than ever that Democrats recover the ability to address—and persuade—a majority of people. And to do so, they're going to have to learn how to "speak American."

This book is about the political language of the Democratic party. It's about what we did wrong during the 1980s, what we can do right in the 1990s, and, most important, how we can speak a common language with the American people. This book will sketch out what could be a cohesive, winning message, but it's not just intended for the tight little community of people who make their livings writing speeches, TV spots, and campaign literature. It's for all those who care about the Democratic party and about the future of political debate in this country.

Now you might say that I'm the last person who should be giving advice on this issue, having been a speechwriter for Walter Mondale as well as Michael Dukakis; I even had a hand in writing both their concession speeches. But while I'm 0-for-2 in presidential politics, I have had the chance to see what works, and what doesn't work, in national political debate. At the very least, my experience has given me an object lesson in the importance of speaking a common language with the American people because, Lord knows, most of the time we didn't. Also, I have been part of several successful efforts at public persuasion, which included two causes that took a beating during the past decade—labor unions and civil liberties. So the question is: Why did we succeed then, but are not succeeding now?

I joined the Mondale campaign after a stint as a traveling troubleshooter for AFSCME (American Federation of State, County, and Municipal Employees). I wrote leaflets for organizing campaigns, handed them out in front of office buildings early in the morning, and met late into the night with the rank-and-file workers. I drafted direct mail pieces and produced radio spots. And AFSCME successfully organized a cross-section of the remarkably diverse people who work in state and local government: from social workers in Chicago to corrections officers (don't ever call them prison guards) at Attica, from hospital workers in Detroit to highway workers in rural Iowa.

There is the notion that people who work in government march in lockstep as yet another liberal special interest group. But those who accept this stereotype haven't talked to too many people who actually do the work on road crews, in welfare departments, and in mental health facilities, much less to the people who work in prisons. No less than people on the "outside" (and perhaps even more so) public employees are painfully aware of how bureaucratic and unaccountable government can be and how disorderly and dangerous public places and public institutions are becoming. And if you ask them about issues like the reckless release of mental patients or the need for metal detectors and police protection in many schools and social service centers, most members of AFSCME don't sound like lawyers for the ACLU.

In fact, AFSCME's appeal, particularly to the white-collar workers we recruited, was on the basis of shared modern middle-class values. We presented the union as something that would make sure that hard work was recognized and rewarded, provide opportunities for education and advancement, and give employees a voice in a large and impersonal system. That's a commonsense approach: people want a stronger voice in decision making on the job, and they want to make better products and provide better services.

For AFSCME, speaking American meant talking to the majority of people we were trying to organize, not just to the discontented minority who would be the first to flock to a union drive. One freezing night in Detroit a few days before Christmas 1978, I was sitting in the union's office being yelled at by a group of social workers who had counted the number of times I'd used the word professional in one piece of organizing literature. "We're not professionals," one of them told me, "we're workers—social workers." Yeah, I thought, and about one percent of your colleagues feel that way, and half of them are here in this room shouting. The rest of the social workers, most of whom had worked hard to earn their master's degrees, appreciated being called professionals. They had no fantasies about the glory or the political correctness of being called a worker. So we kept calling the social workers "professionals," and the militants kept on yelling.

Much of my training in speaking American came from an authentic union militant, Jerry Wurf, AFSCME's national president until his death in 1981. When I wasn't on the road, Wurf would often ask me to help him draft his speeches—my introduction to the craft of speechwriting. Wurf's temper was as legendary as his talents. He would not only edit my drafts, he'd tear them up and throw them in my face. "This is the worst crap you've ever done," he once told me. "It's full of cliches; it's out of the 1930s; it's longwinded. You should write for Hubert Humphrey—or Fidel Castro."

Wurf didn't want to sound like Humphrey, Castro, or what he himself had once been—a socialist street-corner speaker in Brooklyn. Since I was also a Jew from Brooklyn who had dabbled in social democratic politics, I had an easy time capturing Wurf's speech rhythms, but I had a harder time winning his confidence. "I don't want to sound New York, and I sure as hell don't want to sound like some agitator in Union Square," he would say. "I want to sound American." Although he still sounded like a street-corner orator when he harangued AFSCME members, Wurf strived for what he wistfully called "reasonableness" when he addressed outside audiences.

Thus, when we put together his 1978 speech to the National Press Club, in which he criticized President Carter's miserly urban program, Wurf came at the issue from the Left, the Right, and the Center. "Capitalism needs capital, and the cities are starved for capital," he declared. Rejecting as "a proven loser" the old liberal shibboleth of government as the employer of last resort, Wurf called for federal help for education, job training, transportation, and crime control in order to make the cities more attractive for private investment.

Wurf may have been a radical, but he had a strong reality principle. He knew that government workers were up against a terrible problem: Americans hate government. I remember one time when Wurf got wind of the fact that someone was planning a conference in Chicago, where state employees, teachers, and organizations concerned with the plight of the mentally retarded would protest cuts in the state budget. "People are just going to see a bunch of tax-eaters," Wurf warned us. "That's a damn fool idea for a conference." We canceled it.

Wurf was also extremely savvy about social and economic trends. In 1971, he complained to a reporter from the *Washington Post*:

> One of the things that troubles me in my own union is that our older staff guys tend to talk to the workers with a dialogue that was created during the Depression, or created by the generation that immediately followed the Depression and was seriously affected by it . . .
>
> In 1936, most workers were terribly grateful for a union official to tell them where a job is. [Now] an American worker likes to think that he's paying and that the union official has a responsibility to deliver.

Although today few working people take their job security for granted, Wurf's point is well taken. More than a decade before most other union leaders and national Democrats, he understood that working people were becoming middle class, and that you'd damn well better treat them that way.

After AFSCME, I worked on the Mondale campaign, and then became communications director of a civil liberties organization,

People for the American Way (PFAW). I'd been skeptical of the American Civil Liberties Union (ACLU), convinced that the Democrats' biggest problem was their (somewhat deserved) reputation for being soft on crime and hostile to mainstream values. (I should point out now that the criticisms of the ACLU throughout this book are mine and do not reflect the opinion of PFAW or anyone else.) But after talking with Tony Podesta, then president of PFAW, I was reassured. No stereotypical civil libertarian, Tony had learned politics in a tough Democratic ward on Chicago's northwest side, had been a political advanceman (a bully who convinces local people to attend campaign rallies) and a labor lawyer. He'd also served as a prosecuting attorney in Washington, D.C. (his beat was street crime not crooked politicians), and was known for saying things like, "I may believe in the perfectibility of the human species in the abstract, but I don't believe in the perfectibility of an eighteen year old with a .357 magnum."

Listening to Tony persuaded me that PFAW, more than any other group, could defend social liberalism in a way that appealed to, not offended, most people. Indeed, the very name of the organization is premised on a simple insight that seems to elude most liberals: Americans *like* America. Instead of adopting the all-too-familiar liberal posture of carping about this country, People for the American Way has presented itself as a defender of American values against those from outside the mainstream – like Jerry Falwell, Pat Robertson, and Phyllis Schlafly, who, at the time, were trying to keep "controversial" subjects like evolution out of public school textbooks.

Speaking American came naturally to PFAW's founder and guiding spirit, the television writer and producer Norman Lear. The creator of Archie Bunker, George Jefferson, Mary Hartman, and other prototypically American characters, Lear knew that the case for constitutional freedoms had to be made with simple declarative sentences and evocative symbols, not legalistic abstractions. While the ACLU makes its case in courts of law (and often does valuable work defending unpopular clients), PFAW mostly makes its case in the court of public opinion.

Over the years, PFAW has said some surprising things for what the media like to call a "liberal lobbying group." We said that history textbooks needed to tell more about the role religion plays in American life and that schools should teach mainstream moral values and democratic civic values. We commissioned a survey that showed that young people knew everything about their rights as citizens but very little about their responsibilities. By the end of the eighties, with the battles against Falwell fading into the past, Lear told audiences and interviewers that in some ways he was grateful to the religious right. While their answers were mostly wrong, they had called attention to the moral confusion and the spiritual vacuum in American life.

The religious right's undoing was that Americans do tend to be tolerant. And looking back on the debates over social issues during the Reagan era, it seems that when it comes to issues from reproductive choice to the censorship of school textbooks Americans are tolerant. Tolerant, but not permissive—and that distinction is crucial. Unlike Schlafly and Falwell, most people are not concerned with censoring high school curricula. But they do want—indeed, they demand—every possible precaution to keep drugs and guns out of the high schools. And that concern puts most people at odds with the ACLU (which opposed putting metal detectors in Detroit high schools where shootings had occurred). Somewhere between the extreme positions exemplified by those who believe books are dangerous things and those who don't seem to understand that guns and drugs really are, you'll find the great majority of Americans.

Nonetheless, for most of the eighties PFAW was playing defense, sometimes, our opponents would say, with our spikes on. Among PFAW's successes, it was our campaign against Robert Bork's nomination to the Supreme Court in 1987 that had the greatest repercussions and the greatest influence on my own thinking. I wrote the TV spot, narrated by Gregory Peck, that made the case against the nomination. (This resulted in a few interesting moments. One which occurred at the time was hearing Marlin Fitzwater, the Reagan White House press spokesman, denounce the spot against Bork on the intriguing grounds that retired movie actors should stay out of politics. And recently, while in downtown Washington around lunchtime, I was stopped by a friend who introduced me to a co-worker as "the guy who wrote the Gregory Peck spot." The man was a conservative Republican, and he was bigger than me. For a few seconds, he looked at me like he couldn't decide whether he would shake hands, or slug me. Fortunately, he decided on the former.)

To some liberals, Bork remains the devil incarnate, a foe of civil rights, freedom of expression, and everything else that makes today's America more open and egalitarian than the society of a half century ago. But looking across the political divide, it's also clear that Robert Bork is beloved and admired by many conservatives, particularly highbrow types in Washington, as no leading figure has been among liberals since . . . well, I can't remember. For many conservatives, he is part guru, part martyr: the scholar, the independent thinker, the man of principle who was cheated out of his rightful place on the Supreme Court by a liberal smear campaign.

For me, the case against Bork rested on facts that you don't need to be a legal scholar to understand. As a thirty-six-year-old professor at Yale Law School, Bork had opposed the Civil Rights Act of 1964, which outlawed discrimination in restaurants, hotels, and other businesses. He had also criticized a Supreme Court decision outlawing state poll taxes, which history has shown were used not to raise revenues but to keep black people, and sometimes poor people of all colors, from voting. I never thought for a minute that Bork was a racist—he had libertarian reasons for opposing the Civil Rights Act and even more complicated reasons for criticizing the poll tax decision—but I did think he had a peculiar talent for being wrong about issues where most people had been right. While he'd changed his mind about the

Civil Rights Act, I wondered whether he might not make similar mistakes about other issues if he were to take a seat on the Supreme Court.

I accepted that case against Bork, but not the more complex arguments against him—arguments that, as a non-lawyer, I'm not really qualified to understand. Probably, what defeated Bork was the fact that he had initially opposed what most Americans understood at the time was simple justice a century overdue. In fact, Bork was his own worst enemy. In five days of nationally televised testimony, culminating in his final statement that he wanted to serve on the Supreme Court because "it would be an intellectual feast just to be there," Bork painted a portrait of himself as a man more concerned with abstractions than with the impact his decisions would have on actual people. And many viewers must have reached a conclusion similar to mine: He was entitled to a lifetime on the faculty of the finest law school in the land, with all the time he needed to write books and articles and appear on national television, but it would be better for everyone that he stay off the Supreme Court.

Walter Mondale used to say that every defeat contains the seeds of victory and every victory contains the seeds of defeat. Bork's revenge on American liberalism may not have been the reputation he gained as a martyr but the incorrect lessons too many liberals drew from his defeat. We had won the Bork debate on the issues of 1964 (Johnson beat Goldwater once more) but, as Michael Dukakis learned one year later, the defeat of legalistic conservatism did not create a public mandate for legalistic liberalism. Bork lost because he didn't understand Americans—and Americans sure couldn't understand him—but this was a point that escaped many Democrats. In fact, beating Bork probably blinded some, particularly the law professors so influential in the Dukakis campaign, to the potential power of issues like the Pledge of Allegiance, the death penalty, and furloughs for prisoners who had committed violent crimes.

Another erroneous lesson drawn by many Democrats from the

anti-Bork campaign was that they should launch search-and-destroy missions against nominees for every level of the federal bureaucracy. In the spring of 1991, liberal senators devoted an inordinate amount of time and effort to defeating a conservative college professor, Carol Iannone, who had been nominated to the advisory council of the National Endowment for the Humanities, when their time would have been better spent dealing with the economy. The dangers of stressing social over economic issues were pointedly revealed during the Clarence Thomas hearings. While most voters, and most senators, were glued to their TV sets, President Bush quietly vetoed a bill to extend unemployment benefits, which were desperately needed by millions of Americans (eventually an agreement to extend jobless benefits was reached between the Bush administration and the Democratic Congress). For the time being, Bush got the best of both worlds. People concentrated on the Thomas television drama, and most backed Bush's candidate. At the same time they were distracted from the issue of jobless benefits for workers, where Bush's position is unpopular.

For the past dozen years I have worked on and off with the Citizen Action network. This group, with some two million members, has successfully organized around issues like the economy, national health insurance, and toxic waste cleanup. Citizen Action recruits by canvassing door-to-door in the kinds of middle-class communities where voters have deserted the Democrats in national elections. By telling people where politicians really stand on issues, Citizen Action has helped elect progressive populists like senators Howard Metzenbaum of Ohio, Paul Simon of Illinois, and Tom Harkin of Iowa. The example of a successful grass-roots organizing campaign such as this has valuable lessons for the Democratic party. A major reason for Citizen Action's success is that the organizers look people in the eye and talk to them straight about issues that affect them directly.

Civil liberties, government workers, and leftover sixties activists — the causes, constituencies, and co-workers I've spent the past fifteen years with are frequently seen not only as the party's base but as its burden—special interests from which Democrats need to declare their independence. In writing this book, I've tried to cast a critical eye on the kinds of ideas people like me have been promoting, and I've tried to determine which can survive the rigors of public debate—and which can never prevail, and perhaps don't deserve to, even if they are presented more eloquently and effectively than in the past.

Thus I've tried to make this a book about ideas, as well as words and symbols, and to address these ideas with an eye toward the presidential campaigns of the 1990s. By doing so, I hope to develop a way for Democrats to make a case that builds on their basic appeal—the still-surviving sense that Democrats represent the economic interests of the majority of voters. But I'll also discuss how Democrats can address the issues on which they've gotten clobbered, from crime and drugs and moral values to foreign policy and defense. I don't contend that Democrats should abandon their remaining core constituencies. Instead, I believe they can keep that support while regaining that of the voters who left the national party during the seventies and eighties and, in addition, win the support of these voters' children. A thesis of this book is that, whether the issues are social or economic, Democrats should hold on to their traditional concerns but should make them more mainstream, in style and in substance.

Another point I frequently make is that, in order to win, Democrats need to be tougher. In recent years, getting tough with an opponent has too often translated into subtle and not-so-subtle attempts at character assassination. Politicians' public records are—and must be—fair game for free-wheeling public debate, but attacks on people's private lives have no place in a discussion of the issues. Democrats should take the gloves off, but they need not use brass knuckles.

Alert readers will note that my recommendations don't toe the line of either side in the Democratic party's internal debates, a division that some commentators have portrayed as pitting "traditionalists," who preach social and economic liberalism, against "revisionists," who want to take the party to "the center," "the future," or some similarly desirable destination.

For all the worthwhile things that have been said and done on both sides of the Democratic divide, the debate between them sometimes generates more heat than light. Indeed, it often resembles that famous TV commercial for a "lite" beer, in which a crowd at a sports stadium breaks into a shouting match, with some people yelling "Tastes great!" and others screaming "Less filling!" All too often, the Democratic debate is just as unenlightening, with traditionalists shouting "economic populism," and centrists shouting "mainstream values." In fact, just as lite beer should "taste great" and be "less filling," the Democratic party should fight for people's interests and affirm their values. Economic populism and mainstream values are mutually reinforcing — and equally indispensable to what Democrats should tell the voters.

Just as this book is not a manifesto for one side in the Democrats' philosophical debates, it isn't intended as a nominating speech in behalf of — or a stump speech to be used by — any of the candidates for the party's presidential nomination in 1992. Nor does it evaluate substantive proposals about taxes, health care, child care, welfare, job training, education, foreign policy, defense, or any of the other important issues that will be debated during 1992 and the years ahead. And where I've said little about some important causes, controversies, and constituencies, it's often not because I think they're unimportant but because I fear I have little to add to the debate. This is an essay about political language, how Democrats can discuss the issues and the new world of the 1990s in ways people will find comprehensible and convincing, how Democrats can speak American.

1
■ Time Capsules

★ A RAINY MORNING IN MOUNT CLEMENS

My most vivid memory of the Mondale campaign is of standing shivering one morning in Mount Clemens, Michigan, in the
company of a crowd that consisted mostly of middle-aged people
and teenagers. The older folks were wearing nylon union jackets,
and they'd come to cheer Walter Mondale. The younger folks
were mostly from the local high schools and wore letterman's
jackets. They could have been the union members' youngest children or even their grandchildren. But they'd come to jeer
Mondale.

It was the Saturday before Election Day, and I'd been with the
Mondale campaign since September. During the last six weeks of
the race, Mondale had talked less and less about balancing the
budget and, instead, he'd begun to find his voice again. It was a
clear, if unfashionable, voice that preached the gospel of the
world where he'd come of age in the 1930s and '40s.

Mondale spoke of an America where people who made things
were valued as much as people who made money; where people
who had worked hard without striking it rich would feel that their
lives were well spent; where people would help the poor as naturally as small-town folks would help their neighbors; where we'd
give our kids opportunities in the world instead of leaving them
our debts.

Mondale talked about that kind of America to congregations

1 9

at black churches in Memphis and Cleveland, to senior citizens in Brooklyn and Miami, and to small but friendly audiences in factory towns in the Midwest. And the crowds understood and applauded, and we could kid ourselves that Mondale was getting his message across.

But in the evening, when we watched the network news in our hotel workrooms and saw shots of Reagan addressing much larger audiences, we realized that Mondale was preaching to the faithful. How many really did come to our rallies in those midwestern factory towns? A couple of thousand at most, sometimes just a few hundred. Where were their shopmates, the men and women whom the unions couldn't turn out for our rallies? Where were their neighbors, who didn't work union jobs? Where were their kids who didn't want, or couldn't get, factory jobs? Mostly, they were with Reagan.

On the platform that Saturday morning in Mount Clemens were the old bulls of Michigan's Democratic and union leadership—Gov. James Blanchard, Sen. Carl Levin, former UAW president Doug Fraser—and they said that Walter Mondale has always been there for us, and now we're here for him. So the man who was speaking up for those who'd lost out in the Reagan years was himself becoming one more victim to be eulogized. And there was the smell of defeat in the chilly air.

When he came to the microphone, Mondale said many of the right things: President Reagan had done nothing while "more than three million of America's best jobs have left our country," jobs like those the men in the union jackets couldn't pass along to their sons. Republican tax give-aways to the wealthy let Vice President Bush get away with paying less taxes than his janitor. And, looking at that crowd of fathers and sons, mothers and daughters, Mondale said, "I want an America where kids from working families have the same chance to go on to college and vocational school as everyone else." For all the foolishness of a campaign that had proposed raising taxes on people like those in that crowd, Mondale also understood some things that many other Democra-

tic politicians didn't: Most Democrats' kids weren't heading for a
higher education; they were heading down a different path.
But by the end, Mondale sounded more the pleader than the
preacher. Echoing a slogan the state had adopted to woo business
and tourists, he said he'd always been proud to "say yes to Michigan." Unlike Reagan, he'd supported the Chrysler bailout. Unlike
Reagan, he'd stayed in the Midwest. And now it was time for his
friends and neighbors to say yes to him. Unfortunately, however,
what TV viewers from coast to coast saw on the news that night
was Mondale addressing a crowd of people in UAW jackets,
sounding like he was running for governor.

Mount Clemens, just northeast of Detroit, is part of suburban
Macomb County. Political historian Michael Barone, himself a
native of the Detroit area, has written about the extraordinary
growth of Macomb County in recent decades. It's been a movement of Polish-Americans, Italian-Americans, and other children
and grandchildren of immigrants marching from the city to the
suburbs. These new suburbanites were "heavily Catholic, often
blue collar, at least modestly affluent, and ancestrally Democratic."

Those ancestral loyalties were shaken loose during the 1970s
and the 1980s, beginning with a controversial court-ordered
school-busing plan that would have sent suburban kids to Detroit
city schools. In a survey conducted in Macomb and the nearby
city of Warren after the 1984 elections, Democratic pollster Stanley Greenberg found a powerful streak of resentment among these
white suburban voters about busing, affirmative action, welfare,
and other programs they viewed as helping poor blacks at their expense. (I'd seen some of those same tensions when I worked for
AFSCME in Michigan during the late seventies. Even a liberal
union like AFSCME found itself split among factions representing Detroit, the suburbs, and the rest of the state, divisions reflecting race and class as well as geography.)

So, despite Mondale's belated efforts to summon the symbolism of the political faith of their fathers, Macomb County
voters rejected him overwhelmingly, by a margin of over two to

one. And that pattern was repeated all across the country. Mondale prevailed only among voters with incomes lower than $12,500 a year, those who describe themselves as poor. Even among the working people who didn't make enough to risk having their taxes raised under Mondale's budget-balancing plan (those with incomes between $12,500 and $24,999 a year), Reagan won 57 percent of the vote. And Reagan got 59 percent of white-collar workers, 53 percent of blue-collar workers, and 45 percent of voters from union households.

A campaign plane can be like a flying cocoon. Caught up in the excitement of three rallies a day, you can kid yourself that the cheering crowds tell more about public opinion than the poll results. But Mondale's landslide loss shouldn't have surprised anyone who was listening carefully to what he had to say, particularly as it appeared in snippets on the network news. Although he was often portrayed as a pandering politician who promised something for everyone, to most Americans Mondale had little more to offer than a tax increase to ease the budget deficit. His message seemed one of sacrifice, even penance.

Mondale's rhetoric had been caught between that of the Roosevelt years, when Democrats argued that most Americans were decent people who were being exploited by "economic royalists," and that of the late sixties and early seventies, when liberals chastised the middle class for its relative affluence in the midst of those in need. Mondale had begun the primary season with the traditional Democratic appeals: He was a "full-employment Democrat"; he wanted to make sure that all workers and their families would have an "American standard of living"; he respected "people who work hard and play by the rules." This had won him the nomination against the more charismatic Gary Hart, who'd offered unspecified "new ideas," attacked special interests (particularly labor), and emerged as the candidate of the yuppies. Playing effective populist politics, Mondale's strategists cast the primary campaign as a choice between self-indulgent swingers and hardworking families. In the Democratic primaries voters stuck it to the Porsche-driving, quiche-eating yuppies, and voted for the Chevy-buying Democrat.

But after winning the nomination, Mondale started sounding other, discordant notes about tax increases and sacrifice. "This election is about what kind of people we are," Mondale told a Labor Day rally in Merrill, Wisconsin. While he tried to make clear that he thought Americans were good people, he often sounded like he was finding fault with those who disagreed with him. In an otherwise powerful speech at George Washington University, Mondale declared: "I would rather lose a race about decency than win one about self-interest." He didn't specify whose self-interest he was attacking—that of wealthy tax evaders or that of middle-class people who didn't want their taxes raised.

In the primaries, Jesse Jackson had been the candidate of the poor and Gary Hart had been the candidate of the college-educated, affluent young. Mondale was the candidate of working people, and even his cultural symbolism had seemed squarely middle class. But that was in the spring; by the time he faced Reagan, he was trapped in the stereotype of the liberal Democrat who cares mostly about people on welfare.

By that time, the cultural symbolism of the Mondale campaign had changed, suggesting the penitential liberalism of the late sixties and early seventies more than the populist liberalism of the thirties and forties. (In deciding to woo Gary Hart's baby-boomers, possibly his staff had confused affluent "yuppies" with aging "yippies.") Even his road show had the air of a sixties guilt-trip. Musical entertainment was provided by the ultimate folkies, Peter, Paul, and Mary, and Stephen Stills, a member of the seventies rock group Crosby, Stills, Nash, and Young. But we didn't need flower-power, we needed a different kind of power. We needed someone who could sing out his love for America, but like any lover, see and grieve for his loved one's failings.

We're slowly getting split up into two different Americas . . . and there's a promise getting broken. In the beginning the idea was that we all live here a little bit like a family, where the strong can help

the weak ones, the rich can help the poor ones. . . . [E]verybody
was going to have an opportunity and the chance to live a life with
some decency and some dignity and a chance for some self-respect.
Bruce Springsteen said these words to introduce his song
"Born in the USA" (and sometimes his audiences would chant
"USA, USA," just like at Reagan rallies). He stayed out of
presidential politics that year, but if there was one endorsement
Mondale needed, it wasn't from one more governor, one more
mayor, or one more political boss. Springsteen's music spoke to
the young people who didn't show up at rallies in communities like
Mount Clemens (or who showed up to jeer), people who didn't
wonder where had all the flowers gone, but who wondered, even
in that autumn of the Reagan boom, where had all the good jobs
gone.

Maybe, for Mondale, there was some satisfaction in being be-
latedly embraced by the refugees from the sixties Left, who'd
shouted down Hubert Humphrey until the final weeks of his
presidential campaign. And, aside from union members, the
largest contingent at our rallies was made up of people who might
have gone to anti-war demonstrations fifteen years earlier (and
really had warm memories of Peter, Paul, and Mary), those who
went to nuclear freeze rallies, and those who supported anyone
but Reagan.

On the Monday afternoon before Election Day, we had a rally
scheduled at Pershing Square in Los Angeles. For that event,
Mondale's speech was all-important. The night before, the campaign's traveling speechwriters met in an unusually well-
furnished work room in an unusually opulent hotel. I found my-
self thinking of Robert Kennedy, who had been killed in Los
Angeles sixteen years before. As a TV played in the background,
we heard a newscaster report that Reagan hoped to carry all fifty
states, a first. We just might lose worse than McGovern, worse
than Goldwater, worse than poor old Alf Landon.

No matter what we on the staff thought of Mondale's campaign
strategy, we never lost respect for the man himself. We had been

treated to or had observed his many small kindnesses and courtesies. Mondale belied the stereotype of the liberal who loves humanity but dislikes individuals—he genuinely cared for both. So something about the setting and the circumstances made us ask ourselves, how can we help this decent man we work for get through tomorrow with dignity? How can we turn desperation into drama?

For once, we didn't think about strategy or polls. Instead, we turned to the basic texts that Americans use when we want to communicate something of substance: The Bible; Shakespeare. And then someone remembered, this is St. Crispian's Day, when Henry V addressed his outnumbered, ragtag army on enemy territory, the night before the battle they'd certainly lose. At the least, our candidate should draw the audience closer to him and make them part of this moment, when a leader with nothing left to lose becomes one with his troops, and makes them proud to stand with him on the battlefield the next day. "We few, we happy few, we band of brothers."

So at noon the next day in downtown Los Angeles, we stood before an audience of more than 12,000 people. Our sixties folkies sang, and Ed Asner spoke. When Mondale went to the microphone, he seemed to be in surprisingly good spirits, and he seemed at peace with himself. As Joe Morgenstern, political columnist for the *Los Angeles Herald Examiner,* wrote, "Instead of sounding on the verge of tears as he has so often done before . . . he summoned up jubilance from somewhere in his soul." And Walter Mondale celebrated his St. Crispian's Day: "Someone will make history tomorrow—Reagan or us. If they make history tomorrow, they'll give you a future you never wanted. If we make history, you'll be able to tell your children and your children's children that you were here today, on the eve of the greatest upset in American history."

So who stood with us on Election Day? Those Americans set apart by race, religion, culture, poverty, or commitment to the institutions of the 1930s or the causes of the 1960s. Blacks, overwhelmingly. Jews and Latinos, more narrowly; the poor; more women than men, but even so, most women voted for Reagan; and about 55 percent of people in union households. We few, we fading few, we band of brothers and sisters.

In the aftermath of Mondale's defeat, Democrats reached the inescapable conclusion that they no longer had anything to say to most Americans. While Mondale did address middle-class issues, his promises were fragmented, made only to sections of the middle class: autoworkers, steelworkers, and textile workers who cared about import quotas; teachers and government workers; and senior citizens. These were Mondale's special interests. But to middle-class people who didn't belong to an organized group, Mondale looked like he was merely going to hand them a tax bill, along with a sermon about social responsibility.

So it was that Democrats developed a long-overdue curiosity about those of their fellow citizens who are neither rich nor poor nor organized. Someone who's offered some insight into this group is Ralph Whitehead, a social commentator and phrasemaker who began speaking to audiences (on what he's called the "Democratic pep-talk circuit") about the growth of the "new-collar workers." Members of the baby-boom generation, these people are neither blue collar nor white collar and are often the first in their families who don't work in factories. "New collars" work in the service sector, at jobs that mix responsibility and routine, and their paychecks are less princely than those of the yuppies who, as symbols of wealth, had gotten so much attention in 1984.

The new collars were the people who had been ignored by every Democrat seeking the presidency in 1984. Mondale's primary campaign had addressed an America of factories, foundries, and farms, but more people worked in offices, hospitals, and stores. And in his acceptance speech at the Democratic convention Mondale, in a revealing turn of phrase, sought to unite "yuppie and lunchpail," which ignored the lower-paid white-collar workers. While Mondale's general election campaign addressed Jesse Jackson's rainbow coalition of the urban poor, the rural poor, and the collegiate left, and Gary Hart's yuppies, it said little to those in between—the majority of Americans who were suburbanites, many in their late thirties and early forties, who were having a hard time attaining the same standard of living as their parents. "My brothers spent years saying they didn't want to live like our father," recalled Whitehead, who'd grown up in a middle-class Chicago neighborhood. "Now they realize that's no longer an option."

For Democrats, the lessons of the 1984 election were that they should address the economic concerns of this new middle class and run campaigns as different as possible from Mondale's. So, while Mondale's roots were in the Farmer-Labor movements, the 1988 nominee was governor of the state where Whitehead had first found the new collars: Massachusetts, the cradle of the computer, high-tech, and service industries. Whereas Mondale had seemed a creature of the nation's capital, Michael Dukakis had spent his career in state politics. Most important, he was a lifelong suburbanite, a middle-class family man who bought his suits off the rack, took the train to work every morning, and had dinner with his family every evening.

Mondale had embraced the symbolism of the Democratic coalition, but Dukakis addressed the AFL-CIO without saying the word "union," and campaigned in Philadelphia, Mississippi, without even mentioning the three civil-rights workers who'd been murdered there. Mondale's rhetoric was replete with words like "fairness" and "compassion." Dukakis used words like "competence" and "competitiveness," talked about "the middle-class squeeze" (someone on his staff said it sounded like a high-school girlfriend), and offered programs to help people buy their first homes and send their kids to college. Yet, although he was addressing economic anxieties, Dukakis never did that well in the middle-class suburbs. He lost the election largely because he didn't have a clue about middle-class social anxieties.

This, however, didn't really dawn on me until the last week of the campaign. Up until that point I'd been staying at a friend's house in the Dorchester neighborhood of Boston. Then in late October, a friend living in Brookline invited me to use the spare room in her house. As it turned out, her house was just a few blocks away from Dukakis's, so I figured I'd get a look at the area where Dukakis had spent most of his life.

Brookline is a suburb all right, but it's not a typical one. Filled with bookstores, gourmet delis, and theaters showing foreign films, Brookline is home to lawyers (like Dukakis), doctors (like his father), and professors (at nearby Harvard and MIT). A place where you don't have to apologize for being against the death penalty, it has an unusually well-educated—and liberal—population. Brookline was not at all like the countless communities across the country where people who grew up as Democrats were now voting for candidates like Reagan and Bush.

★ A SUNNY AFTERNOON IN BOSTON

On a Wednesday night in late September, I was working in an office in a building next door to Michael Dukakis's campaign headquarters. A group of us writers and researchers were drafting responses to questions he might be asked in his first debate with George Bush. Dinner had arrived (one of the few pleasures of the campaign was that headquarters was just a few blocks from Boston's Chinatown) and we were all walking back and forth between our computer terminals and a table filled with Chinese and Vietnamese food. "Aren't you having a great time working for us?" campaign manager Susan Estrich asked, after I'd made my third or fourth trip to the food table.

At about ten or eleven, Estrich came by my desk again. This time she wasn't jovial, she was frantic. George Bush was coming to town the next day to accept the endorsement of the Boston police union. Once again, he'd be attacking Dukakis as soft on crime, but this time, it would be in front of a cheering crowd of cops from Dukakis's own hometown. This threatened to be a replay of a few weeks earlier, when Bush had taken a boat ride in the polluted Boston Harbor and promised that, unlike the man who'd failed to clean up those murky waters, he would be the "environmental president." The Dukakis campaign had responded with a snippy attack on the Reagan-Bush environmental record, but Bush's boat ride got more news coverage than Dukakis's press release did.

But this time, Estrich declared, we aren't going to be patsies. In fact, even as we spoke, our campaign was putting together its own rally for the same afternoon, which would feature police officers who supported Dukakis and thought of Bush as a Kojak-come-lately. Real live cops—or at least their union leaders—were being flown in from all over America, including Bush's home state of Texas. My friend Robin Wright (at age thirty-one she was dean of the Democrats' advance-people) was putting it all together. Estrich gave me an easier job: write the speech Dukakis would give at the rally, just thirteen hours away.

I left the office and the Chinese food, and walked over to head-quarters, where the campaign's staff experts on crime and drugs were working late. Together we crafted a speech that had some spice, peppered with zingers against Bush. We combined the police-radio jargon I'd heard as a night desk reporter years before and the "Where was George?" refrain from the Democratic convention that summer. And it resulted in a performance that was pretty close to Dukakis's best.

The next day at noon in front of the State Capitol building, Dukakis told his crowd of police officers, "We're here today to investigate a felony—assault and battery on the truth. Because what George Bush is doing to the truth in this campaign is a crime." Then, Dukakis served up a heavy portion of what TV's Sgt. Joe Friday used to call "just the facts." And he counterpunched his rival with a firm command of those facts, along with a fierce contempt for everything about George Bush—from his inactivity as vice president to the viciousness of his presidential campaign.

Meanwhile in East Boston, George Bush was accepting the endorsement of the Boston police union and attacking Dukakis as being "out of the American mainstream" on the issue of combatting crime. Predictably, Bush talked about the man his campaign had made America's best-known criminal, the convicted murderer Willie Horton, who'd raped a Maryland woman while on furlough from a life sentence in Massachusetts. Turning to Dukakis's opposition to the death penalty, Bush insisted that "some crimes are so heinous, so outrageous, so brutal that the death penalty is warranted."

Yet, violent crime had declined in Massachusetts while Dukakis was governor, and, as he frequently noted, it had increased nationally during those same years under the Reagan-Bush administration. Dukakis had increased aid to both state and local police forces, while the Reagan-Bush team had cut federal aid to the states for corrections, law enforcement, and drug treatment programs. Indeed, as Dukakis declared in his speech that day, "Whenever the nation's law enforcement officers needed help from Washington, they put out an all points bulletin for George Bush, but they couldn't find him." And he reminded his audience that while Bush liked to talk about the important "missions" he'd performed, his role as coordinator of the Reagan administration's war on drugs was a mission at which he'd failed abysmally.

The news media presented the day's events as a standoff: Bush hit Dukakis on the now-familiar issues of furloughs and the death penalty; Dukakis finally found Bush's weak spot—his total lack of success in dealing with the problems of crime and drugs. The hometown press portrayed Dukakis as the winner in the day's dueling police rallies. Writing in the *Boston Globe*, Thomas Oliphant concluded that this time Bush had gotten "mugged" on his visit to the big city because Dukakis had made "a full-fledged assault on George Bush's years as Ronald Reagan's quasi-drug czar, on his campaign style and ethics, and on his campaign image as leader in his own right."

While the national media called it a draw, I think the rest of the country had called it in Bush's favor, for the same reasons Bush held his own in the first debate three days later: Dukakis scored on facts and intelligence, but Bush scored on likability and values. This was a problem that became painfully apparent during the disastrous second debate, when Cable News Network's Bernard Shaw asked Dukakis what he'd think about capital punishment if someone had raped and murdered his wife. Dukakis's reply, which began, "Bernard . . . I think you know I've opposed the death penalty . . . all of my life," and concluded with a recitation of the facts and figures of how crime had declined in Massachusetts, completely missed the mark.

What was missing from his answer to that killer question was also what was missing from his speech at the Boston police rally: any indication that he understood the values and emotions that make most people feel so strongly about crime and punishment. My draft had included tough language against crime and Dukakis had used it, but it had all been about what he'd done as governor, what he'd do as president, and what Bush had failed to do as vice president. I hadn't added anything about Dukakis's personal values—his belief that people are responsible for what they do and that crime must be punished.

So why hadn't I written that in my draft? I don't think that I believed in the caricature of Dukakis the Bush campaign had drawn, that he was someone so enamored of legal proceduralism and sociological explanations for criminality that he actually was reluctant to attach painful consequences to evil actions. But as odd as it may seem to have to say it, a campaign and its staff do reflect the personality of the candidate, so in the hectic hours before the rally I was trying to write not the best possible speech but the best possible Dukakis speech. And, for all its tough language, it was like all the other Dukakis speeches, dry and programmatic.

Since the speech was devoid of moral or emotional content, Dukakis was unable to reassure Americans that he too believed that there are moral absolutes, that wrongdoers must be held accountable for their actions, and that he inhabited the same moral universe that most people do, that he felt as they do, that he was one of them.

Several weeks later, the campaign made one more effort to connect with voters on the issues of crime and punishment. One Saturday night in October, Dukakis addressed an audience at Bates College in Lewiston, Maine, his parents' alma mater, and something clicked. Perhaps it was because he couldn't address that audience without talking about his family—and, since he's a devoted family man, he couldn't talk about his family without displaying genuine emotion. In that speech, Dukakis recalled that his father, who had continued practicing medicine well into his seventies, had been beaten and robbed one Saturday afternoon in his suburban office. And he talked about his brother who'd been killed in a hit-and-run accident by a driver who (he'd always assumed) had been drunk or on drugs. So, Dukakis said, he certainly understood the pain and anger of crime victims and their families, and it was a cynical ploy for the Bush campaign to keep saying that he didn't.

Yet this message never persuaded, or more likely it never even reached, most voters. Partly, that was because Dukakis made the point most eloquently on a Saturday night in a college town, so most people never saw it or heard it. But even if they had, it wouldn't have been enough. The real issue was not so much whether Dukakis sympathized with victims of crime but whether he was tough enough to deal with the bad guys who commit the crimes. Just as they wanted more from Dukakis than Sgt. Joe Friday's "just the facts, ma'am," they also wanted more than Phil Donahue-type tears and sympathy. The voters wanted someone like TV's most famous Greek-American, the cop, Kojak. Dukakis never communicated the "tough love" that real American heroes convey: the capacity to care enough to get mad, get tough, and get results.

Crime is a real problem for most Americans. Far from being a metaphor for something else, as some commentators have suggested, crime *is* a legitimate public issue, since protecting people's safety is government's first responsibility. Yet, as a political issue, crime does have many resonances, ranging from the racist (when the Bush campaign used Willie Horton as its sole symbol of violent crime, it was exploiting racial stereotypes), to the reasonable (voters do have the right to conclude that a public official who can't cope with crime won't be able to deal with other difficult problems either). And the Dukakis campaign's failure to satisfactorily address the issue of crime was typical of the national Democrats' failure to convince the voters that we *do* share their values and that we *can* put those values into action.

2
The Music of Words and Symbols

On the Saturday morning before the 1990 Democratic mayoral primary in Washington, D.C., I was standing outside the large building that houses the farmers' market watching the front-running mayoral candidate, John Ray, work a crowd of several hundred. Ray is an affable man with a commanding presence. He rose from poverty to become a successful lawyer and city council-member, and seemed to come straight out of central casting to play the role of big-city mayor.

Meanwhile, in a small art gallery next door to the market, the candidate who'd been running dead last for most of the campaign was earnestly holding forth on her ideas for reforming city government—to a crowd of three people. Watching Sharon Pratt Kelly* spend her Saturday morning talking to her tiny audience, while her leading opponent shook hundreds of hands, I became convinced that, despite her recent endorsement by the *Washington Post,* she had no chance of winning the primary. Moreover, I concluded that her staying inside while all the voters were outside proved that she must have abysmal political instincts.

Three days later, I stood outside a polling place at a junior high school in northeast Washington, D.C., handing out leaflets for Eleanor Holmes Norton, a candidate for the non-voting congressional seat from D.C. Out there with me were volunteers hard at

---

*In December 1991, Mayor Sharon Pratt Dixon married James Kelly. She is now Mayor Sharon Pratt Kelly.

work for all the candidates for Congress and all the mayoral candidates—except Kelly. I wasn't surprised that she wasn't represented, since her campaign seemed to have the least money and the smallest organization of all five mayoral contenders. It wasn't until two hours before the polls closed that a Kelly volunteer finally showed up, but I quickly realized that an upset was in the making. While the dozen-or-so volunteers from all the various campaigns stampeded toward the people approaching the polling place, most voters were friendliest to Kelly's. "I'm bringing my broom," more than one voter told him.

This reference to a broom showed that people were listening to what Kelly was saying on TV debates, evening newscasts, and at community meetings. She'd been promising to "clean house" in city government, fight corruption, and fire political hacks and useless middle managers. From the start of her campaign, Kelly had pledged to "use a broom." Lately, she'd been saying that cleaning up city government would take more than a broom; she'd need a shovel. Later that night, I watched the returns and saw Sharon Pratt Kelly claiming victory—and holding a shovel. And when the newscast showed the crowd at her campaign headquarters, the folks in the front row were gleefully waving brooms.

In hindsight, Kelly was the right woman in the right place at the right time. In the aftermath of Mayor Barry's conviction on drug charges—and in the midst of a serious fiscal crisis in city government—Washington, D.C., voters were ready to turn to an outsider who'd never held public office before. The genius of Kelly's campaign was that she offered a simple message—"I'll clean house"—and memorable symbols—the broom and the shovel. Of all the candidates for any office that primary day, she was the only one whose supporters could offer a rationale for her candidacy, in the second it took to brush off the maniacs who were attacking voters with leaflets for other candidates.

To be sure, Kelly offered more than a slogan, some symbols, and a resume devoid of government jobs. Alone among the candidates, she ran a campaign that appealed to voters' values. She told them that when she'd grown up in Washington, D.C., years before, people had been poorer and had suffered severe discrimination but, nonetheless, they'd had strong values, and she promised to bring those values back. Then there was her pledge to fire paper-pushers and time-servers, not those who do the real work—like teachers, firefighters, police officers, and sanitation workers. Even in Washington, D.C., home of the federal bureaucracy and one of the largest municipal work forces in the country, the idea of cutting fat and sparing muscle is appealing.

Kelly's campaign wasn't the only reason she won. She was a hardworking, energetic candidate, and she's been a hardworking, energetic mayor. But her victory *is* a case study in effective political communication. She appealed to some basic American tenets: a suspicion of large bureaucracies and professional politicians, a nostalgia for the "virtuous" community of the past, and the belief that one honest person can return society to its founding values. Her clear message and down-to-earth symbols reinforced this ideal, as did her public persona: one small woman (she's barely five feet tall) standing alone against entrenched adversaries. All of her rivals held public office, all but one were men, and all were better organized and better financed.

Value-laden words, emotive symbols, and revealing gestures are the makings of a compelling political language. Yet, while Sharon Pratt Kelly was able to use this language effectively and get elected mayor of the nation's capital, the national Democratic party has been unable to move most voters' hearts or minds. But in the past decade, Ronald Reagan and George Bush have been as spectacularly successful at appealing to voters' values as the national Democrats have been spectacularly unsuccessful. What have most Democrats been missing?

During Reagan's presidency, friend and foe alike hailed him as "the great communicator," which suggests that his success with the public could largely be attributed to the skills he'd honed during his acting career. Yet George Bush, who at his best is only a passable public performer, was elected president and has mostly had remarkable approval ratings. Obviously, something more than acting skills has contributed to the Republicans' ability to communicate effectively to a national audience.

Republicans present themselves as America's team. Proclaiming American values, defending American interests, celebrating the American system, they represent Americans as *Americans* – not as members of separate groups. So for Republicans, it's easy to align themselves with American symbols from the flag to the small town, complete with puppy dogs and picket fences.

Even at their shrewdest, Democrats have a harder time embracing American symbols. As the party of outsiders, underdogs, and seekers of social reform, Democrats run the risk of being perceived as way out of the American mainstream. And Republicans have portrayed Democrats as out of the mainstream for the past twenty-plus years, using emotive, symbolic issues like welfare queens, Willie Horton's furlough, and flagburning.

Yet, Democrats can also make a strong appeal. They've always had the sense that America is special because of its attitude toward justice: the belief that justice means equal opportunity and fair play, and its willingness to fight for social justice at home and human rights abroad. These notions of justice are at the heart of American political culture. And from Old Testament prophets to the Sermon on the Mount, there is much in the Judeo-Christian tradition to suggest that, far from being a Republican, God may be something of a bleeding-heart liberal.

Indeed, Sharon Pratt Kelly's campaign shows how Democratic constituencies can respond to mainstream American symbolism. According to the kind of social stereotyping Republican presidential campaigns have exploited, Washington, D.C., is way outside the mainstream. Government is its major industry (and the media may run a close second). It's a predominantly black city, with substantial Hispanic, Asian, and Jewish communities. Yet Kelly won with a campaign that emphasized classic American themes: trimming the bureaucracy, empowering frontline workers, and returning to traditional values of discipline and hard work.

What Kelly did in D.C., Democrats should do all across the country. But first, they need to understand the elements of political language.

★ THE LANGUAGE OF PERSONAL GESTURES

When Michael Dukakis appeared at a Labor Day rally in Detroit wearing a button-down shirt, and a suit and tie, the union people told me they knew his campaign was in big trouble. His appearance perfectly illustrated the voters' fears that he kept himself, as well as his shirt collars, all buttoned up. A month and a half later, when he "came out fighting," Dukakis started coming to rallies with his sleeves rolled up and his tie undone. He'd finally loosened up and become a down-to-earth Democrat campaigning like the scrappy Harry Truman in 1948.

Americans expect their political leaders to be dignified when discharging the duties of their offices, but they also expect that someone seeking office should act like a citizen soliciting the support of fellow citizens—not like visiting royalty. And Democrats, in particular, are expected to act like *democrats*, not aristocrats, autocrats, or bureaucrats.

In fact, if you were Rip Van Winkle and awoke to see silent footage from the 1984 and '88 campaigns, you might conclude that Reagan and Bush were the Democrats and Mondale and Dukakis were the Republicans. Why? Well, you'd see Reagan and Bush outdoors, dressed informally, smiling at the camera, apparently enjoying themselves. And you'd see Mondale and Dukakis indoors, wearing suits, pointing at charts. Reagan and Bush, looking like leaders of the people; Mondale and Dukakis, looking like officials of the government. Guess who won?

But even in the recent past, Democrats have understood the power of the emotionally resonant gesture. In 1976, when Jimmy Carter carried his own luggage and stayed in supporters' homes, he created a powerful image for his anti-Washington campaign.

And when Mondale and Dukakis answered ordinary voters' questions at citizens' forums, they scored points. There is no small irony in the fact that for all their populist imagery, Reagan and Bush rarely appeared in unrehearsed settings, and Democrats need to remind voters of this. But what they really need to do is square their image with their populist message.

★ VALUE-LADEN WORDS

You don't have to be a social historian—you just have to watch TV, go to the movies, talk to your neighbors, or simply search your soul—to get a sense of some of the ideas that have shaped our nation.

Perhaps most important is the idea that America is special, and Americans are special people. A country that doesn't define itself by language or lineage has to set other standards for citizenship, and the classic definition of American nationality includes a dedication to democratic values and a commitment to building a virtuous community—the great American experiment. As social commentator Ralph Whitehead has said:

> I guess that America is the only country on earth dedicated to the idea of building a new Jerusalem. . . .
> It is a belief that the foundation of the American experience is a virtuous one. This society was created as a deliberate break with the old, a break with aristocracy and established religion. . . .
> You really can't expect to effectively lead the nation unless you come to terms with its tradition of exceptionalism.

Far from being academic or archaic, these ideas have echoed throughout two centuries of political debate. While political leaders may disagree about what makes America special, whether it lies in our community or our individualism, the idea that America is a special society, with special strengths and special responsibilities, is the cornerstone of the case every presidential candidate must build. For the past decade, Republicans have been more at home with (and more adept at) the rhetoric of American exceptionalism. "Can there be any doubt that a Divine Providence placed this land, this island of freedom, here as a refuge for all those people of the world who yearn to breathe freely?" Reagan asked in his acceptance speech at the 1980 GOP convention. And in his speech to the 1988 convention, George Bush said of Michael Dukakis: "He sees America as another pleasant country on the U.N. roll call, somewhere between Albania and Zimbabwe. And I see America as a leader, a unique nation with a special role in the world."

During the Reagan-Bush years, Democrats remained reluctant to espouse a similar belief in America's place in the world. Of course, many Democratic party activists—even such national candidates as Gary Hart and Jesse Jackson—were shaped by the protest movements of the 1960s, which ended up concentrating more on America's problems than its promise. Yet Jimmy Carter and Walter Mondale, whose politics weren't formed in the sixties, seemed tone-deaf to the music of American specialness. Indeed, it was Michael Dukakis, almost alone among the national Democrats of the 1980s, who recognized the concept of American exceptionalism. But his tribute, given late in the campaign, was somewhat platitudinous: "America isn't just another place. It's not just a piece of land or just another country. It's the noblest experiment ever undertaken on this planet." Despite Dukakis's love of the country that had welcomed his immigrant parents, little else in his rhetoric suggested a belief in America's special place in the world. It was unfair of Bush to suggest that Dukakis saw America as morally equivalent to Albania or Zimbabwe, but it was not unreasonable to say that he had a less expansive view of its role in the world.

In the debates of the nineties, Democrats would do well to remember that Americans are proud of that role, perhaps even more so since the collapse of communism in Eastern Europe and the U.S.S.R. and the victory in the Persian Gulf. Democrats *should* champion Pentagon budget cuts and hard bargaining with prosperous allies whose defense we subsidize. But if Democrats' rhetoric suggests that "America is in decline" (or, worse yet, seems to delight in that prospect), then they'll remain vulnerable to attacks like Bush's. It would be far better for Democrats to champion our capacity to do good at home as well as abroad, than to give the slightest hint that our world leadership has been a costly mistake. Our country's self-image is not of a city walled off from the world, but in the words of a Puritan magistrate in Massachusetts some 350 years ago, it's "a shining city on a hill"—a new Jerusalem.

In addressing a people for whom the new Jerusalem is a central metaphor, it makes sense to use biblical references. While there is a wide variety of religions and religious practices in our country, it *is* true that the Old Testament is the closest thing Americans have to a common text. During the Reagan-Bush years, Republicans made effective use of imagery from the Bible, yet ever since the defeat of Jimmy Carter, national Democrats (with the exception of the Rev. Jesse Jackson) have avoided using religious references to help make their case. Unfortunately, those who call the shots in national Democratic campaigns seem to believe that the audience is entirely secular, asking speechwriters to quote from the Scripture only if the speech is for a black audience. This gives credence to the charge that all Democrats are secular, and it's a misunderstanding of the electorate that speaks volumes about the mindset of liberal (or, more accurately, white liberal) political operatives.

One liberal political operative who's learned otherwise is David Wilhelm, who managed Chicago mayor Richard M. Daley's successful re-election campaign in 1991. (That fall, Wilhelm became manager of Arkansas governor Bill Clinton's campaign for the Democratic presidential nomination.) During his days as an activist for progressive tax reform, Wilhelm was often asked where he got his crazy ideas and whether he was some kind of socialist. Often without success, he'd try to make his case by citing facts and figures. Then, Wilhelm started quoting the parable of the widow's mite (Mark 12: 42–44), where Jesus observes that a poor widow who threw two mites into the treasury "hath cast more in, than all they which have cast into the treasury; for all they did cast in of their abundance; but she of her want did cast in all that she had, even all her living."

"People understood instantly," Wilhelm recalls. "The Bible reminds people where they got a lot of their notions about fairness."

If the idea that America is a new Jerusalem sounds biblical, then so, too, is the notion that our society is the product of a covenant with God, which is the model for our social contract with each other. From the words of the Declaration of Independence, "[W]ith a firm reliance on the protection of Divine Providence, we mutually pledge to each other our lives, our fortunes, and our sacred honor" to Ronald Reagan's 1980 acceptance speech, where he spoke of "renewing the American compact" between the people and their government, throughout our history political leaders have referred to the idea of the covenant. As the 1992 primary season got underway, Bill Clinton made the idea of a "new covenant" between the people and the government a centerpiece of his campaign. And Nebraska senator Bob Kerrey also spoke about renewing the social contract.

You can hear the American concept of the social contract echoed in the language used by ordinary citizens who intuitively understand the linkage of rights and responsibilities, opportunities and obligations, and rewards and efforts. Thus, Americans talk about a society where people who "play by the rules" can expect certain things in return. In fact, the social programs that are most popular, like social security and Medicare which reward a lifetime of work, are premised on there being a contract between an individual and society.

In the morality plays of American politics, entrenched power is always the villain. Of course, the original American morality play was the Revolutionary War—a people rising, in revolt against distant, corrupt, arrogant rulers. Then the villain was Great Britain. Now, the villain is always named "Big": Big money, big business, and big government are all rhetorical whipping boys for populist politicians. (The story of the California environmental referendum, "Big Green," proves the point. As some commentators observed, the ballot measure lost "not because it was green but because it was big.")

On the other hand, smart Democrats can make good use of the classic conflict between the individual and big government. In his successful campaign for governor of Virginia in 1989, Douglas Wilder found an effective way to attack his Republican opponent, Marshall Coleman, who wanted to make abortion illegal, even in cases of rape and incest. Wilder's television advertisements warned:

> On the issue of abortion, Marshall Coleman wants to take away your right to choose and give it to the politicians . . . Doug Wilder believes the government shouldn't interfere in your right to choose. He wants to keep the politicians out of your personal life.

That argument had resonance in the state that produced that patron saint of individual liberty, Thomas Jefferson. And now, at a time when a conservative Supreme Court may wipe out women's abortion rights, Democrats would do well to remember that this is one issue where it makes sense to speak out against big government.

Just as big is bad, small is good. The classic American stories are about the heroic individual, who climbs from poverty to greatness; the frontier family, who carves a homestead out of the prairie; and the virtuous community of the small town or the city neighborhood, which overcomes disaster. These stories all describe a world of human beings living by human values, where it is possible to succeed despite the harshness of the frontier or the indifference of big institutions. In a country that believes in and derives much of its legitimacy from this possibility of individual advancement, words like "work" and "opportunity" are of utmost importance, for it is through these that people reveal not only their own worthiness but the worthiness of society.

Many of our leaders have played upon these themes. While the aristocratic Franklin Roosevelt could not claim to have risen from poverty, the journalist Henry Fairlie shrewdly suggested that Roosevelt's wheelchair was his log cabin, and his recovery served as a powerful metaphor for a nation trying to get on its feet after the economic collapse of the Great Depression.

★ THE PRESIDENTIAL PARABLES

Under presidents Roosevelt and Truman, Democrats had a simple but compelling message: What's good for working people is good for America. For the generation that came of age during the Depression, served in World War II, and came home to a newly prosperous nation, the Democratic party was America's party. Democrats had breathed new life into the American dream with programs that honored working people—social security, unemployment compensation, the GI Bill, VA and FHA mortgages —and created the college-educated, home-owning middle class.

In the early sixties, presidents Kennedy and Johnson presented themselves as heirs to the New Deal's promise. They created Medicare, which benefits everyone over age sixty-five, tore down racial barriers to full citizenship, and addressed the problems of the poor. Activist government got a bad name only when the Johnson administration was seen as concentrating too much on the poor (stereotyped as black) and excluding the middle class.

Democrats stopped telling the classic Democratic story when those who had opposed Johnson's renomination in 1968 captured the party in 1972. Instead of celebrating America's promise, the McGovern campaign seemed to be urging the people to repent. But the pendulum swung back in 1976. Launching his election campaign from Warm Springs, Georgia (where FDR had recuperated from polio), Jimmy Carter offered the traditional Democratic message. He denounced the "political and economic elite," and declared, "It is time for the people to run the government." But Carter's administration floundered. In fact, Carter may be best remembered for what has been called his "malaise" speech, in which he appeared to blame the people for the failures of his administration (unlike FDR, who told the American people that, despite the Depression, they had not failed).

Carter's "malaise" allowed the Republicans to present him as a drag on the national spirit, and in turn, to appropriate the values and ideals of the New Deal (which was, after all, a story of hope). At the 1980 GOP convention, Ronald Reagan spoke to "all those across the land who share a community of values embodied in these words: family, work, neighborhood, peace, and freedom." These were concepts of the American political tradition, but his words were from New Deal rhetoric. Throughout his presidency, Reagan borrowed more of FDR's themes and phrases, and picked up on his "fireside chat" idea. The symbolism came full circle when the band played Roosevelt's campaign song, "Happy Days Are Here Again," at the 1984 GOP convention. (This strategy worked beautifully at a time when Democrats foolishly believed that the symbolism of the New Deal was a disadvantage.)

And the Republican lock on American values and the vocabulary of the American political tradition continued into the 1988 campaign. George Bush's acceptance speech, which was written by Peggy Noonan, a self-described daughter of the Roosevelt revolution, offered a view of society at once traditionally American and reflective of Catholic social thought:

> At the bright center is the individual. And radiating from him or her is the family, the essential unit of closeness and of love. . . . From the individual to the family to the community, and on out to the town, to the church and school, and, still echoing out, to the country, the state, the nation—each doing only what it does well, and no more.

While Noonan couldn't build Bush a log cabin, she did present this senator's son from Fairfield County, Connecticut (one of America's wealthiest communities), as a member of the postwar middle class—a World War II hero who'd moved to Texas, bought a house in the suburbs, and started his own business. But the kicker came when Bush confessed his yearning for "a kinder, gentler" America. As I heard that phrase, it immediately occurred to me that these were words you'd use to describe a real person. In contrast, most Democratic speechwriters would have had their candidate call for a "more decent, more compassionate society." "Kind" and "gentle" are personal; "decent" and "compassionate" smack of the bureaucratic (however benevolent). One reason why Noonan's team won in 1988 and my team lost was that they were speaking American English, and up until the end, we weren't.

★ SYMBOLIC LITERACY

Symbols have always been part of political debate. In his presidential campaign, John F. Kennedy used the symbol of the rocket to refer to the Soviet lead in space travel and offensive missiles in order to dramatize that the world was changing rapidly and that the United States had to change with it. Jimmy Carter was a Sunday-school teacher, a farmer, and he had a background in nuclear science from his stint in the navy, all powerful symbols he used to reassure Americans concerned about the nation's moral and technological crises.

The reputations of historic figures have been used as symbols, and as noted earlier, Reagan used Roosevelt's. Reagan understood that it wasn't necessary to ally himself with the New Deal philosophy—it was FDR's exuberant vision of a successful America that still has great power for Americans.

The institutions of democracy are themselves powerful symbols for Americans and, in 1987, People for the American Way put that power to work in a television spot for their campaign against the nomination of Robert Bork to the U.S. Supreme Court.

Polls that summer had shown that the last thing people wanted was to hear strident protest, whether from the Left or the Right. In fact, most people approved of both President Reagan (who'd nominated Bork), and the Supreme Court (which Bork had harshly criticized for many of its decisions). But these findings weren't really surprising: Americans like America. (This is a point that cannot be overstressed.) For all our griping about individual public officials, the American institutions of the presidency, the courts, and even Congress are positive symbols for most people.

Thus, the ad I wrote was not sixty seconds worth of diatribe against Robert Bork, and by extension, against the Reagan administration and the Supreme Court. Instead, it showed a family walking up the steps of the Supreme Court building, on one of the pilgrimages Americans make to the shrines of our democracy. The narrator began by saying, "There's a special feeling of awe people get when they visit the Supreme Court of the United States, the ultimate guardian of our liberties." It continued with, "That's why we're so concerned that Robert Bork has been nominated to the Supreme Court," and went on to detail Bork's controversial record. This spot was successful because it grasped the distinction between the public's perception of these offices and the people who occupy them. In the film classic *Mr. Smith Goes to Washington*, politicians are a bunch of crooks and clowns, but the Capitol and the ideals it embodies are portrayed with a kind of awe.

In the fall of 1991, Clarence Thomas was nominated for the Supreme Court seat being vacated by Thurgood Marshall, the Court's only black justice. Thomas is young, with little judicial experience, but he is black, Republican, and he was a loyal and effective member of the Reagan administration. Since the case for confirmation could not be based entirely on his brief record on the federal bench, it was Thomas's character and his compelling, classically American success story (the triumph of the heroic individual) that made the case for him. His supporters made shrewd use of his Horatio Alger story, presenting an array of hometown folks from Pin Point, Georgia, who had aided him in his climb from poverty to prominence. His detractors brought forth leaders of liberal national organizations, which lent credence to Bush's charge that Thomas was being unfairly targeted by elitist special interest groups. Later, Thomas's nomination was embroiled in charges of sexual harassment. Reagan-Bush speechwriter Peggy Noonan called it a contest—"the abstract" versus "the real" America, and the "clever people who talk loudly in restaurants" against "those who seat them." Thomas's opponents lost hands down.

In this case, Washington, D.C., itself, was a symbol. It is the setting for the shrines of democracy, but it also symbolizes the politicians and bureaucrats who have always played the heavies in populist parables—like Thomas's.

New York City also plays several roles in the national mythology. For many, as the site of Ellis Island and the Statue of Liberty, it's the gateway to American opportunity, the home of the urban log cabin and the virtuous community of the ethnic neighborhood. But for nativists, this makes New York less than American. New York has always been a city of minorities, which has made it both a target of and a buzzword for various forms of intolerance. New York itself can be the heavy; it symbolizes Wall Street and the speculators who profit at the expense of productive sectors of the economy—the hardworking middle-class Americans. More recently, New York, as well as other financially troubled cities, has been used in conservative oratory as a symbol of lax liberalism and an unwillingness to submit to fiscal discipline or say no to the special interest groups. As the site of the 1992 Democratic Convention, New York will be the target of Republican attacks, and Democrats will need to portray New Yorkers as strivers, not stereotypes, and conjure up the warmhearted multi-ethnic metropolis of *Moonstruck*, not the decadent overclass and predatory underclass portrayed in *The Bonfire of the Vanities*.

But for at least the past ten years, Democrats have been, and stubbornly so, "symbolically illiterate" (a phrase coined by religion writer Jim Castelli). The dilemma is this: To the lawyers, lobbyists, professors, and policy experts who staff national Democratic campaigns, the use of symbols in political debate is seen as shallow, cynical, and manipulative. So when they do use symbols, they do it shallowly, cynically, and manipulatively. More often, they reject using symbols because they don't want to be shallow, cynical, and manipulative. And they can't recognize a symbol unless it's staring them in the face.

Taking the literal-minded approach, which says that a symbol can only be seen (preferably on a TV screen), the Democrats' 1984 convention in San Francisco put the flag factories on overtime. Each delegate held at least one flag, and waved it at the closest camera. There were flags on the walls, flags on the podium, flags as far as the eye could see. Of course, every national political convention needs flags, but the only thing all those flags symbolized was the Democrats' defensiveness on issues like patriotism and mainstream values. That's how the media reported it. And that's how most Americans must have seen it.

A party that was symbolically literate would have understood that San Francisco was itself a symbol—one to be avoided. Of all the Democrats, only convention keynoter Mario Cuomo realized that and tried, with flare but futility, to redefine this Babylon-by-the-bay as the city named after St. Francis (who is known for the virtues of kindness and compassion, which the Democratic party espouses). Despite his efforts, when Jeane Kirkpatrick gave her speech at the GOP convention a month later, her phrase "the San Francisco Democrats" was immediately understood. And the symbolically illiterate Democrats hadn't even seen it coming.

Four years later, the lawyerly Michael Dukakis and the "experts" around him failed to understand the powerful emotions that surround symbols like the Pledge of Allegiance, and symbolic issues, like the prison furlough of a convicted murderer. But earlier in 1988, some Democrats *had* shown signs of symbolic literacy. During his primary bid, Richard Gephardt calculated that the taxes and tariffs South Korea would slap on a Chrysler K-Car imported for sale would bring the price to $48,000 (for a car that sold for $10,000 in the United States). In his stump speech, Gephardt asked how many Hyundais South Korea would sell here if we imposed comparable fees, and in his TV spot he posed this question as he walked with assembly-line workers. Gephardt had seized on some powerful symbols: hardworking Americans and unfair foreign competition. Furthermore, Gephardt shrewdly combined these with our belief in America's unique role in the world and our value of fairness. He said that even if we did retaliate against unfair trade practices, we would still honor our defense commitments to South Korea "because that's the kind of people we are."

At the 1988 convention Jesse Jackson showed similar understanding when he talked so movingly about the urban poor—who play by the rules and "take the early bus" to work. He knew that if the cause of social and economic justice for black Americans was to regain the moral standing it had held in the national consciousness during the civil-rights movement, riding the "early bus" would have to become as central a symbol in public debate as riding "in the back of the bus" was.

In Democratic presidential campaigns, the worst symbolic illiterates are the policy experts who insist that the only legitimate issues are those where candidates can spell out exactly what they'd do if elected. So in the 1988 campaign these experts were honestly bewildered that George Bush could discuss state and local concerns—like furloughs, saying the Pledge of Allegiance in public-school classrooms, and pollution in Boston Harbor—and get away with it. These were phony issues they said, and almost until the end, Dukakis repeated the same point himself. Even worse, he wasted time defending his record as governor and talking about the trend lines for the crime rate in Massachusetts. Of course, *that* wasn't really the issue.

What the experts didn't understand was that issues such as these symbolized a whole host of deeper questions—from whether our society can defend itself to whether schools can promote values and control behavior. And how a potential president addressed those issues said just as much about how he'd govern as did his ten-point programs on housing or health care.

But these were not the only areas the Democrats failed to identify. The network news was filled with potential targets—like the double-dealers in Washington who left high-paying jobs in the Reagan-Bush administration, where they'd negotiated foreign-trade agreements, to take higher-paying jobs working for those same foreign companies. Sure, you've never heard of any of them, but if Dukakis had picked just one name and lambasted it in every stump speech, that fellow would've become a household word—the Democrats' Willie Horton.

Corporate merger-mania had a lot of potential (especially with barracudas like Frank Lorenzo around), yet it was only raised when Dukakis's program for strengthening anti-trust enforcement could be detailed. His stump speech didn't mention merger-mania at all; even his experts understood you don't detail anti-trust enforcement at a rally. But it was an issue ripe with symbolic potential, and it was lost to the policy experts.

So we missed using insider trading or the lifestyles of rich-and-famous parasites like Leona Helmsley and Donald Trump as targets of righteous wrath. Looking to 1992, I can see a number of symbolic issues Democrats should raise. (Unfortunately, I can also imagine how policy experts would smite them, chloroform them, kill them, and preserve them in legalistic amber.) One emotive issue is the exorbitant salaries of corporate executives, many of whom received lavish pay increases during years in which their companies actually lost money. While Americans aren't extreme egalitarians, we do question whether an executive could possibly be worth a thousand times more than a frontline employee. And rewarding executives whose companies have been losing money is especially repugnant because Americans believe in incentives for success, not failure.

In their stump speeches, it's okay for Democrats to deplore this without detailing how we'd use the SEC, the IRS, and an alphabet soup of lesser-known agencies to deal with it. People believe Democrats know how government works; the problem is, they don't believe Democrats will ever make government work for them. Symbols contribute to public debate and public understanding because when voters hear a presidential candidate railing against exorbitant executive salaries, corporate merger-mania, and Lorenzo-style abuse of frontline workers, they get a sense of the values that candidate might bring to a thousand-and-one decisions involving big business, working people, and the public.

Of course, the use of symbols can be demagogic. It was reasonable for George Bush to talk about furloughs in Massachusetts, but it was irresponsible to use a black man as the only symbol of violent crime in America—just as it would be to make an Italian the only symbol of organized crime, or a Jew the only symbol of financial wrongdoing. Using ethnic stereotypes as symbols is playing with fire. But since they'll be facing a party that represents society's outsiders, some Republicans will keep playing with fire. And the Democrats had better be ready.

So for Democrats in 1992, nothing's more urgent than developing symbolic literacy—or better yet, symbolic fluency. Instead of ignoring the language of symbolism, or whining about "phony" issues, Democrats need to use symbols of their own to deflect Republican attacks. But even more important, they need to paint a picture of how the Democrats would make America better.

3

■ Populism: Better Late than Never?

At his rallies in the final days of his presidential campaign, Michael Dukakis strode to the microphone as the loudspeakers blared a tune by Creedence Clearwater Revival: "Some folks are born silver spoon in hand . . . It ain't me. It ain't me, I ain't no millionaire's son." Dukakis had come a long way from the last week in September when he told me to stop writing speeches attacking "country club Republicans." That was in early fall, when Dukakis still had a shot at the presidency. But by mid-October, in the aftermath of the debacle that was his second debate with George Bush, Dukakis had lost hope of winning and lost confidence in his own instincts. He was willing to try anything, even sounding like a fighting Democratic underdog.

I had a hand in writing a whole new stump speech where Dukakis told his audiences, "I'm on your side," and declared that even though "the Republicans are popping champagne corks in their penthouses," he'd not yet begun to fight. "George Bush is for the people on Easy Street. I'm for the people on Main Street. . . . George Bush is for the people who already have it made. I want to help every American family make it. . . . George Bush is for people with family fortunes. I'm for people who worry about balancing their family budgets. . . . George Bush wants a tax break for the wealthiest one percent of all Americans. I want to help your kids have the chance to go to college."

Dukakis began belting out the old Democratic gospel and gave a damn good speech. He took off his jacket, loosened his tie, and discarded the prepared texts, improvising and improving on what we gave him. Jetting around the country in those frantic final days, Dukakis became the fighter Democrats desperately wanted him to be—proving that a Democrat doesn't have to be Huey Long, Harry Truman, and Hubert Humphrey rolled into one to give a passionate populist speech. Once he got the hang of it, buttoned-down suburbanite Dukakis did just fine.

In that time, Dukakis gained eight points, from a low of 38 percent on October 15, two days after the second debate, to 46 percent on Election Day. The success of that simple message, "I'm on your side," reminded Democrats that their greatest advantage—perhaps their only remaining advantage—was contained in the answer to the oldest question in politics: Who can you count on to represent you?

Ever since the success of those last few weeks of the 1988 campaign, Democrats, like fans of a fighter who refused to come out swinging until the final round (when he closed with an impressive flurry but still ended up far behind in the judges' scoring), have replayed that ending over and over in their minds. Even so, they've seemed unsure of what Dukakis's late conversion meant for the future of the party. Then, in the spring of 1990, Republican strategist Kevin Phillips, an architect of Richard Nixon's silent majority campaign, urged Democrats to rediscover their tradition of representing ordinary folks. In his book, *The Politics of Rich and Poor*, Phillips suggested that Democrats could succeed by attacking the growth of economic inequality in America during the 1980s and the parallel decline of its international economic standing. His advice seemed like the ultimate permission for Democrats to return to their roots.

The kind of politics Truman practiced, Dukakis dabbled in, and Phillips advocates has come to be called "populism." A century after the populist movement mobilized farmers and workers throughout the South and West, terrified the moneyed interests back East, and captured the Democratic presidential nomination for William Jennings Bryan, populism enjoys an ironic afterlife as a word used not by ordinary voters but by political activists and political commentators. While the label "populist" has been applied to anyone from Ronald Reagan to Jesse Jackson who tries to arouse popular anger against entrenched elites, its meaning to most Democratic activists is similar to that offered by political commentator Robert Kuttner: "an advocacy of the economic interests of ordinary working people."

"Populism" has some resonances, both wholesome and unwholesome, that are not completely captured by Kuttner's definition. A populist not only advocates the interests of the great majority of people but fights for them against other, more powerful interests (like the proverbial villains of big business, Wall Street, and the utility companies). Pugnaciousness is intrinsic to populism; perhaps Kuttner's definition should be amended to "an *aggressive* advocacy."

Furthermore, populism suggests an identification with people's values. While liberals and radicals sometimes sound like they want to change the way people live—not only to raise people's standards of living but to make them better people, whether they like it or not—populists present themselves as champions of the people's common sense and common decency. Dukakis's born-again populism was only partly convincing, not only because it was belated but because it seemed incomplete. Throughout the campaign, most people agreed that Dukakis supported their economic interests. But after the Bush campaign portrayed him as a liberal elitist who let violent criminals out of prison and kept the Pledge of Allegiance out of the classroom, most people were not convinced that Dukakis shared their values.

At its worst, populism produces leaders who are demagogic, divisive, or defeated because they celebrate just part of a diverse population, champion crank nostrums, and conjure up baroque conspiracy theories tinged with racial and religious bigotry. At its best, populism produces progressives, like the plebeian Harry Truman or the patrician Franklin D. Roosevelt, who can persuade people that they represent both their needs and their beliefs.

Populism may be the key to an effective political strategy for the Democratic party. The word "liberal" is hopelessly burdened with connotations that have nothing to do with promoting economic justice; indeed, voters are now more likely to identify liberalism with being soft on murderers than with making millionaires pay their fair share of taxes. The phrase "New Deal Democrat" sounds archaic in the 1990s, and suggests a reliance on cumbersome federal programs as ends in themselves. The label "social democrat" sounds European to political scholars and has no meaning at all for most Americans. Although populism is more or less a political in-word, it may best describe the style of leadership that many of us wish the Democrats would practice.

During the Mondale and Dukakis campaigns, I often talked to angry rank-and-file Democrats who had called headquarters and demanded to speak to the speechwriters. First I'd hear their understandable frustration: Why is Mondale talking about tax increases? Why isn't Dukakis fighting back? Why can't Dukakis sound like Roosevelt, or Truman, or Kennedy? But mainly, I'd hear their sense of loss, their nostalgia for the Democratic party's glory days, for the eloquence of its leaders from FDR to JFK, and for two kinds of Democrats who no longer seemed to be around —the "bread-and-butter" Democrat and the "tough" Democrat.

While the two phrases conjure up different images and issues, they are not mutually exclusive concepts, and both fit nicely under the populist umbrella. "Bread-and-butter" suggests what Democrats offered during the years they dominated national politics: a concern for the most basic needs of ordinary people, and the ability to promote an agenda that allows the economy to prosper so government could meet those needs. The rhetoric of bread-and-butter politics is down-to-earth; it doesn't deal in abstractions or technicalities. The Harry Truman of 1948, who talked about keeping food prices down and providing decent housing for veterans and their families, was a bread-and-butter Democrat. And Hubert Humphrey, when he boasted in 1968 that the Democrats had brought unemployment down to its lowest rate in fifteen years, was promoting himself as a bread-and-butter candidate. The "tough" Democrat was a species that seemed particularly endangered in the fall of 1988. When Michael Dukakis was accused of being soft on crime and defense, he seemed to justify the Republican charges by his refusal to counterpunch. The Democrats who called Dukakis headquarters spoke longingly of Truman and Kennedy, two who got respect on the world stage *and* gave the Republicans hell. But those men had served a quieter America, and a growing list of social anxieties in recent years has lent a new dimension to the "toughness" people want in their leaders: the willingness and the ability to protect people's safety in public places and to set standards for behavior in public institutions.

If those rank-and-file Democrats I spoke with could have put together their ideal candidate, that candidate would have been liberal on bread-and-butter issues, credible on foreign policy and defense, and tough enough to draw the line against behavior that defies common decency—from crime in the streets to insider trading on Wall Street. And for many of them (and for many of us on the staffs of both campaigns), the prototypical tough Democrat for the modern era was Robert Kennedy, who in the turbulent year of 1968 campaigned as a crime fighter and as an advocate of the poor and for civil rights.

So, while those worried callers didn't use the word "populist" (a role that fighting underdog Democrats have sought to play, with varying success), it was clear that they wanted a Democrat who would best fit the definition of that word.

Political buffs remember that Harry Truman won an upset victory in 1948 by touring the country in a railroad train, stopping at every community, large and small, and haranguing the crowds from an improvised podium on the caboose. Fewer people remember how shrewd and disciplined his strategy was. Truman didn't talk about his merits as an individual, didn't make personal attacks on his Republican rival Thomas E. Dewey, and didn't emphasize foreign policy and defense. Instead, he stressed the partisan differences between Democrats and Republicans. "The Democratic party," he said, "is the people's party." And he added (in what is now a somewhat ironic turn of phrase), "The Republican party is the party of the special interests, and it always has been and always will be."

The real genius of Truman's campaign was in his reminding voters that partisan differences were also class differences. The Republicans, he warned, were in cahoots with "Wall Street reactionaries" and the "gluttons of privilege." As for the Democrats, their philosophy was: "If the working people of this country are well off, whether they work in factories or on the farms, in offices or in stores, the country will get along all right."

To be sure, the electorate has changed enormously in the past forty years, but the Truman campaign still holds some lessons for today's Democrats. He faced a far more difficult task than merely reassembling the New Deal coalition, and he was a far different man from Roosevelt.

Truman was a product of the Democratic party as it had existed before it was reshaped by Al Smith and FDR who had organized the urban ethnics and inspired industrial unionism. A farm boy from a small town, Truman had built up a successful clothing business: the little guy who had made it. And his campaign was geared toward all the little guys of America, no matter what type of work they did, and against the big institutions that pushed the little guys around, no matter what those institutions were. So, although he was a man of the pre-New Deal era, Truman should not be dismissed by Democrats wondering how to address a post-New Deal America. Truman appealed to impulses that have been part of America since its founding—before the days of big government, big cities, and big labor—and these impulses remain strong today: Americans still believe that hard work should be rewarded and that ordinary men and women are the backbone of America and deserve a fair shake. Indeed, Republican strategists, recognizing the potency of Truman's rhetoric, have shrewdly used it in their attacks on the special interests. The man from Independence, Missouri, would have recognized that kind of talk.

The next Democratic presidential nominee, Adlai Stevenson, also came from a small town with a wonderfully resonant name—Libertyville, Illinois. But, as the literary critic Irving Howe observed, far from campaigning as a populist, Stevenson "did not speak in the name of the poor or the workers" and did not use "Truman's 'antiplutocrat' vocabulary."

Twice defeated by Dwight Eisenhower by landslide margins, Stevenson's campaigns nonetheless reveal what the Democratic party is and what it is not. In spite of his emphasis on foreign policy, post-election surveys showed that only 2 percent of Stevenson's supporters voted for him because of his foreign policy expertise. Intriguingly, the polls found that most of those voting for him did so because they believed that the Democratic party was on their side on domestic issues—the very issues his campaign seemed to be avoiding. These people were really voting for Truman or Roosevelt, not Stevenson himself, and even though that kind of Democrat wasn't on the ballot in 1952 and '56, economic issues were still at the heart of the Democratic party's appeal.

John F. Kennedy had a charismatic personality and a special appeal to Catholic voters, but the decisive factor in his election may also have been the traditional appeals of the party itself, whether he made them or not. Post-election polling showed that, in spite of Kennedy's discussion of the "missile gap" and communism, voters who cited foreign policy as the major issue supported Nixon. However, Kennedy won by two-to-one among those whose chief concern was domestic economic policy and by five-to-one among those specifically concerned with unemployment. Clearly, Kennedy's "we can do better" theme was most resonant when applied to bread-and-butter issues.

In his 1964 campaign against Barry Goldwater, whom most people perceived as a right-wing extremist, Lyndon Johnson enjoyed the support of moderate Republicans and corporate chieftains. While understanding that he couldn't bash big business and Wall Street when they were in his corner, Johnson realized that he could—and he did—embrace the little guys. Typical of his campaign was this nationally televised talk in which Johnson attacked "those" (Goldwater) who would get rid of government programs that help ordinary citizens:

> We are now told that we, the people, acting through government should withdraw from education, from public power, from agriculture, from urban renewal and from a host of other vital programs . . . strip labor unions of many of their gains, and terminate all farm subsidies. Too many have worked too long and too hard to let this happen now.

Four years later, when a month before the election Democratic candidate Hubert Humphrey found himself trailing Richard Nixon by twelve points, Victor Fingerhut, one of the campaign's pollsters, sent a memo to its high command advocating a strategy that concentrated on partisan differences on economic issues, particularly on which party fights for working people. He advised de-emphasizing everything else from civil rights to the Vietnam War to the personalities of the two candidates (despite the fact that Humphrey was more likable than the brooding Nixon).

In the final weeks of the campaign, Humphrey took Fingerhut's advice and began echoing Truman in a passionately populist stump speech:

"What has Richard Nixon ever done for old folks?

"What has Richard Nixon ever done for schools?

"What has Richard Nixon ever done for workingmen?

"So what are you going to do for Richard Nixon?"

To which the crowd shouted, "Nothing!"

And, he reminded audiences that "our Republican friends have fought every piece of social legislation that has benefitted this country."

By Election Day, Humphrey had so narrowed the margin that he lost by only seven-tenths of a percentage point. By some estimates, Humphrey had gained eight million votes in the final three weeks of the campaign.

George McGovern, the party's nominee in 1972, has been described as a "prairie populist." Yet he disregarded Humphrey's advice to champion "the little guys against the big guys," and instead stressed his opposition to the Vietnam War, his concern about the Nixon administration's corruption, and his own support for school busing to promote racial integration. While Humphrey spent the home stretch of his campaign sounding like a New Deal populist, McGovern closed out his race sounding like an Old Testament prophet, urging Americans to "change those things in our national heritage which turned us astray." He lost to Nixon by a record-setting twenty-three points.

By 1976, in the aftermath of the Watergate scandal, the country was ready for a prophet who combined Old Testament anger and New Testament mercy. Unlike McGovern, who suggested the people themselves had gone "astray," Jimmy Carter campaigned on the premise that a virtuous people had been betrayed by corrupt elites. His acceptance speech included some of the most resonantly populist rhetoric in contemporary politics:

> Too many have had to suffer at the hands of a political and economic elite. . . . When unemployment prevails, they never stand in line looking for a job. When deprivation results from a confused and bewildering welfare system, they never do without food or clothing or a place to sleep. When the public schools are inferior or torn by strife, their children go to exclusive private schools. And when the bureaucracy is bloated and confused, the powerful always manage to discover and occupy niches of special influence and privilege. An unfair tax structure serves their needs. And tight secrecy always seems to prevent reform.

Carter's appeal was masterful because it combined the more mainstream elements of the populisms of the Left and the Right. Liberals heard Carter bemoaning unemployment, poverty, and government secrecy. But alienated working-class and middle-class voters heard Carter voicing their resentments. "Public schools torn by strife" sounded like a reference to the school busing controversy, and the attack on elitists who send their kids to "exclusive private schools" was an effective jab at "limousine liberals" insulated from the consequences of their pieties. Adding the word "exclusive" was particularly shrewd because it made clear that Carter wasn't talking about parochial schools, yeshivas, or other places where good Democrats might send their kids.

Indeed, the Jimmy Carter of 1976 was a more effective populist than Hubert Humphrey had been in 1968. Unlike Humphrey, Carter understood that people resented social engineering by big government as much as they resented the economic machinations of big business. A populist of values as well as interests, Carter presented himself as a tolerant social conservative, a born-again Christian who believed that the civil-rights movement had redeemed his native South, a small-business man from a small town, a man of high moral standards whose youthful aides posed for pictures in the music tabloid *Rolling Stone.* Jimmy Carter was a man of the people for the America of 1976, the year when rock-and-roll fused with country-and-western.

When Carter faced the voters in 1980, it was not as a shrewd populist but as a failed president. With the Soviets invading Afghanistan and American hostages held in Iran, Carter's foreign policy was a failure and, with inflation and unemployment on the rise, it was those with modest incomes and meager bank balances who were hurting the most. And Carter hadn't delivered on his populist promises: national health insurance, tax reform to help the middle class, and welfare reform to help people get off public aid and into the work force.

Carter's last pitch came one hour before midnight on the eve of Election Day, when he told a rally in Seattle:

> I'm proud to be a Democrat because I believe in the heritage and mission of the Democratic party. . . . Every great advance . . . in the nation, in the private lives of our citizens for the last half-century, from collective bargaining to the minimum wage, from social security to Medicare, every single one has been made possible by Democrats over the opposition of Republicans.

But his appeal came too late. Unlike other Democratic presidents from FDR through LBJ, Carter hadn't produced a single "great advance" in the lives of most Americans. Indeed, his administration had broken the main promise of the Democratic party since the New Deal: to use the full powers of the federal government to protect the people from economic hardship.

★ UNILATERAL RHETORICAL DISARMAMENT

In 1984, the man who had been Carter's vice president, Walter Mondale, was burdened by conflicting symbolism in his futile pursuit of the presidency. A Minnesotan, Mondale's politics were shaped under the tutelage of Hubert Humphrey and the Democratic Farmer-Labor party. With union support, he won the Democratic nomination in a hard-fought campaign.

Yet, when I joined his campaign in late August, I was struck by how few of his campaign staffers had any connection with the unions or with grass-roots politics. Instead, Mondale's headquarters, on the outskirts of Washington's fashionable Georgetown neighborhood, was filled with former staffers for the Carter administration, some of whom had joined centrist think tanks like the Brookings Institution. And, just as he clinched the nomination, Mondale's campaign took a turn, suggesting that he was now taking his cues from the Brookings Institution, not the Bricklayers Union.

While it has become conventional wisdom that Mondale's landslide defeat was a repudiation of "New Deal liberalism," this is a misreading of the real message of the 1984 campaign.

Mondale had won the nomination campaigning as a bread-and-butter liberal — despite carrying the baggage of the unpopular Carter administration, in spite of such charismatic opponents as Gary Hart and Jesse Jackson, and in spite of most people's preference for the new and exciting over the old and familiar. His primary victory should have persuaded his staff of the potency of the theme of economic populism, which had defeated Hart. But like the Portuguese soldiers who converted to Marxism while fighting liberation movements in their African colonies and then tried to generate a similar movement back home in Portugal, Mondale's lieutenants became converts to Hart's post–New Deal politics and pursued a "yuppie strategy" in the general election. Partly, this may have happened because so many of Mondale's staffers were yuppies themselves; quite likely, many of their friends outside the campaign had been for Hart during the primaries. These staffers felt they had spent the primaries "pandering" to people like auto workers, steelworkers, and garment workers, and now, in the general election, they would try to win over their law school classmates.

Even more foolishly, they became fixated on winning the moderate Republican vote, on the theory that these affluent but tolerant voters were offended by Reagan's embrace of the religious right. Going against his own best instincts, for much of the summer and early fall Mondale pursued this fruitless strategy.

It had started with his acceptance speech at the Democratic convention, when Mondale said that after Carter's defeat:

I heard you. Our party heard you. We began asking you what our mistakes had been. . . . Look at our platform. There are no defense cuts that weaken our security; no business taxes that weaken our economy; no laundry lists that raid our treasury.

With that speech, Mondale accepted not only the Democratic presidential nomination but the Republican terms of debate as well. By implying that government programs were "laundry lists that raid our treasury" and progressive tax reform was "business taxes that weaken our economy," Mondale engaged in unilateral rhetorical disarmament before the battle had even begun. And his defensive tone also validated voters' suspicions that he was some kind of weakling.

In fact, the Mondale campaign's post-convention strategy reflected a bizarre misunderstanding of Democrats' strengths and vulnerabilities. Whatever the Carter administration's mistakes were, they weren't "laundry lists" for liberal causes or additional taxes on business. In spite of his promise of progressive tax reform, the only change in federal tax policy during the Carter administration was a capital-gains tax *cut.*

Mondale's speech didn't address the Carter administration's real failures—he just apologized for "mistakes." Indeed, his only solid promise was to maintain a strong national defense, although he found an extraordinarily weak way to say it.

What people remember most from Mondale's acceptance speech and his campaign was his classically Republican emphasis on cutting the deficit. His plan to balance the budget by raising taxes, starting with Americans making more than the median income ($25,000 a year for a family of four in 1984), was unpopulist and predictably unpopular, since it would have raised taxes on those who were the mainstays of Mondale's support in the primaries. Especially when coupled with his pledge not to raise business taxes (which many voters heard as a pledge not to raise taxes on the rich), Mondale's tax plan was hardly looked at favorably by working people. The leaders of traditional Democratic constituencies understood that this proposal was way out of line, but none had been asked for their advice, and they weren't informed ahead of time. In fact, the first union leaders heard about the tax plan was when they watched Mondale announce it on TV. They were horrified.

Things did not get any better after that. Several weeks into my stint as a speechwriter, I was called on the carpet by a campaign higher-up—a former New Jersey state official with no background in media—who represented himself as the "message czar." This message czar ordered me to rewrite my draft of a speech to the Machinists Union as a challenge to President Reagan—a where's-your-plan-to-cut-the-budget-deficit speech. Coming at a time when memories of the 1982 recession were still painful, the machine-tool industry was in the doldrums, and many machinists were out of work, the last thing union members wanted was to hear a lecture on the federal deficit.

By October, Mondale began to shift his rhetoric back to the populism of his primary campaign. He stopped talking about balancing the budget, instead, he attacked corporations that got away without paying any taxes at all, and called for protecting working people and retirees. Mondale gained five points, moving from 36 percent on October 23 to 41 percent at the ballot box on Election Day. His campaign was hardly a test of the effectiveness of traditional Democratic populism.

Four years later, Dukakis rode a roller coaster in his campaign, and populism produced his late rebound. After an upbeat convention, he led George Bush by a remarkable seventeen points, but his acceptance speech, with his now-famous declaration that the election was about "competence, not ideology," failed to define any terms of debate except that Dukakis was a better administrator than Bush. With a withering attack on the "Massachusetts miracle," Bush overtook Dukakis and had a six-point lead by their second debate. Several days after that debate, polls showed Bush leading 51-to-38. In the last three weeks of the campaign, however, Dukakis found populism, came out fighting, and gained eight points for a 46 percent finish.

From Hubert Humphrey in 1968 to Michael Dukakis in 1988, trailing Democrats have staged remarkable recoveries in the polls when they've adopted populism, even as a last resort. But they haven't gone far enough, fast enough, to win the presidency. For Democrats now pondering their political strategy, the questions seem to be: If last-minute populism is good for a last-minute "kick," how far could we go if we ran as populists from the start of the race? And if populism has its drawbacks as a Democratic identity, is there any other identity that's more effective?

★ THE 45 PERCENT SOLUTION?

Back when the Mondale high command was planning its strategy for the general election, the pollster Victor Fingerhut had a meeting with a Mondale campaign strategist and suggested that

Mondale take a populist stance right away and hammer away on issues like taxing the big corporations, protecting social security and Medicare, and getting tough on unfair trade policies practiced by countries like Japan.

"Those are labor issues," the campaign strategist told Fingerhut. "They will only get us up to forty-five percent of the vote, but no further."

"Well, let's use these issues to get us up to forty-five percent, and then we'll discuss the last five points," he replied. (Years later, Fingerhut commented, "You can't get to fifty percent without passing through forty-five percent first.")

Fingerhut's strategy was ignored until it was too late to make much difference. Four years later, Michael Dukakis, who went populist earlier than Mondale, got to 46 percent, five points ahead of Mondale.

The argument has been made that, despite Dukakis's showing, in the end populism is self-defeating for Democratic presidential candidates. In *Minority Party*, journalist Peter Brown maintains that the Democratic party has lost white middle-class support because of its close identification with black people, particularly poor blacks, and that economic populism will not bring white voters back. According to Brown, economic populism sounds too downscale for most middle-class people, and reminds them of things that make them uncomfortable—from poor urban folks to their own blue-collar roots. Therefore, Brown says, while Dukakis's last-minute "On Your Side" campaign theme consolidated the Democratic base, it also "confirmed the feelings of a much larger group of middle-class voters that he wasn't their type of guy."

While Brown's book is filled with data, he offers no hard evidence to show that Dukakis's belated populism offended more voters than it attracted. The closest Brown comes to supporting his point is to report that Dukakis's pollster, Tom Kiley, had insisted all along that the populist approach was an obsolete "forty-five percent strategy," ultimately doomed to defeat. Kiley, however, doesn't agree with Brown's description of his views or with Brown's analysis of the effectiveness of Dukakis's "On Your Side" message.

Kiley maintains that his skepticism about using a populist message in the 1988 campaign was largely based on his uncertainty about whether the low-key Dukakis could carry it off. Kiley himself believes in a populist approach, as long as it conveys a sense of national purpose and is tempered by the understanding that America is a predominantly middle-class society.

As for the effectiveness of the theme "On Your Side," he says, "It was the only way we make a respectable showing at all. It definitely helped us bounce back in those last few weeks. And it scared the Republicans." Kiley closely followed poll results during the home stretch of the campaign, and didn't see any indications that "On Your Side" scared off potential supporters.

This conclusion is supported by a survey of the news coverage of the final weeks of the campaign and the post-election analyses of the results.

For example, *Washington Post*/ABC News pollsters, with the help of the marketing firm Claritas, compiled data from interviews with voters who had just cast their ballots. The voters were organized into twelve demographic groups and the results were analyzed.

They found that none of these voters had become disenchanted with Dukakis during the three weeks before the election. Interestingly, his gains were greatest among the group called "mid-scale families," which the *Washington Post* described as "the demographic middle of middle America: solid citizens living in stable families." While they voted for Bush by a narrow margin, Dukakis's "uptick late in the campaign came mainly from this group who may have been attracted by his populist message."

Similarly, a *New York Times*/CBS News poll, conducted during the final days of the campaign, found that those who had made their decision in the two weeks before the election favored Dukakis by more than five to four and "voters who said they had made up their mind in the last few days were choosing Mr. Dukakis by an even larger margin."

That survey also showed that Dukakis had made substantial gains among voters earning from $12,500 to $35,000, while he suffered small losses among those with incomes greater than $50,000. This last reference is the only one I've seen that suggests Dukakis lost support. More important, this survey makes clear that "On Your Side" helped much more than it hurt. In fact, another post-election report, compiled by Democratic pollster Peter Hart and Republican pollster Linda Divall, suggests that Dukakis's last-minute populism was just about the only thing he had going for him.

So it looks like Peter Brown got it wrong: "On Your Side" was much more of a plus than a minus for Dukakis.

Of course, all this doesn't mean that if the 1988 campaign had gone on another week or so Dukakis would have won. A survey conducted two weeks after the election found that, by 52 to 26 percent, voters did prefer Dukakis on "helping the middle class and the average working person" but, unfortunately, they preferred Bush on almost everything else, particularly on handling "crime and law enforcement" (47 to 19 percent), "the federal budget deficit" (34 to 27 percent), and "national defense and military issues" (64 to 16 percent).

This survey suggests all the reasons why Dukakis lost: He had let a violent criminal out of prison; in the second debate he'd shown no emotion when asked what he'd do if his wife was raped and murdered; he had little experience in foreign policy and defense; he had looked silly riding in a tank. But there was no evidence that he'd hurt himself by declaring he stood with the people on Main Street, not the people on Easy Street.

Indeed, in just about every survey of political attitudes taken since the election, in fact, in most surveys taken since the Great Depression, the Democrats' strongest point (perhaps their only remaining strong point) is their traditional advocacy of average working families as opposed to the super-rich. It's an issue on which the Democratic party has always run even with, or better than, the GOP.

This raises two important points: One is that the identification of Democrats with working people's economic interests has such deep roots that even when the party has been seen as inactive or ineffective it can be revitalized on the strength of this issue alone. During the 1990 budget negotiations, congressional Democrats initially waffled on the issue of taxing millionaires rather than the middle class. But when they finally proposed this an NBC/*Wall Street Journal* poll found that they led Republicans, 47 to 18 percent, on the question of which party better represents the middle class. The second point (which may have some bearing on Democrats getting from 45 to 50 percent – plus one) is that perceptions about "who represents who" can spill over into perceptions of "who is more effective." Thus, before the budget debate, the NBC/*Wall Street Journal* poll found that Republicans led Democrats by ten points on the more general question of which party could manage the economy better. But afterward, Democrats led by 5 percent on the same question. (Significantly, Democrats win on this issue when it is perceived in populist terms, like it was after the budget debate, but lose when it is perceived in managerial terms, as it has been for most of the Reagan-Bush era.)

Perhaps the best case for making "On Your Side" the Democratic message is to consider the alternatives. Virtually every other Democratic identity offered during the past two decades has either failed – or relied on accidents of history. Dukakis's emphasis on good management was rejected by the voters and, in the end, by the candidate himself. Mondale's emphasis on fiscal responsibility was even more futile and, in the last weeks of his campaign, he returned to his roots as Hubert Humphrey's heir, not Jimmy Carter's. As for Carter, his appeal in 1976 as someone who would "never lie to you" depended on the special circumstances of Watergate, but the success of his populist appeals has more universal applications. George McGovern's definition of

Democrats as dovish (which haunts the party to this day) is a proven loser. So is the "rainbow coalition" concept of the Democratic party as a gathering of the "damned and disinherited" (in Jesse Jackson's phrase), which has been used by Republicans to scare the hell out of the middle class.

Economic populism may only bring national Democrats 45 percent of the vote, but except in unusually favorable situations (such as Watergate), there's no other theme that gets Democrats even that far. Indeed, there may not be any single definition of either political party that draws more than 50 percent of the national vote. For instance, during the Reagan-Bush era, Republicans presented themselves as hawkish, pro-business, and socially conservative. None of these identities, alone, can be counted on to attract more than half the electorate, but taken all together they won majorities for both Reagan and Bush.

The lesson here is not that Democrats should start pounding away at populist themes in the last *four* weeks of presidential campaigns; they should do it all year 'round. Democrats should start their national campaigns with the solid 45 percent of the vote that even critics of populism concede it attracts. Furthermore, it is the populist Democrats, with their aggressive style and substantive concern with bread-and-butter issues, who are best able to project themselves as tough on crime and credible on defense. Toughminded, bread-and-butter Democrats can go from 45 percent to 50 percent—plus one.

★ **POPULISM IS POPULAR**

Still, many are wary of a populist approach, and three common misconceptions need to be addressed.

■ **MYTH #1. *Populism is anachronistic.***
It has been argued that populism is a throwback to an era when most people worked in factories, foundries, or on farms, lived in big-city neighborhoods, and listened to their union delegates and

their Democratic precinct captains. Commentators like Peter Brown have said that populism is anachronistic now: More people work for Federal Express than U.S. Steel; more wear blue jeans on Saturday nights, not Monday mornings; and the gang from the old neighborhood has moved out to the suburbs.

If populism is presented entirely in industrial or agrarian terms, then the doubters are right. But even Michael Dukakis's last-minute populism had the potential to draw together the country's work force—it was the "computer operators" and the "lathe operators" against the "sharp operators on Wall Street."

Modernizing the rhetoric is necessary, but it's certainly not the only point. Populism has been around since before the industrial age, and it persists despite the fading of "smokestack America." Its premise does not rest on Marxist notions of class struggle but on prototypically American attitudes: Americans believe that self-reliant working people are the moral center of society. Americans believe that prosperity requires opportunities for people in the middle and at the bottom, not special privileges for people at the top. And, while Americans believe in private enterprise, they also fear that it favors the rich and the big corporations, and they believe that the rest of us need a strong voice in the political system.

For Democrats, the challenge is to be that voice—for today's Americans, not yesterday's.

■ MYTH #2. *Populism is divisive.*

Republican orators and conservative commentators can be counted on to condemn Democratic populists for "dividing America" and stirring up "the politics of envy," as George Bush did during the final days of the 1988 campaign. The shrillness of such attacks suggests that Democratic populism works—and Republicans know it. Certainly, they haven't forsworn first use of *their* populist arsenal. While attacking alleged Democratic demagogy, Republicans gleefully practice class-baiting of their own.

Thus, they attacked the Family and Medical Leave Act as a "yuppie benefit" for affluent couples who could afford unpaid leaves and, in an amazing bit of fancy footwork, Bush administration officials argued for eliminating the deductibility of state taxes from federal taxes on the grounds that this would tax the rich. There was a purpose to this high-sounding rhetoric. As George Bush's campaign manager, the late Lee Atwater, explained:

> [Y]ou have . . . two establishments. . . . If the people are thinking that the problem is that taxes are too high and government interferes too much, then we [Republicans] are doing our job. But, if they get to the point where they say the real problem is that rich people aren't paying taxes . . . the Democrats are in pretty good shape.

Typically, Republicans practice cultural, not economic, populism, as in 1988, when they branded Michael Dukakis an elitist from the "Harvard Yard boutique," and contrasted him with George Bush, the regular guy who loves country music and pork rinds. Recently, round one of Clarence Thomas's confirmation hearings for the Supreme Court found Republicans shrewdly manipulating populist symbols. They paraded ordinary Americans from outside official Washington as character witnesses in his behalf, while the liberal coalition ineptly made their case with official spokespeople from established institutions.

Curiously, in both sets of hearings, Thomas's critics allowed him to duck several issues that were potential populist flashpoints. The first round was supposed to focus on his constitutional philosophy. However, we never found out, for example, if his belief in "economic rights" for businesses lead him to oppose the minimum wage, job safety, and other protections for working people. Lost in round two was a basic fact about sexual harassment: It isn't just something men do to women, it's something bosses do to workers to keep them in their place, and Thomas was his accuser's boss. But its potential as a working women's issue was ignored, and liberals lost a battle of populist images.

Looking to November 1992, there's little suspense about

Republicans' populist hit list: members of the "permanent" Congress who have bounced checks and gotten free lunches; unionized bureaucrats in federal, state, and local governments; "politically correct" professors in ivory-tower "boutiques"; and liberal elitists, who didn't want Clarence Thomas to make the climb from Pin Point, Georgia, to the nation's highest court.

Rather than just stand there and take it, Democrats need to respond with populist appeals of their own.

■ MYTH #3. *Populism turns off swing voters.*

Commentators like Peter Brown have further suggested that populism hurts Democrats by reminding voters of the party's links to unpopular constituencies, particularly racial and ethnic minorities and welfare recipients.

In fact, only an inept populism can be mistaken for guilt-ridden limousine liberalism. An effective populism doesn't focus on the abject poor, but on the striving middle class. It stresses words and symbols, like "working people," "the middle class," and "family budgets," that counteract the racial, cultural, and class stereotypes right-wing populism exploits. It can make a compelling case against the Republicans' "top-down" appeal, but it can't do it with the old-fashioned Democratic "bottom-up" coalition. What Democrats should try to do is develop a more modern strategy, employing a progressive populism that builds a "middle-down" coalition.

Indeed, research suggests that the swing voters attracted to right-wing populism are potentially responsive to this progressive populism. Victor Fingerhut's research has shown that while Democrats who supported Ronald Reagan in 1980 and '84 favored his stands on foreign policy and social issues, they believed, just as firmly as those who stuck with Carter and Mondale, in raising taxes on the rich, defending social security and Medicare, limiting imports of foreign products, and establishing national health insurance.

Similarly, in a survey of Louisiana Democrats taken after

"former" Ku Klux Klansman David Duke's surprisingly strong 1990 race for United States senator, Garin/Hart Strategic Research found that, by a margin of 63 to 26 percent, these Democrats believed that the middle class is more severely squeezed by "tax breaks for the rich and unfair advantages for big business" than by "the cost of welfare programs for the poor and unfair advantages for minorities." And 57 percent faulted Democrats for paying too much attention to "the wealthy" and "big business," compared to only 27 percent who faulted Democrats for favoring "minorities" and "the poor."

Reagan Democrats—and even Duke Democrats—are still Democrats. And they're fervent populists. The national Democratic party can regain their loyalty not by muting its populism—but by turning up the volume.

The only danger lies in merely making more noise and creating more static. Populism needs to be loud, but more important, it should make a contemporary, not an anachronistic, sound. It should be a populism that sounds right for the post-urban, post-industrial middle class.

4
■ The Search for the Tough Democrat

Sometime during the final days of the 1988 campaign, Michael Dukakis's chief adviser tried to fire up his weary candidate. "Get tough," John Sasso told Dukakis. Trying to make sure Dukakis understood the urgency of this, Sasso started pounding the radiator next to him. "Get tough," he said.

"Get tough on what?" Dukakis asked. "Get tough on the radiator?"

That story (first told in *Newsweek*'s instant history of the campaign) sums up the Democratic party's identity crisis. And when party activists and sympathetic commentators write about what people find lacking in the national Democratic party, they use the word "toughness" more than any other.

"Tough liberals win, soft liberals lose," political analyst William Schneider wrote after the 1988 election. Seeming "soft" was a big reason why Dukakis, Mondale, McGovern, and Stevenson lost their presidential bids. Being tough was a big reason why Johnson, Kennedy, and Truman won theirs.

When people talk about toughness and softness, psycho-sexual metaphors are never far from the surface. Back in 1987, in a 107-page treatise, Democratic pollster Patrick Caddell warned that "we must face the sensitive question—Is the Democratic party perceived as a 'feminine' party—and the GOP a 'masculine' party—not only on policy issues but rather on characteristics such as 'strong,' 'tough,' 'forceful,' and 'leadership.' "

In 1991—after the Democrats had lost one more presidential

election and the Republican administration had won two more wars—syndicated columnist Christopher Matthews speculated that the Democrats had become the national "mommy," providing social services at the state and local levels, while the Republicans played the part of "daddy," defending the nation and managing the economy. (In fact, political analyst Elaine Ciulla Kamarck has said, only somewhat sardonically, that the 1992 presidential campaign "will be about testosterone level" and that the Democrats should nominate a "tough combative risk-taker.")

But without an understanding of the substance and the symbolism of toughness, Democrats will remain bewildered, wondering, as Dukakis did, where to target their toughness.

★ WHY DEMOCRATS SEEM SOFT

If Democrats are thought of as soft it's because there's a perception that they are unwilling or unable to defend America at home or abroad—from people like Saddam Hussein or Willie Horton.

Two weeks after the 1988 election, a Democratic polling firm found that George Bush had held a four-to-one advantage over Michael Dukakis on national defense and a greater than two-to-one advantage on crime and law enforcement issues. And those perceptions have only been bolstered by what has happened in America and the world during the first three years of George Bush's presidency: Most of Eastern Europe became free and the Cold War finally ended, with the failed Soviet coup and the subsequent collapse of the Communist party, all of which have seemed to vindicate the Reagan administration's tough stands on foreign policy and defense. After Saddam Hussein invaded Kuwait, proving there were still "bad guys" in the world, there was bipartisan support for protecting Saudi Arabia and imposing sanctions on Iraq. But when the issue was military action against Iraq, 45 of 56 Democratic senators and 180 of 266 Democratic representatives voted no. After the international coalition led by the United States won the war in 44 days, many Democrats said, sounding somewhat lame, "We'll never know if sanctions would have worked." Right after the Persian Gulf War, Republicans held a 68 to 17 percent advantage on the question of which party could maintain a strong national defense. Remarkably, it was the same four-to-one advantage Bush had held over Dukakis. And it would not be surprising if, on the national level, Republicans still enjoyed their two-to-one advantage on law enforcement after the war as well.

Understandably, defending national security and defending personal security occupy adjoining areas in the public mind. Both conjure up similar images and similar rhetoric. Thus, during the Cold War, hawks spoke of the Soviet Union as "a burglar testing every door on the floor, trying to find one that isn't locked." During the Persian Gulf War, just about everyone referred to Iraq's invasion of Kuwait as "rape." And from the fifties on, many have used the image of the United States as the "world's policeman."

Unfortunately, national Democrats seem less like police officers than they do social workers. So, a party whose purpose is to represent the less-privileged segments of society—and the gentler side of the human spirit—needs to display a rare order of toughmindedness to avoid seeming too soft.

Liberals believe that people are perfectible. And it's a belief the American experience has vindicated because we've taken the world's "teeming refuse" and made them into some of the most decent and productive people on earth. However, a too-optimistic view of human nature can veer off—or look like it's veering off—into thinking that there's no such thing as a bad person and refusing to recognize evil when it exists. By the same token, liberals also believe in the peaceful resolution of conflict—and what sensible person doesn't? But someone who seems to think sweet reason can resolve every dispute can look like an easy mark for those who believe that might makes right. Liberals also believe that ends don't always justify means, but an exaggerated concern for the purity of your means can prevent you from attaining those ends, or doing much at all.

Democrats don't need to repudiate liberalism or to deny (as Dukakis seemed to deny for much of his campaign) that they have any philosophy at all. What they need is to state clearly, as New York mayor David Dinkins did in his successful 1989 campaign, that they "know where to draw the line."

Declaring that you "know where to draw the line" has several implications. First, it acknowledges that there is a line between acceptable and unacceptable behavior. It implies that your philosophical principles are balanced by a reality principle, which recognizes things as they are as well as how they should be. Democrats need to demonstrate that they know there is evil in the world and that even innocent situations may become dangerous, in which case, if the power of persuasion fails, you are willing to use the persuasion of power. And if people believe that you know where to draw the line, they will trust you to protect them. A party that people don't trust to defend the national security and their personal security is a party with two strikes against it.

Aside from the perception that you can't trust Democrats to defend you, another one is that you can't trust Democrats to run things.

Running things requires a different dimension of toughness — the ability to give orders, set priorities, and often, cut budgets and fire people. Unsurprisingly, the language and the symbols that people use to talk about running things are almost as macho as those used to describe national defense and law enforcement. Managers are "take charge," "hands on," and "no nonsense." The image is of the brass plate on Harry Truman's desk, the one that said, "The buck stops here." Softness is out of place in the head office. You don't want a manager who can't make a decision, or who can't stand by a decision. Most of all, you don't want someone who can't say no.

And it is the perceived inability to say no that may best sum up voters' reservations about letting Democrats run the country.

Being dominated by special interests is a stereotype that has dogged the Democrats for at least a decade, even though Republicans are at least as beholden to their special interests.

There are reasons why the Democrats are stuck with that label and the Republicans aren't, and they may lie in the styles of the two sets of special interests, as well as the styles of the parties themselves. Democratic interest groups—labor and civil rights, for instance—make their demands in public and have the nasty habit of speaking forthrightly about what their members want. Republican special interests—corporate executives and wealthy investors—are more comfortable lobbying in private, and have the knack of claiming (with a straight face) that what's good for the Fortune 500 is good for America. The Republican party presents itself as America's team: undifferentiated Americans addressing the national interest. But the Democratic party looks like a feuding assortment of factions, caucuses, and tribes. Thus, when George Bush endorsed a cut in the capital-gains tax, the public hadn't seen him being pressured by a Wall Street caucus. But when Walter Mondale selected Geraldine Ferraro as his running mate, he looked like he had given in to the National Organization for Women, not like he'd just made history.

To beat the rap that we "can't run things," Democrats need to do more than boast of their "competence," as Dukakis did. Such claims are likely to arouse skepticism. As United Mine Workers president Richard Trumka said: "If I think I'm taking it on the chin, and you keep telling me how competent you are, then I just figure that if you take over, I'm just going to keep on taking it on the chin—competently." Moreover, as we learned with Dukakis, nobody in public office at any level has been right all the time, and making exaggerated claims merely narrows the debate to a close examination of your record.

So, as with the perception that Democrats can't defend society, refuting the perception that Democrats can't run things requires a fresh look at the Democrats' philosophy—and how that philosophy must be presented to the public.

As the party of social reform, Democrats stand for the idea that there are things wrong with society that need to be fixed. And Democrats should embrace that idea, not run away from it. But they should not give the impression that they're bound, philosophically or politically, never to say no to the organizations that represent society's underdogs. And, when Democrats do support those organizations, they should take a leaf from the Republicans and present themselves as representing the national interest, not a special interest. (Indeed, this is also good advice for the groups that tend to support Democrats; they should learn from their corporate counterparts and start explaining why what's good for them is good for America as well.)

So, the next time Democrats announce a public works or public service jobs program, they shouldn't make the presentation in front of a union audience—then it'll be viewed as just another boondoggle. The program should be announced to those whose needs for public facilities or services will be met by the jobs program. The broader public interest will be addressed and job creation will be seen as a bonus. Furthermore, while Democrats work towards social justice, they also need to demonstrate their concern that society's institutions are successful as well as fair. Yes, Democrats should be tough on those who pollute, discriminate, or exploit. But they need to convince the public that the success of businesses and public institutions will be enhanced by meeting higher social and environmental standards.

This brings us to another aspect of "toughness": the willing-- ness and the ability to set standards. And a reluctance to set standards is another accusation against Democrats.

As *Washington Post* political reporter E.J. Dionne, Jr., notes in his discussion of recent presidential elections:

> The problem was not that Dukakis (or for that matter, George McGovern) held personal values that were outside the mainstream; they did not. Rather, liberals were seen as unwilling to uphold a set of public values; they were plainly uneasy about using government

to promote, encourage, and—where violent crime was at stake—enforce the community's shared moral commitments.

Although violent crime is perhaps the most visible example of a society's failure to "enforce the community's shared moral commitments," there are many other examples of "liberals" (which overlaps with "Democrats") being unwilling or unable to set standards.

For instance, in the education debates of the past decade, liberals often took a stand for spending more money, but were unwilling to test students or teachers, set requirements for school curricula, expel incorrigible students, or require any kind of accountability for how that money was spent. While this last generalization does not apply to Democrats across the board, it is a reasonably accurate, if harsh, summary of what most voters thought they were hearing from many Democrats on the national scene.

Another example is the simple matter of civility in public places. When the issue was raised about whether unruly homeless people could loiter in public libraries or beg on the subways, civil libertarians often said that it was a constitutional issue, and that society shouldn't do anything to defend itself. But some leading Democratic mayors have understood the difference between toughminded liberalism and extreme libertarianism: David Dinkins of New York has removed squatters from a city park; Richard Daley of Chicago has assigned police officers to city schools; Maynard Jackson of Atlanta has prohibited panhandling in the city's downtown. But while national Democrats frequently seize the opportunity to stand in solidarity with the leaders of urban America, few if any, have praised these mayors for trying to keep their cities civil as well as safe.

It wouldn't be difficult for national Democrats to talk about enforcing civility in public places in ways that achieve a balance between toughminded and tenderhearted. After all, the wealthy send their kids to private schools, take taxis, and buy hardback books; it's the working class and the poor who need public schools, pub-

lic libraries, and public transportation. There are plenty of emotive stories Democrats could use to illustrate their point. Imagine
a garment worker going home after a hard day's work. She could
be the mother of a young Geraldine Ferraro or a young Colin
Powell (both of whose mothers were garment workers). Shouldn't
she be able to ride home unafraid of being menaced by someone
harassing her for money? Or a young James Baldwin, stopping off
at the local library on his way home from school. Shouldn't the
library be his oasis from the mean streets — not an extension of
them? Unfortunately, national Democrats rarely talk that way.
"Liberal Democrats are morbidly afraid of setting standards,"
concludes Tony Podesta, a former prosecuting attorney and
former president of People for the American Way.

This issue of standards often came up when I asked people
what they thought was wrong with the Democratic party. While
their feeling that the party lacks strong standards was not surprising, what very different people were saying about it *was* surprising. A leading television writer from Los Angeles, a Democratic
ward committeewoman from Chicago, the campaign manager for
the mayor of Chicago, and several liberal academicians and political analysts from Massachusetts — all told me that the Democratic
party is "too secular."

Most people I talked to don't want Democrats to switch sides
on such church-state issues as whether to allow organized prayer
in public schools. But they would like Democrats to recognize the
role religion plays in American life, to address people's sense of
a moral breakdown in society and, most of all, to make clear that
they *do* believe in absolute standards of right and wrong, for individuals as well as for society. As Democratic senator Joseph
Lieberman of Connecticut, an Orthodox Jew, said in an interview
with the conservative Heritage Foundation:

> I believe that people have enormous potential for good, that we are
> all touched by the Divine. But we're also all imperfect, and we have
> the capacity to do great evil. And part of the answer to that evil, ac-
> cording to my religion, is the role of law as an attempt to create or-

der . . . to express our best aspirations for ourselves and deter our worst instincts.

In many people's minds, secularism leads to softness, because someone who doesn't believe in God-given moral principles probably doesn't believe in absolute standards of right and wrong. And people who don't believe in those standards themselves won't be able to set standards for society. The Democrats who have managed to be both "liberal" and "tough," like Robert Kennedy, Jimmy Carter, and Mario Cuomo, have drawn upon their religious backgrounds to talk about right and wrong.

Finally, Democrats too often seem soft on yet another menace to America: their Republican opponents.

Michael Dukakis's presidential campaign has become a metaphor for the passivity of the Democratic party of the 1980s. When the Republicans started pummeling him, he didn't counterpunch, or even try to protect himself; he just stood there and took it. Americans love an underdog, but they have nothing but contempt for someone who won't even fight back. Linda Williams, a political analyst, remembers that after the 1988 election a cab driver in Boston started carrying on about how angry he was at Dukakis. "What he couldn't stand was that Dukakis let Bush take unanswered shots, not just at him but at the state of Massachusetts," Williams recalls. "He felt personally betrayed."

One reason why Democrats still dump on Dukakis is that his defensive crouch so closely resembles the party's posture for most of the eighties and early nineties. During President Reagan's first term, the party rarely offered an attack on, much less an alternative to, the administration's social and economic policies. The same has been true during most of President Bush's first term, prompting some folks to complain that the Dukakis campaign had never ended. From 1981 through 1990, there have only been three times when the opposition party has been an effective opposition: the defeat of the Bork nomination in 1987; the 1988 session of Congress that dared the president to veto its social legislation—from raising the minimum wage to requiring advance notice of plant closings; and the budget negotiations of 1990, when congressional Democrats finally challenged President Bush to raise taxes on millionaires, not the middle class.

The Democrats' aversion to political combat emerged once again during the confirmation hearings of Clarence Thomas to the Supreme Court. When allegations of sexual harassment against Thomas came out Democrats looked sneaky (they had declined to pursue the charges until someone leaked the story to the press) and weak—dragged reluctantly into battle only after women's groups had rightly raised hell. The hearings became a classic courtroom drama. Republicans on the Senate Judiciary Committee played a defense that looked like an offense, questioning the character of his accuser. But the Democrats didn't know whether to be prosecutors or judges, so they neither cross-examined Thomas effectively nor appeared to be judging him fairly.

The problem wasn't that Democrats wouldn't fight dirty; the problem was they wouldn't stand up and fight publicly, in full view of the American people. (Their behavior called to mind a malapropism attributed to John P. O'Brien, a machine politician who served briefly as mayor of New York early in the 1930s: "I will not be partial in this dispute, but neither will I be impartial.") Democratic senators seemed simultaneously insensitive to women's concerns but not manly enough to fight for what they believed. In the aftermath of the battle, the publisher and the editor of *National Minority Politics*, Willie A. Richardson and Gwenevere Daye, summed up what many people felt: "If you are in a fistfight, be it physical or ideological, whom would you want on your side—Republicans or Democrats?" Clearly, the answer was: the Republicans.

There may be structural reasons why Democrats show little taste for political combat in the national arena. Kept out of the White House for twenty of the past twenty-four years, the Democrats have settled for dominating Congress. And, in the psychic dichotomies of politics, if the executive is the hammer, the legislature is the anvil. A president proposes; Congress disposes. A president acts; Congress reacts.

Today, it's even less likely that a party based in Congress rather than the presidency will really stand up and fight on national issues. Both parties are dependent on campaign contributions, whether from wealthy donors, corporations, or political action committees. And since lobbyists are often from the same groups that contribute to their campaigns, congressmembers often look like they're responding to special interests, and frequently, that's just what they're doing. Unfortunately but unsurprisingly, congressmembers do tend to pay more attention to their contributors than their constituents.

★ A CONTACT SPORT

Locked out of the White House and hiding out on Capitol Hill, in statehouses, and city halls, Democrats probably can't help seeming soft. And ironically, the very revulsion against political rough-and-tumble that emerged in the aftermath of the 1988 campaign may, in fact, reinforce this softness, and encourage a replay of the attitudes that made the Dukakis candidacy a punching bag. (Like many who suffered through that campaign, I remember those attitudes all too well.) Now the danger is that the professors and policy experts, those who tend to advise presidential campaigns, may make political passivity a point of principle!

There's been a lot of discussion since 1988 about how to improve the conduct and coverage of political campaigning. Lord knows, there's a lot of room for improvement. (Of course, some real improvement could be made in campaign financing—by somehow reducing the dependency of candidates and political parties on large donations. For Democrats, this dependency has been especially harmful since their wealthy contributors don't want the populist economics Democrats espouse. Often, like the savings-and-loan operators, they want special favors; or, like some affluent liberals, they want a permissiveness on social issues, which mainstream voters don't want.) But amidst all the articles, reports, books, and conferences about how to improve campaigning itself, some sensible ideas have emerged. One of these would require television networks to provide free time during the final weeks of the campaign—perhaps five minutes on alternate nights—for the major parties' presidential candidates to speak directly to the voters. This might force the contenders to engage in a serious discussion of the issues, which was so lacking last time. After all, every other night they'd have to find something to talk about—for a full five minutes.

But where the discussion has gotten dreamy, and potentially dangerous for those political practitioners who take it seriously (and I'm afraid only liberals would take it seriously), has been the suggestion that something can or should be done to make presidential politics less combative. Newspaper columnists, university professors, and stray political consultants have taken turns deploring the nasty things that candidates say about each other in 30-second paid advertisements or the even shorter soundbites that appear on the nightly news. Unless the networks themselves refuse to accept political advertising or decide to lengthen the news segments they broadcast during presidential campaigns, the only alternative to those sleazy spots and soundbites is to *require* that the networks provide some free air time. And Democrats should fight for that "five-minute fix" (a phrase coined by *Washington Post* reporter Paul Taylor), not as pacifists squeamish about political combat but as populists who want more information for the people and less influence for the big-money types.

What Democrats shouldn't do is accept the fashionable notion that there's something wrong with attacking your opponent, or with doing it in a 30-second spot or a snappy soundbite. The fact is: Political debate has always been about attacking your opponent. And it's always been about ideas that can be reduced to short sentences and compelling symbols. All that's changed are the media through which these ideas are communicated. Indeed, those who bemoan these spots would do well to remember that the same number of words—no more, no less—made up the headline of the handbill or the tabloid news story that, decades ago, were major media for political communications. In those days, political leaders were able to communicate compelling ideas: Lincoln's warning that the Union could not survive "half-slave and half-free"; Teddy Roosevelt's promise to "bust the trusts"; and FDR's "New Deal." These phrases succinctly framed the issues, and an electorate less educated than today's understood those issues and made its choices.

Of all the chroniclers of the 1988 campaign, only E.J. Dionne, Jr., got beyond the conventional pieties on the inherent evils of the attack ads. "The problem is not the spots themselves," Dionne wrote, "but what is said in them." However, even a commentator as sophisticated as Dionne missed the point about the part "issues" play in political debate:

> [P]olitics these days is not about finding solutions. It is about discovering postures that offer short-term political benefits. We give the game away when we talk about "issues," not "problems." Problems are solved; issues are merely what politicians use to divide the citizenry and advance themselves.

But it would be more accurate to say that issues are those subjects about which political parties and political leaders disagree, and these have always been the currency of political debate. What better way for voters to choose among competing candidates than by judging their views on the issues and the skill with which they defend those views? Asked to offer an example from the finest moments in American politics, most people wouldn't cite some candidate's position paper on how to solve some problem. They'd most likely point to Lincoln and Douglas—or Kennedy and Nixon—debating the issues of their times.

Democrats need to understand that the best issue is one where they can *take issue* with someone—Republican opponents, privileged special interests, or even the liberal shibboleths that

Democrats need to shuck off. Controversy is what generates news coverage; controversy is what gets the public's attention. And getting the public's attention is the only way to move public opinion, which decides elections. Looking back, the Dukakis campaign got very little news coverage when we offered a program on home ownership, science education, or some other subject where we sketched out our views but failed to criticize Bush. But Dukakis got great coverage, got applause, and moved up in the polls when he called Bush's proposal to cut capital-gains taxes a bonanza for the rich. And by doing so, Dukakis gave voters a much better idea of the differences between him and Bush than when he offered more detailed, but less newsworthy, proposals for problem-solving. Certainly, a campaign's position papers do play an important part in political debate, but it's an illusion that political battles can be fought with ten-point programs. Furthermore, position papers only benefit by including substantive criticisms of the opponent's record and programs.

And Democrats shouldn't cry foul whenever Republicans hit them anywhere near the belt. For a party that's already perceived as too soft to defend itself—much less defend America—the last thing Democrats need is to sound like wimps and whiners. And, for all the bemoaning of recent Republican campaign tactics, there's little evidence that voters believe these were unusually unfair. In a national survey taken just before the election, Democratic pollster Victor Fingerhut found that "by a margin of 66–25 percent," the soft Bush voters and the undecideds believed that "the Democratic campaign has been just as dirty as the Republican campaign." So, far from summoning the media's "campaign cops" to defend them against Republican attacks, Democrats should counterpunch and, indeed, should try to beat Republicans to the punch.

Today's Democrats, in particular, need to remember two things: First, as vice presidential candidate Lloyd Bentsen kept telling the Dukakis campaign, American politics is, and always has been, "a contact sport." American culture is combative (football outdraws tennis on TV), and Americans expect candidates to attack each other's records, programs, and philosophies—actively and aggressively. Folks figure, not unreasonably, that a candidate who can't take the heat of campaigning probably can't withstand the rigors of the presidency.

People want politicians to *debate*, but not *defame* each other. After hearing ad nauseam about the personal habits of Gary Hart, Edward Kennedy, John Tower, Clarence Thomas, and other public figures, people are fed up. A lack of passionate debate on the issues leaves a vacuum, which is often filled with personal attacks, and voters are aware of this.

Following the debacle of 1988, many Democrats did display a determination to play politics as a contact sport. For instance, in the 1989 New Jersey gubernatorial election, Democratic candidate Jim Florio was attacked for failing to support a ban on flagburning. A navy veteran, Florio surrounded himself with fellow veterans, including a former prisoner of war, and held a news conference at the Trenton War Memorial. Addressing his Republican rival, Florio said, "If you are challenging my patriotism, come out and say it like a man." And in his 1990 Senate campaign, Democrat Tom Harkin of Iowa, a Vietnam-era veteran, had a strong response to a Republican challenger who attacked him on flagburning but who'd never served in the military himself. "Before you wrap yourself in your country's flag," Harkin declared, "you should be willing to wear your country's uniform."

Among the most remarkable examples of the advantages of beating your opponent to the punch is the recent experience of Frank Annunzio, a thirteen-term Democratic congressman from Chicago. Aged 75, Annunzio faced a formidable challenge from Republican Walter Dudycz, a right-wing populist who'd won a seat in the state senate by appealing to middle-class voters angered by high taxes and permissive social policies. To many observers, Annunzio, who'd entered politics as a labor organizer, looked like an anachronism from an earlier era—and an easy mark for a more vigorous challenger who knew how to play on today's social and racial resentments.

But Annunzio showed that he had some fight left. With the help of a few campaign consultants, Annunzio fought back. One Annunzio campaign brochure featured photos of a revolver, a razor blade, and some suspicious white powder under a headline reading "Drugs and Guns." Inside, it pointed out that Dudycz had voted against drug education programs, opposed gun control, and accepted campaign money from the National Rifle Association. Another flier asked, "Why are your property taxes so high?" and charged that Dudycz was a "ghost worker" in the county sheriff's department, collecting paychecks for days when he was also claiming per diems as a state legislator. Yet another piece showed an elderly women being "EVICTED!" from a nursing home and charged that Dudycz had voted against health-care cost controls and stricter nursing home regulations. Annunzio won, proving that some Democrats still know how to fight back—and how to talk to anxious middle-class voters.

★ TOUGHNESS: STYLE AND SUBSTANCE

The Democrats' search for toughness didn't start in the aftermath of 1988. For the past four decades, Democrats have sought that image, and their prototype has been the plain-spoken and decisive Harry Truman, for whom the style and the substance of toughness were inseparable. A gleeful and pugnacious campaigner, Truman made toughness his trademark during the 1948 election.

A staunch anticommunist, Truman welcomed the opposition of "Wallace and the Communists" when Henry Wallace, who sought an accommodation with the Soviets, ran on a third-party ticket. When Southern Democrats protested a platform plank endorsing civil rights, Truman let the "Dixiecrats" leave the party. He called the Republican-dominated Congress "do-nothing," and denounced Wall Street and big business before crowds in the industrial heartland and the farm belt. Harry gave 'em all hell and beat his heavily favored Republican opponent, Thomas E. Dewey.

In contrast, the prototypical soft Democrat was the party's next presidential nominee, Adlai Stevenson, a patrician intellectual. Against the beloved "Ike," Supreme Allied Commander in World War II, anyone would have had an uphill battle, but Stevenson's problem was that he wouldn't fight at all. Critic Irving Howe observed that even at the height of his following, Stevenson lacked the joy of battle and shunned the party's populist message, and therefore found it difficult to rouse blue-collar voters. Nobody yelled "Give 'em hell!" because he wouldn't even give 'em heck. Indeed, a young political operative named Robert Kennedy, who was traveling with Stevenson in 1956, was so appalled by his candidate's indecisiveness that he voted for Eisenhower.

Stevenson was the forerunner of a new breed of liberal that runs the risk of seeming bloodless, if not gutless. And partly in reaction to him, the Democrats of the Kennedy-Johnson era prided themselves on their toughness. For the war hero John Kennedy and the consummate political professional Lyndon Johnson, toughness was second nature, and it was revealed in their determination to contain communism. Still, they were wary of Stevenson's legacy, and they developed rhetorical styles to reinforce their toughness. Kennedy's best-remembered oratory consists of simple words in simple declarative sentences, with the eloquence coming from his characteristic device of turning sentences and phrases upside down. Thus: "Ask not what your country can do for you. Ask what you can do for your country." And: "We shall not negotiate out of fear. But we shall not fear to negotiate."

As for Johnson, even Kennedy's clipped, staccato style wasn't plain enough. Richard Goodwin, a speechwriter for both presidents, has said that Johnson's preference was for "simple, straightforward, unadorned language."

The endless, fruitless war in Vietnam gave tough-minded liberalism a bad name, and for a time, the generation of Democratic activists who entered politics in opposition to the war preferred candidates whose personal styles, as well as their views, seemed the opposite of Johnson's and Kennedy's conspicuous toughness. Anti-war presidential contenders Eugene McCarthy (who had the guts to challenge a president from his own party) and George McGovern (a bomber pilot in World War II) showed courage in opposing the war. But, as Clifford Adelman notes in *No Loaves, No Parables,* his study of the liberal political rhetoric of the late sixties and early seventies, McCarthy, McGovern, and their speechwriters favored a style that stereotyped them as soft: long words, lengthy sentences, passive construction, and an aversion to aggressive, active verbs.

At that time, the one exception was Robert Kennedy, who argued against the war with the same clipped cadences that his elder brother had used to commit America to the struggle against communism. But Kennedy also capitalized on his career as a tough senate investigator and even tougher attorney general, who'd probed and prosecuted organized crime. This helped Kennedy win blue-collar support in the 1968 presidential primaries.

However, by the early seventies, Democrats were being attacked as unpatriotic and "soft on crime." Journalist Sidney Blumenthal has noted that the seventies became "the age of toughness," and Democrats scrambled to find symbols and slogans to match their Republican rivals. Blumenthal interviewed Democratic political consultant David Garth, whose clients have included governors Hugh Carey of New York and Dan Walker of Illinois, California senator John Tunney, and mayors Tom Bradley of Los Angeles and John Lindsay and Ed Koch of New York. Garth said:

> What happened with toughness was that we got involved with a lot of campaigns in 1970 when the right wing was coming on very hard on law and order. We came up with the idea of using the word tough to provide an answer to the right-wing attack. We started to use the word tough in our commercials.

Garth cleverly constructed Democratic toughness by max-
imizing the party's strong point—fighting the fat cats—and
minimizing its weakness—seeming soft on crime and defense. His
slogans included: "It's the second toughest job in America" (for
Lindsay) and "The big boys have enough friends. You need a
fighter in your corner" (tailor-made for Tunney, son of a heavy-
weight champion).

At the tail end of the seventies, the newly elected Democratic
president, Jimmy Carter, metamorphosed from tough to soft in
full view of an increasingly contemptuous country. Carter's election campaign had brilliantly balanced the rhetoric and symbolism
of toughness and softness. A nuclear physicist (so he hinted) and
a naval officer, he seemed tough enough to defend America. A
peanut farmer, small-business man, and a cost-cutting former
governor, he seemed tough enough to run a government and han-
dle the economy. And Carter was a born-again Christian, so he
seemed both tough enough to set standards and soft enough to
"translate love into simple justice."

But by 1980, with the cost of living soaring, the Soviets invading Afghanistan, and Iranian extremists holding American
hostages, Carter's toughness was forgotten and his softness was
despised. Voters yearned for a strong leader and thought they'd
found one in Ronald Reagan. And as Democrats ruefully con-
ceded by decade's end—and while Reagan, himself, was worri-
some because he lacked many important qualities—nobody
doubted the toughness of the man who'd survived an assassin's
bullet, busted the air traffic controllers union, tamed inflation, and
won the Cold War.

★ THE SHORT UNHAPPY LIVES OF SOME SEMI-TOUGH
DEMOCRATS

During the Reagan-Bush era, as Democrats questioned the defense buildup, opposed military action in Grenada, Panama, and
Kuwait, and supported social programs against budget cuts, they

found themselves increasingly on the "soft" side of policy debates (honorable stands, but unfortunately, stereotypically soft).

Soft in substance, Democrats took increasingly desperate measures to seem tough in style. Those who took the wisest (and most effective) course updated the slogans of the seventies and presented themselves as populists who combined strength and sensitivity. Frequently, the most skillful candidates were women, who knew they had to combat stereotypes based on gender as well as partisanship. In 1990, former San Francisco mayor Dianne Feinstein ran a strong race for governor of California, using the slogan "Tough and caring." One effective television spot showed her taking charge as mayor after the assassination of her predecessor. Another showed her speaking in support of the death penalty. That same year, Ann Richards was elected governor of Texas after a campaign in which she refused to be out-toughed by rivals who stressed their support of the death penalty for murderers and work gangs for drug offenders.

However, other Democrats were so desperate to prove their political manhood that they were led to acts of foolish, sometimes fatal, machismo. The Mondale campaign in the summer of 1984 was a perfect example. During the primaries, Mondale had been unfairly labeled as an overcautious, uncharismatic organization man—in short, a wimp. In fact, Mondale had shown real courage in the Senate as a supporter of school integration, child care, and farmworkers' rights. He'd shown guts and endurance in winning the nomination after Gary Hart had almost knocked him out in the New Hampshire primary. But the symbolism of Mondale's candidacy—he was the choice of the Democrats' "special interests" and a loyal supporter of Hubert Humphrey and Jimmy Carter—did not suggest courage.

Then, once he was the nominee, the supposedly cautious Mondale embarked on a risky, almost reckless, strategy. To my mind, one of his risks was wise while the other two were foolish. First, he selected as his running mate the first woman ever nominated by a national party—a decision that made history and expanded people's sense of what's possible in America. Then in his acceptance speech, he promised to raise taxes, a position that haunted him for the remainder of the campaign. Next, for most of July and August he campaigned *not* in the relatively friendly territory of the Northeast and the Midwest, but in the South and the Southwest, Reagan's stronghold. Then, he revealed that his tax increase plan would start with families earning $25,000 a year. Mondale had gotten tough, all right—on those people who should have been his strongest supporters!

By early fall, Mondale was headed for his fate. "With Mondale, it was a self-inflicted wound at every level," Democratic political consultant Robert Shrum said after the campaign. "It wasn't a wound, it was stigmata." Sometime in mid-September, the campaign finally began to reach the sensible conclusion that if Mondale must be a martyr, let it be for a better cause than balancing the budget. Mondale eased off talking about his tax plan and started, in the time-honored Democratic way, attacking Reagan for giving tax breaks to the rich.

But at least one leading Democrat seemed to envy Mondale's martyrdom. In 1988, former Arizona governor Bruce Babbitt based his primary campaign on a call for a tax increase. Mondale's tax proposal had been basically progressive (he wanted big tax increases for the wealthiest families, but he never recovered from headlines reporting that he'd impose small increases on families making as little as $25,000). But Babbitt barely mentioned fairness at all; his message was what a brave man he was, and he'd ask his audiences to "stand up" and show their support for a tax increase. In a debate with other primary candidates, he asked if they had the guts to "stand up" with him. When they didn't, it proved to his satisfaction, if not the voters', that he was the only stand-up guy in the race. Campaigning as the last honest man, Babbitt became the favorite of the traveling press and some sympathetic commentators—but not the favorite of Iowa and New

Hampshire Democrats. He finished near the bottom in both states—and sat down in February.

Then there's the case of New Jersey governor Jim Florio. Here is one political leader who shouldn't have to prove how tough he is. A veteran, son of a shipyard worker, and former amateur boxer, Florio is a living reminder of the simpler, happier days when Democrats were the tough guys and Republicans were the "effete snobs." Elected in a landslide, he courageously and commendably went to work tackling the problems left by his Republican predecessor. In one legislative session, Florio pushed through an agenda that might have been four years' work for a less aggressively ambitious governor: lower insurance rates, strict gun control, redistribution of state education funds from the wealthier to the poorer school districts, and (more dangerously) a Mondale-style tax increase that started with the middle class but rose rapidly for higher-income households.

As journalist John Judis has observed, Florio seemed the model of the "tough liberal." He was decisive, effective, and seemingly fearless in confronting such powerful interests as insurance companies, the gun lobby, and the teachers' association. And yet, while he must have communicated his courage, he failed to make his case for tax increases and school-funding reform. (Maybe he couldn't have sold those policies anyway, but it seemed like he cared more about pushing them through than promoting them.) By the fall of 1990, the voters were so angry at Florio that he was blamed for the near-defeat of the state's popular Democratic senator, Bill Bradley. And in the fall of 1991, Democratic candidates for the New Jersey state legislature were defeated, and Florio faced a Republican-dominated legislature in 1992.

You don't have to be David Garth to imagine how Florio could run for re-election as "A Governor with Guts, Who Made the Tough Decisions and Took the Heat." Maybe he'll win—people like a fighting underdog. But still, his experience suggests that pugnacity alone isn't enough.

★ WHO EVER HEARD OF A SOFT POPULIST?

For Democrats desperately seeking to project their toughness, the first part of the prescription is populism. Liberals seem soft, but populists seem tough. As Dukakis learned in 1988 (or as he may have understood to begin with, since he shunned the word *liberal*), liberalism no longer means Medicare, social security, and the GI Bill. Instead, a liberal has come to resemble the portrait the Bush campaign painted of Dukakis: someone who would put violent criminals back on the streets, oppose needed defense systems, and keep the Pledge of Allegiance out of the classroom. The primary meaning of a liberal has become cultural, and it's now defined as one who is overtolerant of antisocial behavior and hostile toward mainstream values. While a liberal has traditionally been seen as a supporter of the economic interests of ordinary people, even that idea has been turned around. Now, the word *liberal*, in its economic sense, is beginning to resemble its old-fashioned dictionary definition, "the quality of generosity," meaning generosity with money, mostly *other* people's money. As a former union activist from Canarsie (a middle-class neighborhood in Brooklyn) told sociologist Jonathan Rieder: "A liberal is a giveaway: too much, too fast, too easy."

In communities like Canarsie, liberalism is perceived as a creed for the elite. The "limousine liberal" is someone wealthy enough to send his tax money to the poor, guilt-ridden enough to want to send the poor *your* money, too, and privileged enough to be insulated from what you're up against — street crime, school busing, and hiring quotas in a stagnant job market. Thus, "liberalism" means softness — soft policies from people who have soft lives.

But if liberals are soft, populists are not. And reclaiming their populist tradition can save liberals from charges of softness in several ways.

First, of all the traditional postures of liberalism, its strongest stance has always been in its populist identification with the causes of the working man and woman, the productive middle class, and the deserving poor. To the extent that Democrats are still perceived as people in touch with the harsher realities of life, they aren't seen as too soft to survive in this cruel world. Thus, Daniel Patrick Moynihan claims that, more than most liberal intellectuals in the Kennedy administration, he understood the dangers of the world because he'd grown up in the gritty Manhattan neighborhood of Hell's Kitchen. When you come from a place called Hell's Kitchen, people believe you understand that there's evil in the world.

Second, populism is in the cultural mainstream. It celebrates people who work hard and support their families, who are looking for a fair shake, not a special favor. These are the very standards Democrats need to advocate and be willing to set for society.

Next, populism tells a story about villains, as well as heroes. Populists don't just stick up for ordinary folks; they stand up to powerful special interests: wealthy people who don't pay taxes, greedy corporations that poison the air and water, heartless utility companies that cut off elderly customers' gas and electricity. To combat the perception that Democrats don't set standards of right and wrong, populist Democrats can demonstrate their standards by condemning crime in corporate suites as well as violent crime in the streets.

Finally, the populist style is inherently aggressive. The ultimate populist parable is David and Goliath: The little guy takes on the big guy—and wins. Indeed, while liberalism connotes caring for casualties, populism suggests fighting back. (And, as David Garth pointed out, populist political slogans almost always use a word like tough or fight.)

During the final weeks of the last few presidential elections, while the Democratic nominees staggered toward defeat, pollster Victor Fingerhut asked voters: "If Dukakis [or Mondale in 1984, or Carter in 1980] were more of a traditional Democrat in the tradition of Roosevelt, Truman, and Kennedy, fighting for working people, would you be more inclined to vote for him?" Not surprisingly, each year overwhelming numbers of voters said, yes, they'd prefer the "fighting" Democrat to the current model.

Fingerhut, who has close ties to the labor movement, concludes — correctly, I think — that his survey results show that voters would prefer Democratic presidential candidates to take a more populist approach. But voters also want Democrats to be tougher on foreign policy, defense, social issues, and in their campaign styles as well. Toughness and populism can reinforce each other. Think about it. It's easy to imagine a "soft liberal." But isn't a soft populist as rare as a wimp from Hell's Kitchen?

★ "THE TOUGH GUY WITH A BIG HEART"

Americans don't want one-dimensional leaders who are all toughness, no tenderness. All this talk about toughness is because it's the quality people miss most in the Democrats, not the only thing people want in a president. In fact, voters are just as likely to reject political leaders for being *too* tough. In 1964, Republican presidential candidate Barry Goldwater criticized social security before senior citizens in New Hampshire, and the Tennessee Valley Authority in front of an audience in Tennessee. That was foolish, but he also talked about lobbing an atomic bomb into the men's room of the Kremlin and sawing off the Eastern seaboard. None of that scored him any points; it just scared people half to death.

Then, on the Democratic side, there's Jim Florio. He's probably shed the "soft liberal" stereotype forever. But his confrontational style hasn't made his tax increases popular.

What Americans want in a leader, and particularly in a president, is someone who resembles what *Time* magazine called "the tough guy with a big heart." What's needed to play that part is a combination of strength and soul, caring and courage. Americans respect someone who cares deeply enough about other people to take risks in their behalf; someone who lives by a moral code and fights for it; someone who would not only visit you when you're sick, but take your side against an angry mob. In the movies, that part was perfected by both Humphrey Bogart and Lauren Bacall, the hardboiled hero and heroine. Cynical on the surface, they usually ended up doing the right thing, particularly when there were fascists to be fought. More recent exemplars are the TV cops Kojak, Cagney and Lacey, and Lt. Furillo of "Hill Street Blues." They not only capture criminals, they comfort the victims.

In fact, while Democrats are obsessed with toughening their images, Republicans are set on softening theirs. Retired actor Ronald Reagan, of course, had decades of practice playing the nice guy with the common touch. Presiding over a military build-up, cuts in social programs, and a painful recession, Reagan smiled benevolently and reminded people of his Irish heritage, his working-class upbringing, and his years as a union president and active Democrat. As journalist Garry Wills observed, Reagan's public manner suggested "relaxation" and "friendliness," while his advanced age "soften[ed] Reagan, taking sharp edges off."

In the 1988 presidential campaign, George Bush accomplished what seemed impossible: he both toughened and softened his image. Branded a "wimp" because of his patrician upbringing, his preppy mannerisms, and the enforced subservience of the vice presidency, Bush had to show Americans how tough he was. Books and TV spots appeared that emphasized his war record. And in a televised confrontation (that seemed more orchestrated than spontaneous) he demolished Dan Rather when he questioned Bush's knowledge of the Iran-Contra affair. However, once he won the nomination, Bush faced the familiar Republican problem of proving that he cared about people less privileged than himself. Fortunately for him, he had Peggy Noonan, the enormously talented speechwriter who'd scripted his convention speech, and she was also instrumental in shaping the images and symbols that filled his campaign: Bush as "the education president"; Bush, the inspiration of a "thousand points of light"; Bush yearning for a "kinder, gentler" nation.

Once, Noonan was asked to defend that last phrase by a campaign staffer who didn't get it, and she proved her perfect understanding of the image that Bush, or any presidential candidate, needs to project. "Listen," she said, "only a man utterly comfortable in his own strength can talk like that, only a strong man can say this." And this same image of gentle strength was carried over into Bush's TV ads: the young George Bush, fighter pilot; the older George Bush, holding a grandchild above his head.

For the Democratic party, and for most Democratic candidates as individuals, the challenge is similar to the hurdles Bush cleared: First, prove your strength; then, remind people you have a heart.

If the Reagan and Bush campaigns exemplify how Republicans can combine the characteristics people want in a president, then the Robert Kennedy of 1968 shows how Democrats can play the role of "the tough guy with a big heart."

Almost a quarter-century after his death, Robert Kennedy remains an enigma for a generation who never fully understood what manner of man he was and who will certainly never know what kind of leader he could have become. Those who mistrusted the man because he worked for Joseph McCarthy, or who despised him for offering to give blood to the Viet Cong, have had their doubts vindicated in the recent revelations about the Kennedy brothers' public and private lives. For those of us who still have photos of Robert Kennedy on our walls (and it must mean something that Murphy Brown, the hardboiled but idealistic television journalist of the popular situation comedy, has his photo in her home), the man we honor is, most of all, the man who might have been.

Americans caught a glimpse of that man in the Democratic presidential primaries of 1968, and apparently they liked what they saw. With the exception of Oregon, in every state where he competed, Kennedy put together a remarkable coalition that included working-class whites, poor blacks, and a significant number of middle-class liberals. Some voters were drawn to Kennedy because of his advocacy of peace in Vietnam and social justice at home. But, as Republican speechwriter William Gavin observes in his memoir, *Street Corner Conservative*, others voted for the "ruthless" Bobby:

> What the liberals failed to understand was that the man who voted for Bobby and who also liked George [Wallace] was not doing anything but voting for the guy he thought could best clean up the urban mess, i.e. get tough with lawbreakers. . . . It wasn't the 'compassionate' Bobby of the liberal myth for whom the blue-collar workers voted but the "ruthless" Bobby, the tough-on-crime, bitter, determined little bastard.

To be sure, Kennedy's campaign did emphasize those portions of his resume: the crimefighter and the shrewd political operative who'd managed his brother's presidential campaign. But Kennedy also projected toughness by saying and doing things that conveyed his compassion. Unlike other liberals, who went around telling their traditional Democratic constituencies what they thought they wanted to hear, Kennedy told them what he believed they *needed* to hear. And Kennedy's message—which was remarkably similar, no matter whom he was addressing—emphasized that all Americans share a responsibility for each other's well-being and for our society's success.

Thus, Kennedy told medical students that they should serve the poor; he reminded white working people of his support for civil rights; he told black audiences that he opposed civil disorder and supported the rule of law. And, decades before it was fashionable to talk about "new paradigms" for social policy, Kennedy expressed his skepticism of federal bureaucracies and his belief that local problems could best be solved by community action, private enterprise, and state and local governments.

Of course, Kennedy also told people what the more conventional politicians did. But his credibility was enhanced by the fact that he was also willing to tell unpleasant truths, a quality that made people believe that he was not only honest, but strong.

Almost twenty years after Kennedy's death, in discussions

with voters from white middle-class suburbs of Detroit, researchers read one of his statements urging Americans to honor society's obligations to blacks, who suffered through slavery, segregation, and discrimination. Asked what they thought, the focus group participants reacted with vehement disagreement and offered such responses as: "I'm fed up with it, man" and "I really feel that they have had so much handed to them." Told that the statement had been made by Robert Kennedy, one participant said, "No wonder they killed him."

We'll never know whether the people in that focus group, or others with similar views, would have reacted differently to that statement had they heard it from a contemporary political leader who was already known to be "ruthless . . . tough-on-crime." Surely, if there were any kind of public figure who could preach the gospel of racial liberalism to voters like those in that focus group, it would be someone whose credentials, personality, and philosophy add up to Robert Kennedy's meld of toughness and tenderness.

Indeed, that combination is necessary: Common decency requires that society provide everyone with opportunities for a healthy start in life, good schooling, and job training or a college education. But common sense requires that society provide a combination of incentives and sanctions—carrots and sticks—to encourage people to make the best use of their opportunities to be productive and self-sufficient. If Americans are ever to support progressive social policies, and if these policies are to succeed, they should embody the principles of "tough love," which Robert Kennedy seemed to advocate more compellingly than any other political leader in recent years.

It is not an easy stance, and the Democrat who would lead must take risks, be willing to seek and speak the truth, challenge Democratic allies as well as Republican adversaries, and set high standards, for *every* segment of society.

5

■ "Tough and Caring"

Democrats need to show a combination of toughness and tenderness—to show that they can provide services and set standards. This is especially important when they address three seemingly unrelated issues: crime and drugs; education; and foreign policy and defense.

★ BE CAREFUL OUT THERE

In the 1984 presidential campaign, Democrats didn't take advantage of the fact that their ticket consisted of two former prosecutors: Walter Mondale had been attorney general in Minnesota and Geraldine Ferraro had been an assistant district attorney in Queens. Both had sent their share of criminals to the slammer. But you'd have to be a student of political trivia to know that.

As a speechwriter for the Mondale campaign, I drafted his only major talk about crime for a congressional hearing on drugs chaired by Charles Rangel, who represents Harlem and Manhattan's Upper West Side. If Rangel hadn't asked him to speak, Mondale might not have addressed the issue at all, in spite of the fact that crime and drugs were serious problems in the early eighties.

Silence is golden, but it won't help win elections. And the Mondale campaign's near-silence on the crime and drug issues spoke volumes about liberals' reluctance to address those issues. Since Reagan wasn't attacking Mondale as soft on crime, we didn't have to counterpunch, and instead we could have come out swinging, listing the Reagan administration's failures. But crime and drugs are issues most liberals won't discuss unless they have to—even if they have solid credentials, even if their opponents are vulnerable.

It's been a quarter-century since Republicans started attacking Democrats as soft on crime, and too many Democrats have foolishly found themselves insisting that crime is unmentionable in public debate, calling it a "phony issue," or even a "code word for racism."

The first national Democrat in the modern era to take a sensible stance on crime was Robert Kennedy. When he campaigned as a fighter for "law and order with justice," some supporters of Eugene McCarthy, his rival in the primaries, suggested that Kennedy had turned conservative, even racist. But Kennedy carried more than 90 percent of the black vote in the primaries and also won the votes of working-class whites.

Two years later, Hubert Humphrey, another national Democrat with solid civil rights credentials, gave a well-publicized speech urging liberals to "condemn crime and riots and violence and extreme social turbulence." Attacked by the *Minneapolis Tribune* for making "a rightward shift," Humphrey replied: "I've spent a lifetime trying to point out that you can't have civil order without civil justice."

Unfortunately, most national Democrats didn't learn from Kennedy and Humphrey. For instance, Ramsey Clark, attorney general in the Johnson administration, the 1974 Democratic nominee for senator from New York, and a very visible liberal activist, declared:

> Poverty, injustice, idleness, ignorance, human misery, and crime go together. We cultivate crime, breed it, nourish it. Little wonder we have so much.

Forgetting that crime hurts poor people more than anyone, some liberals seem to condone it as an understandable response to deprivation. But concentrating on the "root causes of crime" is offensive to most voters, especially to those who are poor themselves but who proudly live within the law. "Don't say give everyone a good job, and they won't be doing crime, because that won't impress people," says political analyst Linda Williams.

Democrats like Ramsey Clark make a perfect punching bag for Republicans. Most Democrats haven't sounded that soft, but the sense that they weren't tough enough either was one of many perceptions that helped Nixon and Reagan win the White House. And in 1988, when George Bush told voters that Michael Dukakis had let a convicted murderer run loose, that made sense because it confirmed what they already thought about liberal Democrats.

In addressing the emotionally charged issues of crime and drugs, Democrats should keep in mind a few rules and heed the watchword of "Hill Street Blues" and "be careful out there."

■ **RULE #1.** *Make clear that you live in the same moral universe as most Americans.*

As Democratic pollster Mark Mellman explains, "Crime is about values. People see the link between actions and consequences has eroded, and the public wants the connection restored."

There's room for debate about the death penalty, defendants' rights, criminal rehabilitation, and how much government money to spend on law enforcement. But, if Democrats don't show that they share the basic belief that there must be a "link between actions and consequences," they'll be losers.

In his successful 1989 mayoral campaign in New York City, liberal Democrat David Dinkins got it right:

Every crime must be punished. I don't care if it's your first offense. I don't care if you just stole a car for the night or if you just took a few dollars. . . . If you commit a crime and are caught, you'll learn to respect the law and the system. . . . You will because you will be punished, no excuses, no apologies.

The death penalty, of course, is the most conspicuous example of the "link between actions and consequences." If a Democrat sincerely favors the death penalty, he or she should say so—loudly and clearly—particularly before liberal audiences for whom that's not an applause line. At the 1990 California state Democratic convention, when gubernatorial candidate Dianne Feinstein proclaimed her support for the death penalty, the crowd jeered her. But she used a film clip of that jeering crowd in an effective television spot to document that she was "tough but caring." Feinstein's forthrightness was fine for a political leader who sincerely supports the death penalty.

As for Democrats who sincerely oppose the death penalty (as I do), they should make clear that their feelings come from the heart and soul, not from a textbook. Dukakis lost out on the death penalty issue because he cited cerebral rather than visceral reasons for opposing it. "Capital punishment is not an effective deterrent," he would say. In contrast, Mario Cuomo has always explained his opposition to capital punishment in terms of personal moral conviction, and he's also managed to show a gut-level understanding of people's fear and anger about crime. He's expanded New York's prison system and has refused to reduce prison sentences for murderers and perpetrators of other violent crimes.

Illinois Democratic pollster Michael McKeon observes, "Cuomo is against the death penalty, but they never laid a glove on him. As long as you understand the problem at a personal, emotional level, it almost doesn't matter how you frame the solution."

Cuomo also understands that there's only one alternative people might accept instead of the death penalty: life without parole. Locking up murderers for life not only makes people feel safer, but it satisfies their sense of justice. Thus, in a *Boston Globe*/WBJ poll conducted in September 1990, 71 percent of Massachusetts voters initially said they wanted the death penalty but, when presented with the choice, 42 percent supported life without parole, while 44 percent continued to favor capital punishment.

■ **RULE #2.** *Keep in mind: The real crime may be in the stereotypes.*
Republicans have been willing, even eager to exploit harmful and inaccurate stereotypes about crime. Two weeks before the 1988 Democratic National Convention, while Michael Dukakis was interviewing possible vice presidential candidates, George Bush's campaign manager, the late Lee Atwater, gave a talk to southern Republicans:

> I can't wait until this Dukakis fellow gets down here [the South]. . . . Can you imagine him trying to answer how in the world . . . he was in favor of this weekend furlough program that allowed first-degree murderers and drug pushers to go on weekend vacations where they could murder, sell drugs, and do all the rest of this stuff? There is a story about a fellow named Willie Horton who for all I know may end up to be Dukakis's running mate. . . . The guy [Dukakis] was on TV about a month ago and he said you'll never see me standing in the driveway of my house talking to these candidates [referring to Mondale's protracted search in 1984 for a running mate, interviewing prospects at his Minnesota home]. And guess what, on Monday, [who] I saw in the driveway of his [Dukakis's] house? Jesse Jackson. So, anyway, maybe he'll put this Willie Horton guy on the ticket after all is said and done.

Atwater's free association of convicted murderer Willie Horton with presidential primary contender Jesse Jackson shows that the Bush high command knew very well what it was doing: exploiting anxieties about color as well as crime. More than any other issue, crime is tangled up in people's minds with stereotypes of every kind.

Democrats suffer from stereotypes that not only link them with Hortonesque criminals but with "turn 'em loose" judges, "bleeding heart" ACLU attorneys, and irresponsible governors and mayors who favor foolish ideas like prison furloughs. Democrats have to prove they can be trusted to fight crime. So they need to introduce some counter-stereotypical symbols and ideas into public debate.

For starters, it's way past time to remind people who's most vulnerable to crime. In 1989, a New York City police department tally found that 57.1 percent of murder victims were black, 34.8 percent were Hispanic, and only 10 percent were non-Hispanic whites. Nationally, U.S. Justice Department statistics show that blacks are six times as likely as whites to be murdered, and are much more likely to be victims of burglary and robbery as well. Other groups more likely to be crime victims include women, senior citizens, and people who work for low wages, work nights, or live in inner cities. If you want to conjure up an image of a typical crime victim, she might be a woman who works evenings cleaning office buildings in midtown Manhattan. She takes the subway home to the Bronx every night, and she's thankful for every night she gets home safely.

"Limousine liberals" may be squeamish about being tough on crime. But leaders whose constituents ride city buses and subways feel differently. For instance, Dennis Rivera, president of Local 1199 of the hospital workers union in New York City (one of the most militant and progressive unions anywhere), recently admitted that it's hard to get the members to attend evening meetings in the union's mid-Manhattan headquarters. He said many hospital workers "don't like to go out in the dark."

Liberal politicians often go before Local 1199's delegate assembly, pleading for their support. While talking tough about corporate tax cheats and union-busting bosses is fine, the next time a big-name Democrat addresses Local 1199, he or she should talk tough on crime, too. That will earn applause from the delegates who ran the gauntlet to get to the meeting. And if the media are there it will help change the stereotypes about who's really concerned about crime.

In a funny way, this will give Democrats more credibility as crime fighters with middle-class suburbanites, because nothing will shake their idea that, for better or worse, Democrats care most about people like the members of Local 1199. So Democrats may as well make clear that nobody cares more about cracking down on crime than someone who takes the subway home every night.

In general, Democrats would do well to redefine many of their stereotypically "liberal" attitudes as being the kinds of commitments that make them tough on crime.

For instance, during her successful gubernatorial race in Texas, Democrat Ann Richards was accused of being soft on crime by her Republican opponent, Clayton Williams (who had joked that the weather was like rape—you should just relax and enjoy it). Richards responded:

Clayton Williams has absurdly suggested that because I am female that I might be soft on crime. And yet as a woman, I am part of the population that is the most victimized by crime. We are the ones that are raped. We are the ones that are beaten. We are the ones who are abused. So maybe it's going to take a woman to get tough on crime.

Democrats need to make symbolic connections not only with crime victims but with the police as well. In his 1985 race for lieutenant governor of Virginia, Democrat Douglas Wilder was accused by his Republican rival of having "the criminal's interest at heart." Wilder's response became a political classic. Campaigning in the small town of Kenbridge, he found a police officer—and loyal Democrat—named Joe Alder, described by political reporter Dwayne Yancey as "a beefy, slow-talking white Southern lawman, straight out of the stereotype." A Wilder TV spot showed him with Alder, who endorsed him as a friend of the policemen who daily put their lives on the line. If there was one image of Wilder that voters remembered on Election Day, it was his standing alongside that portly policeman in blue. In 1989, he became the first black to be elected governor—of any state. And as a contender for the 1992 Democratic presidential nomination, he continued to emphasize his tough stand on crime.

Of course, Democrats' embrace of the police should be substantive as well as symbolic. While Republicans give police lip service, Democrats should offer resources and respect. And they have solid reasons for creating a link in the public's mind between themselves and the police: Both have seen the seamier side of life, both protect the most vulnerable people in society and, at their best, both project a tough kind of caring. After all, that's what people found so admirable about Lt. Frank Furillo, the weary, wise, and compassionate TV cop. Think about it. It's a lot easier to imagine Mario Cuomo or Douglas Wilder filling in for Lt. Furillo than to visualize George Bush or Dan Quayle in a grimy precinct house.

■ **RULE #3.** *Remind voters that public safety is a public service.*

Once Democrats counter the stereotypes about themselves and clear the hurdles of values and symbolism, they need to get people thinking of public safety as a service government provides. And providing public services is the Democrats' strong suit.

Tough Democrats, by pointing out that what has seemed like "softness" in the criminal justice system is often really just a shortage of resources, can convince people that the rhetoric of revenge is mere rhetoric, and that the only way to really do something about crime is to provide the money needed to fight it.

For instance, Joe Biden, chairman of the Senate Judiciary Committee, has pointedly criticized the Reagan and Bush administrations for failing to put their money where their mouths are on solving the problems of crime and drugs. For all their tough talk, these Republicans have been relatively stingy in helping local, state, and federal law enforcement agencies to police the streets, treat drug abusers, try defendants, and imprison convicted criminals.

Indeed, Democrats do best when they present public safety in populist terms. Mario Cuomo did when he attacked President Bush for declaring a war on drugs without providing the troops with ammunition. Better still, Cuomo linked the federal government's shortchanging of law enforcement with the Reagan-Bush administration's tax breaks for the wealthy:

> It doesn't take a tax genius, just a school parent or someone who lives in an unsafe neighborhood to realize that billions of dollars that might be used for falling bridges and the drug war will end up in minks and Jaguars when the top rate drops to 28 percent.

Democrats usually lose out when they fall into Republican rhetorical traps, like getting sidetracked in congressional debates about creating harsh new punishments for obscure crimes. But when Democrats draw people's attention away from Capitol Hill to the city streets, they can shift the terms of debate from whether to get tough to deciding on what the real problems are and finding solutions for them.

Police departments are laying off, not hiring, officers; streetlights break down and aren't being repaired; people who ask for drug treatment often have to wait months for an opening in a rehab program; court calendars lag behind arrests; jails are overcrowded, so defendants awaiting trial are sent back out on the street and then their cases are plea bargained. Then there's the shortage of prison cells (which makes a mockery of the "tough" talk to put more criminals away for longer terms). Fixing these problems costs money. So does the quality of our police.

The training of law enforcement personnel has recently become an issue in the wake of such shocking examples as the behavior of the Los Angeles police under Chief Daryl Gates. People need to feel confident that their local police respect all the people they're sworn to protect. An unlikely coalition of House liberals *and* conservatives (ranging from Massachusetts Democrat Joseph Kennedy to California Republican Robert Dornan), support a national "police corps," which will provide a college education for 25,000 new officers a year. Georgia Democrat John Lewis, a veteran of the civil rights struggles of the sixties, has called this bill "vital to black Americans. . . . The police corps represents a commitment to check and reverse the tide of insensate violence that has crippled so many black communities."

Aside from money, getting results also means getting smart. Democrats should embrace new ideas, such as "community policing," which puts cops back on the streets walking neighborhood beats. New York's Mayor Dinkins has experimented with this, and people like it. Fred Siegel, a historian who lives in Brooklyn in a neighborhood where people worry about street crime, has called it "the most hopeful thing in New York in twenty years. People see the cops walk by, and they smile."

★ "REWARDS FOR RESULTS"

By the beginning of the 1980s, "education reform" was not only a catch-phrase for editorial writers but an important movement in our society. Like many movements, it started at the state and local level, particularly in southern and border states where people understood they needed a highly skilled work force to attract high-paying jobs.

Standards and accountability are the watchwords. Education reformers demand greater accountability for students *and* teachers. They have rewritten school curricula to make sure a high school diploma means that a student has acquired basic skills and mastered a basic course of study, and they've proposed merit pay for teachers, so that the best ones are recognized and rewarded.

The strategy behind the reform movement is simple and sensible, embodying the American concept of the social contract: rewards for results. Before states pour more money into education, taxpayers want solid evidence of improvement; they want to be sure schools are doing the job right.

Governors from both parties have built national reputations as education reformers. Among the best known are Republican Lamar Alexander of Tennessee, who is now secretary of education in the Bush administration, and Bill Clinton of Arkansas, a contender for the Democratic presidential nomination in 1992. In 1983, Gov. Clinton offered an education reform proposal that included competency tests for teachers, a pay raise for the teachers who passed, and a sales tax increase to finance it.

Although the minimum-competency test merely required teachers to demonstrate the same levels of competence expected of *students* in the eighth grade, the Arkansas Education Association resisted Clinton's program. And its parent organization, the

National Education Association, tried to get national Democratic leaders to persuade Clinton to soften his standards.

In general, the NEA's influence as a lobbying group is one reason why the national Democrats have been slow to get on the education reform bandwagon. For example, in the 1984 campaign, Walter Mondale proposed increasing federal education spending, but he didn't address the issue of raising standards for students, teachers, and school systems. Nor did Michael Dukakis in 1988. This made it easy for Ronald Reagan and George Bush to capitalize on the demand for improving education without offering any solid programs of their own.

The release of the Department of Education's 1983 report, *A Nation at Risk*, underscored the public perception that American schools are mired in mediocrity. So, under the leadership of education secretaries Terrel Bell and William Bennett, the Reagan administration could assume the voice of populist critic of the educational establishment. Republicans have sounded like parents' advocates, while the national Democrats, with their links to the NEA and the school bureaucracies, have sounded like defenders of an unpopular status quo. Thus, George Bush was able to campaign successfully as the candidate who would be "the education president," although he offered no plan and no money for improving the schools.

Now ten years old, the education reform movement has taken hold, and more Americans than ever are demanding that schools measure up. In May 1991, a national *Time*/CNN survey found that 37 percent of Americans believe the public schools are doing a "poor" job. Another 18 percent rated the schools "very poor."

Similar attitudes emerged in "Battleground 1992," a study of public opinion conducted jointly in June 1991, by Republican pollsters Tarrance and Associates and the Democratic polling firm Greenberg-Lake. Asked how to improve education, 26 percent favored testing teacher proficiency and 18 percent emphasized teaching "values," compared to 16 percent who said smaller classes were needed. Only 10 percent wanted salary increases for teachers.

Invariably, Democrats score better than Republicans on domestic issues, from child care to social security. But on the question of who is doing a better job for education, Republicans were running even with Democrats. It's a sure sign that the GOP is doing something right, or the Democrats are doing something wrong.

Around the time these polls were taken, the Bush administration finally announced an education program. It stressed radical change in the status quo but offered no federal resources to aid reform and, indeed, it appeared to be bypassing public schools. The emphasis was on "school choice"; states would pay for parents to send their kids to any school they select, public or private. However, the administration promised to raise funds from private corporations to develop experimental public schools in every congressional district.

Critics of the Bush plan make the obvious point: Public schools could end up like public hospitals—poverty wards for people who get turned away everywhere else. But to effectively critique Bush's policies, the Democrats have to stop sounding like defenders of a discredited system. Democrat Richard Gephardt, the majority leader in the U.S. House of Representatives, and Albert Shanker, president of the American Federation of Teachers (the smaller of the two teachers' unions), understand this.

Gephardt proposes financial incentives for states whose high school seniors meet international standards in math and science. Calling his plan "rewards for results," Gephardt said:

> One of the problems in the past is we say to taxpayers, "We're going to take money from you, but we don't know if we're going to get results." [Now] we're saying to taxpayers, "You're going to achieve the results you want."

I'd offer one kicker for "rewards for results." "Results" should mean how much schools can improve students' achievement, not just how well the students do. Taking kids who are flunking out and helping them pass English and math—that's getting results. Maybe the students would just get Cs and Bs, but that school deserves an A-plus.

Shanker's organization has shown more flexibility than the NEA on the issues of competency testing and national certification of teachers. While the AFT rejects merit pay plans that would give administrators arbitrary power to play favorites, it endorses promoting the best teachers to the position of "master teacher," and having them mentor their colleagues. AFT locals in Rochester, New York, Dade County, Florida, Cincinnati and Toledo, Ohio, and Hammond, Indiana, have led experiments in "school-based management," where teachers help run the schools, thus cutting back on costly and cumbersome administrative bureaucracies, or conduct peer review of their colleagues, thus assuming responsibility for the quality of teaching.

In effect, the AFT is proposing a social contract that says we want high standards and want to help achieve them, but give us the raises, respect, and recognition we deserve.

As for the NEA, it's an effective union, with a powerful political mechanism that turns out voters and volunteers in communities across the country, particularly from its base in suburban and rural areas, where Democrats are weak. (The AFT is equally effective, especially in the urban areas that are its base.) Yes, Democrats should *court* the NEA and the AFT. But they should also *challenge* teachers' unions to seek "rewards for results."

Public schools need more money. And teachers need pay raises. But for Democrats to champion these issues they first have to show they're tough enough to set standards and get results.

★ AMERICA FIRST?

Often marginalized on the dovish or isolationist end of the political spectrum, Democrats have been getting clobbered on foreign policy issues for years. Throughout the postwar era, Democrats who have won the presidency haven't been militaristic, but they have stood for idealistic activism, at home and abroad. Today's Democrats need to demonstrate not only that they are principled, but that they are tough enough to put those principles into effect.

While Americans' economic concerns were the major factors in 1948, Harry Truman ran not only as an economic populist but as a toughminded anticommunist as well. And in 1960, although those who cited foreign policy as the major issue voted for Nixon, Kennedy's attack on the Eisenhower-Nixon administration, that it had allowed America to become flabby and complacent, was a critique of its international role as well as its domestic policy. By capitalizing on anxieties about American decline, from the missile gap to Castro's emergence in Cuba, Kennedy probably convinced swing voters that he was tough enough to lead America.

It works the other way, too. In 1964, Lyndon Johnson marginalized Barry Goldwater as a dangerous bomb-thrower. And until he escalated the Vietnam War, Johnson occupied the middle ground on foreign policy: tough enough to stand his ground against the Soviets, sensible enough to seek – and keep – the peace.

The last Democrat to win the presidency, Jimmy Carter in 1976, also campaigned as a toughminded idealist, contending that the Nixon and Ford administrations hadn't been tough enough on human rights violations from the Soviet Union to South Africa. Now that the Cold War is over, many Democrats think they can benefit from the shift in public sentiment. In a *Washington Post*/ABC News survey conducted in October 1991, 70 percent of Americans agreed that President Bush "spends too much time on foreign problems and not enough on problems in this country."

Democrats can and should capitalize on this, but they need to keep several points in mind.

■ **POINT #1.** *Americans want a foreign policy.*

The Persian Gulf crisis, the failed Soviet coup, the continuing turbulence in Eastern Europe and the Middle East – all remind Americans that the world remains a dangerous place, and that we must maintain an influence on what happens beyond our borders. The overwhelming advantage Republicans enjoy on foreign policy and defense (64 to 15 percent in the "Battleground 1992" survey) still constitutes a formidable barrier for Democrats seeking the presidency.

■ **POINT #2.** *The first line in a president's job description is "Commander-in-Chief."* Voters want a president who will keep America strong and use force, when necessary, against foreign foes. Indeed, precisely because Democrats should be talking about cutting the defense budget and using the money for middle-class tax relief or domestic investment, they need to sound like sober advocates for America's new needs in the nineties, not like stereotypical sixties peaceniks.

■ **POINT #3.** *Democrats don't make convincing isolationists.* Traditionally, isolationism is a close cousin to nativism: the view that America was a better place some time before 1917, when people who weren't white Anglo-Saxon Protestants knew their place, and our country avoided foreign entanglements.

But Democrats are primarily folks whose families came over in steerage or on slave ships—not on the Mayflower—and who feel familial and philosophical ties to freedom fighters like Poland's Lech Walesa and South Africa's Nelson Mandela (the most sought-after speakers at labor conventions in 1989 and 1990). Democrats have always believed that we need to take care of our own flesh and blood, but as the party of inclusion, they have never believed that the rest of the world should go to hell. And people know it.

That's why Virginia governor Douglas Wilder's slogan for his 1992 presidential campaign sounded strange. "America First" was used in the 1930s by right-wing isolationists who, mostly, didn't like African-Americans or any other kind of "hyphenated American." Democrats do better with slogans like Richard Gephardt's in 1988: "Let's Make America Number One." This suggests that

America should compete aggressively in the world economy, not withdraw from the world stage.

■ **POINT #4.** *Democrats should attack President Bush's indifference to domestic problems on populist, not isolationist, grounds.*

In the fall of 1991, a sure-fire applause line for Democrats was to attack President Bush for spending too much time abroad and not dealing with America's domestic problems. But the logic of that line could ultimately be self-defeating because it feeds the perception that Democrats don't care about foreign policy and defense. Worst of all, it implies that Bush is basically a good guy who would do the right thing on domestic issues if he spent more time in the White House and less time on Air Force One. In fact, Democrats should be saying that Bush is a country-club Republican who would veto unemployment compensation, family leave, and anything else that's good for working people, even if he weren't distracted by foreign events!

■ **POINT #5.** *Democrats should criticize the Bush foreign policy for failing to advance American interests and democratic values.*

Just as Democrats don't make convincing isolationists, they don't make convincing militarists. But Democrats' domestic strengths do make them convincing idealists, populists, and environmentalists on the world as well as the national scene.

Like Carter in 1976, Democrats should emphasize their principled idealism as the reason for criticizing Republican foreign policy blunders. And Bush's record offers some very tempting targets: cozying up to Saddam Hussein almost up to the day he invaded Kuwait and then letting him massacre the Kurds after the allied victory in the Gulf War; cozying up to the Chinese gerontocracy after the bloodbath at Tiananmen Square; and giving the cold shoulder to Boris Yeltsin just before the attempted Soviet coup. Indeed, the human rights issue offers the best basis for promoting trade policies that defend American businesses and American workers. Democrats seized the moral high ground in the debate over most-favored nation trade status for China when Senate Majority Leader George Mitchell pointed out that many of the products covered are made by slave labor and child labor. "Protectionism" may be a loser among media elites; but Americans agree with the argument that our country shouldn't grant favorable trading status to—and our workers shouldn't be forced to compete with—countries whose products are cheap because their workers are denied basic human rights.

■ **POINT #6.** *Democrats should take pride that America won the Cold War and the Gulf War.*

Whatever our political affiliations, Americans are proud that our country kept the world safe from communism and from thugs like Saddam Hussein. And, whatever their value as applause lines, voters ultimately don't appreciate remarks like Democratic presidential contender Paul Tsongas's comment that the Soviet Union and the United States fought the Cold War, and Japan won.

Most people are proud that, thanks in large measure to the policy of containing communism that Democrats initiated, leaders like Yeltsin now hold power in Moscow. So Democrats should lend a moral dimension to their economic nationalism by pointing out that trade rivals like Japan didn't do their part in the Cold War and the Gulf War.

As the 1992 campaign got underway, Sen. Bob Kerrey of Nebraska got it right. Kerrey was a Medal of Honor winner in Vietnam, who became a critic of the war when he came home. In announcing his presidential campaign, he said that hearing Eastern European leaders like Lech Walesa and Vaclav Havel address the U.S. Senate made him proud of most of what America had done during the post-World War II era. And, after being attacked by Republican leaders for initially opposing the Persian Gulf War, Kerrey said: "I choose to participate in the prideful sense that America has just done something good, even if I am not invited by the RNC [Republican National Committee] to do so."

Kerrey's point is that Americans should stop arguing about the past, and should look back in pride, with the understanding that it's time to move on. And that's a good point for Democrats to make.

6
Putting the Middle Class at the Center of the Argument

★ TWO CITIES, NO SUBURBS?

In the fall of 1984, three times a day at virtually every rally, his voice increasingly hoarse, Walter Mondale would shout his indictment of the Reagan administration:

The rich are getting richer. The poor are getting poorer. And the middle class is standing on a trap door.

Four years later, in his clipped, staccato delivery, Michael Dukakis told the crowds at his rallies:

The rich are getting richer. The poor are getting poorer. And the middle class—and that means most of us—is getting squeezed.

Mondale and Dukakis were each telling a story in which the middle class seemed to come last. Mondale's "trap door" referred to the federal budget deficits that were endangering the economy but his metaphor was obscure, and the middle class sounded like an afterthought. Dukakis's words reflected a somewhat more sophisticated strategy, which recognized that the middle class is "most of us," and that we're "getting squeezed." But not until the end of the campaign did Dukakis make plain what he intended to do for "us": "I want to be the president who stands up and fights for middle-class working people."

However, Mondale and Dukakis weren't the only national Democrats who had trouble addressing America's middle-class majority. Most Americans still remember New York governor Mario Cuomo for his eloquent keynote speech at the 1984

Democratic convention, where he told "a tale of two cities" to indict the inequities of the Reagan era. Cuomo is one of the party's most gifted orators, but his metaphor must have bewildered, or even offended, many listeners.

Taking the image of America as "a shining city on a hill," which Reagan used in his acceptance speech that year, Cuomo told his audience that "relative few . . . live in its good neighborhoods," and instead, in "another part of the city, some people can't pay their mortgages, and most young people can't afford one . . . students can't afford the education they need and middle-class parents watch the dreams they hold for their children evaporate."

So far, Cuomo was talking about the middle class, and he called them "the heart of our constituency . . . people not rich enough to be worry-free but not poor enough to be on welfare, those who work for a living because they have to." But then he continued, "In this part of the city [presumably, where the middle class lives], there are more poor than ever, more families in trouble, more and more people who need help but can't find it." There were the elderly "who tremble in the basements," the homeless "who sleep in the city's streets," and those in "ghettos where thousands of young people, without an education or a job, give their lives away to drug dealers every day."

What Cuomo's "two cities" metaphor seemed to be describing was a neighborhood with only two districts—one high-rent, one low-rent, with nothing in between—where the middle class lives next door to the poor as well as the homeless and drug abusers. While that image may have made sense to middle-class people in places like Manhattan's Upper West Side, for those who lived on the outskirts of major cities, or miles away in the suburbs, Cuomo, eloquent as he was, wasn't talking about any place they knew.

It's somewhat ironic, because Cuomo was personally and painfully aware of the fears conjured up by the idea of the poor moving next door to the middle class. More so than most other office-seekers who call themselves "citizen-politicians," Cuomo is the real thing. He's spent his life in neither the shining city of the wealthy nor the ghettos of the poor, but in New York City's Queens County, a borough of working- and middle-class neighborhoods, where people *are* anxious about meeting mortgage payments and affording college educations for their kids. Prior to being appointed to public office at the age of forty-three, Cuomo worked as a lawyer, often representing community groups against city officials who wanted to gut neighborhoods. He first gained major attention as the mediator between residents of Forest Hills, Queens, and the city government, which wanted to build a low-income housing project in that middle-class community. He crafted a compromise between residents and the city, and the Forest Hills Housing Project was built in 1971. So Cuomo knew firsthand that any American city has many neighborhoods. And he also knew that the folks in these middle-class neighborhoods are anxious to keep their distance from the miseries he'd so movingly described.

For all the acclaim he received, Cuomo later seemed embarrassed by his speech. Indeed, he stopped using the "tale of two cities" metaphor, as well as his image of Americans as a family, "feeling one another's pain, sharing one another's blessings . . . recognizing that at the heart of the matter we are bound to one another . . . " Perhaps it's because Cuomo had learned from his own experience that, far from living in the same neighborhood with the poor, much less regarding the poor as kinfolk, the middle class had largely left the city and moved to the suburbs.

Cuomo's keynote and Mondale's and Dukakis's stump speeches all show the failure of the national Democrats to address the middle class. Instead, much of the most moving Democratic oratory of the eighties was about its victims. At the 1980 convention, Sen. Edward Kennedy roused the crowd with stories of suffering: jobless steelworkers and miners in Pennsylvania, a hard-pressed farm family in Iowa, an elderly woman in California who couldn't afford a telephone. (Now Kennedy's speech reads like a standard Democratic indictment of Republican heartlessness, but his target was the party's nominee, President Jimmy Carter. Kennedy had lost the primary race earlier that year, in spite of the economic problems that he and the Republican nominee Ronald Reagan so eloquently, but so differently, described.)

As the 1984 campaign got underway, Democrats had a more tempting target: a Republican in the White House who had presided over a recession just two years earlier. For much of the campaign season, Walter Mondale's stump speech featured a litany of the administration's unfairness:

> In Reagan's America, if you're rich they give you tax cuts. If you're poor, they give you cheese. . . . If you're a woman, they blame you for unemployment. If you're Hispanic, they say you enjoy overcrowded housing.

And in his campaigns in 1984 and '88, Jesse Jackson urged listeners to join together on "economic common ground," which he usually defined as a ground of economic disasters—farm foreclosures, factory closings, picket lines, and unemployment lines.

Kennedy, Mondale, Cuomo, and Jackson were all addressing issues that should be the concern of Democrats as well as all Americans. In the America of the eighties, only the most privileged were insulated from the problems they described. Yet many in the middle class must have wondered: What does this mean for those of us who are working, who aren't homeless, whose factories are open, whose farms haven't been foreclosed, who aren't on strike, and who aren't victims of discrimination?

As public opinion surveys showed, Democratic rhetoric was being interpreted in ways we didn't want by middle-class voters. Hearing calls for compassion for what sounded like a litany of losers, many people concluded that Democrats cared mostly about the poor, particularly the black poor, and that the party no longer cared about them.

Consider the difference between what the Democrats of the 1930s and '40s offered Americans and what the Democrats of the past quarter-century haven't. The programs of the New Deal were for everybody, not just the poor. Any requirements for participation conformed to society's values: work or military service. The most noteworthy exception was Aid to Families with Dependent Children (AFDC), which began as a temporary Depression-era expedient, but has mushroomed into today's "welfare." And experts on public opinion agree, so closely is the New Deal linked with respect for work, that the Roosevelt years are not identified with welfare but with the WPA and the Civilian Conservation Corps, programs that put people to work, even if it was "make-work." Indeed, one pollster recently heard strong nostalgia for Roosevelt—*he'd* put welfare recipients to work.

The last major Democratic program applicable to the middle class was enacted in 1965: Medicare, which provides health-care coverage for just about every senior citizen. Since then, Democrats have been identified with "means-tested" programs intended exclusively for the poor: Medicaid, food stamps, and AFDC. These programs often offended the middle class, not only because they weren't beneficiaries, but because the eligibility standards seemed to be the absolute opposite of society's standards: People got rewarded for having broken homes and not working, and punished for having a job or an intact nuclear family. And as champions of civil rights, Democrats became identified with controversial efforts at racial integration, such as busing and affirmative action, which added to middle-class estrangement.

But to make things even worse, Democrats lost sight of who was paying the bills. As their incomes rose, because of both prosperity *and* inflation, federal taxes on the middle class grew to rates originally designed for the wealthy. Meanwhile, since state and local governments were getting a smaller share of the federal pie, their need for more revenues resulted in increased sales and property taxes, which also hit moderate-income workers hardest. (Property taxes were particularly infuriating since they taxed the only asset most families owned.) Thus, when many in the middle class heard Democrats talk about "fairness," they didn't think it meant a better deal for people like them. They thought it meant hiring quotas, school busing, rising property-tax bills, and even something as unlikely as welfare recipients living high on the hog (as in Reagan's apocryphal anecdotes). And Democrats exacerbated middle-class anger with a rhetoric that seemed to tell them that they were doing well enough, and that their concerns and problems were peripheral compared to those of society's *real* victims.

By the end of the eighties, many congressional Democrats had learned their lesson, and just prior to the 1988 presidential election they promoted an ambitious agenda. While their bills served different segments of society, they all benefitted people who work: day care for the children of working parents, minimum wage increases, the family leave bill, tougher trade policies, and a sixty-day notification requirement before plant closings. All were good old-fashioned bread-and-butter issues, and all scored well in public opinion surveys. More recently, some Democrats in Congress began championing tax cuts for the middle class, to be paid for by tax increases on the wealthy.

Along with their rediscovery of middle-class issues, some Democrats started trying to speak a more contemporary political language that no longer relies on the party's old rhetorical habits: like the age-old battle between rich and poor, which leaves the middle class in the middle, getting shot at by both sides; or the image of America as an industrial city divided into a working-class section where "our people" live and a ritzy neighborhood where Republicans live. Democrats had used this rhetoric long after it no longer made sense, perhaps because these old dichotomies make for such stirring speeches.

Michael Dukakis was the first Democratic presidential nominee to pitch his campaign explicitly to the middle class, but he didn't reach, much less rouse, most of his intended audience. At times, the Dukakis campaign seemed simply to change the sociological mix in the roll call of victims. We stopped talking about the failing farmer, the laid-off steelworker, and the hungry child.

Instead, we talked about the family that couldn't let its son play Little League baseball because they'd lost their health insurance, the young couple who couldn't afford to buy their first home, and the middle-class teenager who worried about being able to afford college. Worthy issues all, and post-election polls showed Dukakis had scored on each of them. Yet we failed miserably at addressing middle-class social anxieties: fear of crime and drugs, anger about paying more taxes for fewer services, and their sense that society was losing respect for the virtues that Americans need in order to make the most of their opportunities and win a measure of security. We failed to pluck the violin strings in most voters' hearts—their ambitions for themselves, their regrets about the strains on their families' lives, and their yearning to see their values reflected in their communities and their country.

Putting the middle class at the center of the argument starts with understanding that the middle class is at the center of the American idea—and knows it.

★ A MIDDLE-CLASS NATION

"You're middle class if you work for a living, if you don't clip coupons, if you depend on your own personal skills to make a living. And, if you work hard, if you play by the rules, then you deserve a chance to own your own home, have a nice car, send your kids to college, and feel you've achieved something in this life."

That's a fair definition of what it means to be middle class. But the speaker is Richard Trumka, president of the United Mine Workers, and if anybody might say they're "working class" rather than "middle class," it's the members of his union. Proud of their union's reputation for militancy, they work at one of the most dangerous jobs in America and might be expected to question the notion that our society is solidly middle class. Yet, as Trumka explains (with some exaggeration), "Ninety-nine point nine percent of the people in this country think they're middle class — whether they truly are is another question."

Indeed, the fact that Trumka heads this union is a sign of how much working-class and middle-class consciousness have melded. A third-generation miner, Trumka paid for college and law school by working summers in the mines. He served on the union's legal staff, returned to the Pennsylvania coalfields to organize a challenge to the union's president, and in 1982, at the age of thirty-three, Trumka was elected to the post. He campaigned in a three-piece pinstriped suit, vowing to challenge "the stereotype of the coal miner as an unskilled pick-and-shovel laborer."

While most people haven't made a journey as dramatic as Trumka's, the American creed has always held that it is not only possible, but unremarkable. So while Trumka's degree of success is unusual, the way he achieved it is not. And in fact, his path epitomizes both what it means to be middle class and what it means to be American.

Being middle class has a moral dimension: You work for a living; your life is your responsibility; you deserve credit for your success, having achieved it though your own skills. All are classic American virtues, and the middle class needs those virtues to survive. And they resent those like the "idle rich," who were born on third base but think they've hit a triple (to paraphrase the populist firebrand Jim Hightower), and the "undeserving poor," who don't work and live off the dole.

The American economy, buffeted by international competition, has changed enormously. As the political economist Robert Reich has pointed out, the most affluent segment of society no longer depends upon the American economy for its success. Working as investment bankers, lawyers, lobbyists, and advertising and PR consultants for multinational or even foreign-owned corporations, the "overclass" can still prosper even if their fellow citizens suffer. On the other hand, the "underclass" seems assured of a minimal livelihood — at the taxpayers' expense. This leaves middle-class working people virtually alone in the patriotic, but less and less rewarding, position of relying on the uncertainties of the American economy for their livelihoods, which has left the middle class feeling that their hard-earned position is somewhat tenuous. In order to make it and maintain their footing, the middle class needs discipline and self-restraint. Understandably, they see themselves as the keepers of society's values, and all they ask from society is a fair shake.

The concept of a fair shake is key to middle-class consciousness. Unlike other countries, where your future is determined the day you're born, here you can go as far as your talents can take you. There is nothing more American, or more middle class, than a Horatio Alger-type story. "America is still wide open," says Republican speechwriter Peggy Noonan, expressing a view shared by Americans across the political spectrum. "You can come here from anywhere and do anything." Then Noonan makes a point I first heard from the late socialist Michael Harrington: The United States is so egalitarian that it is the only country on earth where you call the waiter "Sir."

To most Americans, egalitarianism means the opportunity to achieve; responsibility and individualism make America work, and America is working if the middle class is large, growing, and secure. In the 1830s, French writer and politician Alexis de Tocqueville toured the United States. His discovery of a thriving middle class strengthened his faith in American democracy. "Such folk owe no man anything and hardly expect anything from anybody. They form the habit of thinking of themselves in isolation and imagine that their whole destiny is in their own hands."

If the American creed (or the middle-class creed) can be summed up, it is in that simple idea, new in Tocqueville's time: Your whole destiny is in your own hands. This translates into an even simpler phrase—"self-reliance." The chance to make something of yourself requires the wherewithal to make the most of that chance, and the willingness to be responsible for your actions. So important is this idea that the elements of the American dream—a home, a car, and an education—all reward your hard work and make you even more independent.

Historically, self-reliance has been the goal of America's progressive economic policies. For example, the Homestead Act of the 1870s, which guaranteed 160 free acres of land to settlers on the frontier, was premised on a fundamental American principle: Government can give you the resources, but then it's up to you. FDR's New Deal rewarded work with the security so desperately needed, and in the postwar era universal programs were added, which opened opportunities for education and home ownership.

Interestingly enough, it was the Truman administration's programs that kicked off the journey from the cities and farms to the suburbs. Now, even allowing for the fact that it under-counted city dwellers and the poor, the 1990 Census tells the story of a middle class that has pretty much completed that journey. The new suburbs, with populations greater than one hundred thousand but fewer than a million, are the fastest-growing communities in America. And these are new because they are no longer the classic bedroom communities of the past—they are places where people work and shop as well as sleep. More and more middle-class working people call these communities home.

Democrats used to kick off their campaigns on Labor Day at Cadillac Square in downtown Detroit. Now, however, the downtown resembles a ghost town (except for a mall called "Renaissance Center"), and Cadillac Square is no longer a central symbol for working people in that area, much less for the entire nation. In recent years, Detroit has lost more than a quarter-million people. The middle class, both white and black, has marched out to the suburbs.

Of the twenty-nine cities across America that passed the one-hundred-thousand mark for the first time during the eighties, eighteen were in California. As Tony Podesta, former president of People for the American Way and Michael Dukakis's California campaign manager, notes, "In California, the 1988 campaign was decided in communities that barely existed when Kennedy ran in 1960." And in Texas, Florida, and other sunbelt states, similar communities, not so much suburbs as new post-industrial cities, grew dramatically, and they now hold the balance of political power.

Too often during the 1980s, Democrats scripted TV spots and stump speeches similar to those of thirty years ago, offering them to an audience that has moved out of hearing range. If Democrats seemed slightly bewildered, it was because a result of suburban migration has been that "our people," the middle of the middle class, aren't our people anymore.

In a paper presented to the centrist Democratic Leadership Council, the political scientist William Galston noted that in the 1988 presidential election (as in 1980 and 1984), Democrats lost that "heart of the middle class," the voters with family incomes between $25,000 and $50,000, who account for fully 40 percent of the electorate. In 1976, 51 percent of them supported a victorious Jimmy Carter. By 1988, only 43 percent backed a defeated Michael Dukakis. People's pockets were pinched, and if they didn't think Republicans had their best interests at heart, they didn't think Democrats did either. Why not?

★ "NOT RICH ENOUGH TO BE WORRY-FREE"

In his devastatingly effective closing remarks in his 1980 campaign debate with President Carter, Republican challenger Ronald Reagan suggested to voters, "It might be well if you would ask yourself: Are you better off than you were four years ago? Is it easier for you to go and buy things in the stores than it was four years ago? Is there more or less unemployment than there was four years ago?"

With these words Reagan showed rare understanding of how candidates should discuss pocketbook issues. Rather than *tell* voters that the cost of living was rising and unemployment lines were lengthening, which they already knew, Reagan treated the electorate as adults who understood the facts of their own lives and who were prepared to render a judgment based on the evidence of their own experience.

Now, almost a dozen years and two recessions later, most people are as anxious as ever about their condition—and the country's. Indeed, for much of George Bush's presidency (and even before the economy sank into recession), public opinion surveys have shown that people have the same worried view of their families' finances and the nation's economy: It's bad, and it's in danger of getting worse. In a bipartisan public opinion poll taken after the victory in the Persian Gulf War—a moment when most people might have been expected to be optimistic—48 percent said things are on the wrong track economically, while only 32 percent felt the country is moving in the right direction. Fifty-one percent said they fell behind last year, 53 percent said they don't expect to do any better next year, while only 23 percent thought they would be better off. Pessimism deepened as the recession dragged on.

The conditions causing that anxiety are commonplace at kitchen-table discussions as well as in media coverage and political debate. Stagnant family incomes and rising costs for housing, health care, child care, and college mean more overtime or a second job—facts of life in the nineties. So while economists, demographers, and sociologists debate how much people are hurting, voters will pass judgment on the economy the way candidate Reagan had shrewdly asked them to—not by studying the statistics but by examining their own experience.

And when the middle class has examined their experience, Democrats will find that there is a large pool of voters they could attract—the majority who say they've been running in place or falling behind in recent years. And in reaching out, Democrats should demonstrate concern, but should *not* draw parallels between these voters and the most abject victims of the past twelve years. Voters will listen to Democrats who understand that they're just getting by but (in Mario Cuomo's phrase) are "not rich enough to be worry-free."

So Democrats need to build their case on the bread-and-butter concerns of the great majority of Americans. In particular, studies by the Economic Policy Institute (EPI), a liberal think tank funded largely by labor unions, are required reading for an understanding of what the Reagan-Bush years have meant for the federal budget *and* family budgets. But studying the statistics about the difficulties of maintaining a middle-class life is only a start. People want more than a recitation of problems with which they're more personally and painfully familiar than even the best-intentioned leaders, candidates, or wanna-bes. They want an understanding of the texture of their lives, a sense of how their stories fit in with events around them, and a plausible explanation of how things might get better.

During the 1980s, for most American families incomes grew slowly, or not at all. According to the EPI, average hourly wages actually fell between 1980 and 1989, and any gains families made were because more members worked, and worked longer hours. Not only did more mothers work, but more fathers (and some mothers, too) took on second jobs and more teenagers got after-school jobs. And to many it still seemed like the ground was cracking underneath their feet—and for good reason. Not only were middle-class families working longer hours at lower hourly rates but their tax burden had increased as well.

It seems that only the wealthiest families came out ahead. Sorting through the welter of data about changes in the federal tax structure in the past fifteen years, the EPI has calculated that, in 1990, the top 1 percent of Americans got a tax cut averaging $45,565. The next richest 4 percent received, on average, an $881 tax break. However, looking at what happened to the rest of us, the other 95 percent, the EPI found that in 1990

> The lowest [income] fifth of families had a small tax hike of $15 . . . the second fifth . . . [paid an] increase of $193; and the middle and fourth fifths paid $186 and $269 more. . . . Even the

bottom half of the top fifth paid $446 more . . . and the next 5 percent paid $411.

This is because payroll taxes, which hit hardest at the middle class, were increased during the Reagan years, while federal tax rates for the richest households were drastically reduced. This shift in the tax burden, coupled with the cut in capital gains taxes during the Carter administration, created a bonanza for the wealthiest segment of society. On top of all this, state and local taxes (which take the biggest bite out of the middle class and which are not factored into the EPI statistics cited above), increased during the 1980s, largely because the federal government was handing responsibility for social programs over to the states. While both parties have had a hand in cutting taxes on the wealthy and raising them for the rest of us, populist Democrats can make a convincing case that these tax policies flow from prototypically Republican economic and social policies. (After all, it's Republicans, not Democrats, who wax eloquent about the need to cut taxes on wealthy investors.)

Democrats can follow the example of Rep. Tom Downey, a congressman from a middle-class district on Long Island, who talks about how the tax system has become increasingly unfair for "people who work very hard but don't make a lot of money." He points out that between 1977 and 1990 the tax rate of the richest one percent has dropped 23 percent, which has nearly doubled their average incomes to $550,000. Downey, after telling his audiences these facts, says: "I dare say there's nobody in this room who has had their incomes go up and their taxes go down. Most middle-income people have had their taxes go up and their real incomes go down, and their spouses go to work."

The parents of many people in Downey's audiences, the generation that went to work after World War II, could count on certain things — a job that offered security, health insurance, and a safe and satisfactory pension. But that social contract was broken for their children. Democrats have had much to say about the decline of basic industries with strong unions that provided good pay and solid benefits. Republicans have replied that more new jobs have been created, and they've claimed that these new jobs pay about as well. But one obvious fact gets less attention: The new jobs are less secure and offer fewer benefits.

The wrenching economic changes of the eighties not only closed factories, devastated communities, and stranded workers, it left many working Americans coping with quieter crises: Some companies started passing along part or all of the cost of health insurance to their employees; others cut back on pensions, until, by the end of the decade, fewer than half of all workers were covered by retirement plans; still others cut their work forces and replaced full-time employees with part-timers, often at lower pay and without benefits.

And people did what they've always done: adapt to their new environment. But this has been accompanied by new worries. According to pollster Celinda Lake:

> People were afraid of losing their jobs for a different reason from what you'd hear in the past. They were saying, "If I lose my job, I can probably get another one. It probably won't pay as much, but that's not the real problem. What scares me is, my new job won't have health insurance."

A new, anxiety-ridden breed of worker has emerged, one as familiar with the rapid pace of economic change as their fathers were familiar with the rapid pace of the assembly line. In the aftermath of the recession of the early eighties, the social commentators Ralph and Barbara Whitehead went around the country talking to young people who had been jostled from job to job. Ralph Whitehead recalls:

> We had a pizza in Parma, Ohio, with a young couple. He's 35; she's 31. After high school, he worked five blue-collar jobs and was laid off in each job—chiefly because the companies were going down the drain, or changing hands. . . .
>
> He and wife sort of pieced together one good job between them. . . . They believe lifetime job security is a thing of the past.

Yet those in this predicament don't necessarily blame the nation's leaders for their plight or think things will get better if a different party moves into the White House. Indeed, the congressional district that includes Parma voted for Reagan in 1984 and Bush in 1988. And during those campaigns, those of us working for Mondale and Dukakis could see why our arguments about Republican-caused economic dislocation might not draw these voters back to the Democratic party.

People remembered that the economic doldrums began back in the seventies, during the Carter-Mondale administration (if not even earlier, with the 1973 Arab oil embargo under President Nixon). As one of the speechwriters traveling with Mondale in the fall of 1984, part of my job was to call various contacts from the campaign staff, the party, and the labor unions to try to learn what was on people's minds in the places where Mondale would be speaking the next day. And in cities like Flint, Michigan, or Youngstown, Ohio, where steel and auto industries had taken a terrible beating in 1979 and 1980, I'd be warned that Mondale wouldn't get too friendly a reception because folks remembered when their troubles really began.

But at one question-and-answer session with a skeptical crowd in a high school auditorium in Youngstown, Mondale masterfully disarmed their anger by beginning with an apology for the Carter administration's failure to do enough for the steel towns. The crowd appreciated his frankness and they applauded when he attacked Reagan for doing even less, and they listened to his program for saving American steel. And Mondale carried Youngstown. If he could have answered questions in high school auditoriums across America, he'd have given Reagan a real race.

So it's not that people blame any president, past or present. They understand that what's happened to them and their communities is largely the result of global competition and technological change, and they don't want empty promises. This was brought home to me during the 1988 campaign, when I was calling Democrats and union people in the Pennsylvania steel town of McKeesport, where Dukakis was speaking the next day. "For God's sake, don't have Dukakis tell them he's going to bring the mills back, like in the old days," someone told me. "People know better than that."

But this doesn't mean that Democrats have nothing to say to those still feeling the aftershocks of the economic traumas of recent years. People want to know why the Reagan-Bush tax revisions have resulted in a middle class that pays *more* taxes while the rich pay less. And they want *their* stories told. When Sen. Tom Harkin of Iowa spoke about a family where the husband lost his $14-an-hour job and had to take a $7-an-hour job, while his wife had to work a $4-an-hour job, which left them working twice as hard for less money, people recognized themselves. And they applauded.

But more than applause lines, people want a sense of security in uncertain times. Since the Depression, that's been the Democratic party's unique selling point—fighting for worker protection in times of economic adversity. So Democrats need to promote expanded unemployment compensation, protection of pension benefits and, for people whose careers have been bumped around for the past decade, ideas about job training and retraining.

And there are the problems the political system has barely begun to address. Sixty percent of Americans want "fundamental change" in the health-care system. They worry about being able to afford health insurance—and if their coverage will really, fully, protect their families. Significantly, health care was one issue where a bipartisan poll in the spring of 1991 found that Democrats already held a 31 percent advantage—and the party hadn't even offered a health-care program. Similarly, middle-class families are looking for help with problems like day care and long-term care for elderly relatives.

When Democrats press these issues, they need to talk about the human realities behind the numbers. The fabled "middle-class squeeze" is more of a stretch—of people's time, energy, and resources. With longer work hours, less time at home, fewer and shorter vacations, and credit cards at the limit, many people feel they're at the edge—financially and psychologically. At least market researchers understand this. A typical advertisement (appropriately, for an antiperspirant) shows a tense young woman saying, "Between work, kids, the house, I'm stressed out." As one New Jersey man explains:

> I get on this goddamn train and travel two hours to go to work, so my kids can live in a nice clean place. Things at work are really bad, so work is just awful, and I come home, and between my taxes going up, my health insurance going up, and schools costing more, I don't know how I'm going to make it. What more do they want from me?

That man might see a little of himself in Al Bundy, the father in Fox Television's cynical situation comedy, "Married . . . with Children." At the beginning of each episode, Bundy, a shoe salesman in a Chicago suburb, is shown sprawled out on his sofa, as one by one, his wife, his son, and his daughter walk by. Reaching wearily into his pocket, he hands each of them some money, and when his dog walks by, he reflexively hands him some money, too.

Democrats should remember that the last thing Al Bundy wants is to hand out yet another wad of bills—especially to a tax collector to give to those "less fortunate." As Marge Laurino, a Democratic ward committeewoman from a middle-class area on the outskirts of Chicago, puts it, the people in her neighborhood and in the nearby suburbs feel that "I wasn't put on earth to pay for everyone's problems."

If you're working two jobs and your wife's working and your kids are working after school, then you're not likely to feel too generous toward those you believe don't work as hard as you, much less toward those who don't work at all. As Celinda Lake points out, workers whose health insurance is being cut back are often resentful that welfare recipients have free coverage provided by Medicaid (and working people's tax dollars).

So, today's middle class may feel more put-upon, more proud, and ultimately, more virtuous than ever. Democrats need to recognize that feeling and show some empathy for it. (The 1984

Reagan campaign did with its TV spot featuring people talking about how hard they work just to make ends meet. "Mondale must think you don't work hard enough already," the announcer said. "He wants to raise your taxes.") Democrats should understand that sustaining a middle-class life is a real struggle, and that the effort itself is central to middle-class identity.

People place such great value on having some degree of control over their lives that it extends to how they talk about their "money situation." To tell yourself that your paycheck is shrinking and that you're not doing any better than years ago comes perilously close to calling yourself a failure. But attributing your family's financial squeeze to the soaring cost of living is a more comfortable—and dignified—way to talk about the same problem. Today, people say they are more anxious about rising prices than at any time since the double-digit inflation of the late seventies. And costs *are* rising.

Particularly for that essential element of the American dream—a home—the news hasn't been good. The Economic Policy Institute reports that during the 1980s, a combination of high interest rates and rising home prices resulted in a drop in home ownership. Rents increased across the board and households with children were especially hard hit.

Michael McKeon, a Democratic pollster from the blue-collar community of Joliet, Illinois, sums it up:

You have more and more young people . . . in their twenties and even in their thirties, and they're still living with their parents. They've tried jumping through all the hoops, but they can't find a decent job, and they can't make enough to move out of the goddamn house they grew up in.

This leads us to another problem. What a lot of these young (and no-longer-so-young) people are missing is a college degree, which is the ticket to the best-paying and most secure jobs. And many don't have a degree because it, too, has been priced out of reach: State colleges are cutting back; student aid for all but the poorest is being curtailed; and tuitions at private colleges are zooming into the stratosphere. This is a powerful, emotional is-sue. As one middle-class man from a Detroit suburb said, "What happens is you're creating an elite, those families that can afford to put their children through college. They're going to run the country."

★ THE MIDDLE-CLASS SQUEEZE: MORAL AND MATERIAL

Rising prices and stagnant incomes have put middle-class voters in an economic vise, but equally important is their feelings of being squeezed between the two extremes of the economic spectrum: wealth and welfare.

After almost ten years of talking with middle-class voters in small discussion groups, or focus groups, pollster Stanley Green-berg concludes:

> The middle class today perceives itself as "squeezed" between the rich and the poor, neither of whom play by the rules, but seek their reward through shortcuts or special claims—tax breaks, windfalls, and welfare.

The sense that they follow the rules but others don't is a com-mon complaint of the middle class. They work hard for their money, pay more than their fair share of taxes, show personal re-straint, and try to raise their children right. They uphold their end of the social contract while others don't; indeed, they feel they carry the rich and the poor on their backs. But when it comes to their place in the political process, middle-class people often sound ambivalent. They're angry that nobody speaks for them yet they're proud of their self-reliance—they don't make special claims on society. Thus, when they do talk about their situations it is often in tones of a beleaguered morality. One middle-class voter put it this way: "The average person . . . is supporting both ends. You have the extremely rich who pay a very low tax, and you have the poor who are paying none, and you [the middle class] are right there."

The sociologist Jonathan Rieder, during his interviews with residents of Canarsie, a middle-class section of Brooklyn, found "a self-professed conservative Democrat" who expressed a similar view:

> It's okay to talk about the welfare classes, but the real problem is the middle-class squeeze. You get it from the top and bottom. It's not only welfare, but the multinational corporations who are ripping us off, taking our jobs away. . . . The middle classes are the lost people.

Despite their economic worries, where the middle class feels most painfully squeezed, and the most distressed ethically, emotionally, and economically, is not in the workplace, the marketplace, or the political process, but in the home.

When it seems there's no time for families to spend together, when it's difficult to find child care you can trust and afford, when the public schools seem less than adequate, when higher education is unaffordable, and when high-paying jobs are more difficult to find and keep, it is children who become the focus of people's worries, regrets, and even guilt. Throw in the social anxieties— from crime and drugs to popular music that celebrates sexual sadism—and it seems like both the economy and the culture are at odds with family life. Social commentator Barbara Whitehead has learned from her focus groups with middle-class parents that people feel their families are caught in a "cultural squeeze":

> This surfaces as parents talk about the pressure on their grade-school children to buy $65 Reeboks and $50 stone-washed jeans . . . they are losing the struggle to pass on their values to their children— losing it to an aggressive and insidious consumer culture. In their eyes, their children are no longer acquiring an identity as much as they are attempting to buy one in the marketplace.

Many Americans regard the two decades after World War II, when living standards rose steadily for an expanding middle class, as a golden age. And many Democrats seem to misunderstand the focus of that nostalgia. Much Democratic rhetoric suggests that we long for the days when most Americans worked in basic industries, as if there were mass nostalgia not only for secure paychecks but for the sound of the factory whistle.

In fact, people's nostalgia is not for the work life but for the home life of that era. While the majority recognizes that women are in the workplace to stay, and support equal pay and equal opportunities for women, husbands and wives also want to spend more time with each other and with their children. Barbara Whitehead notes that in speaking of the family life of the recent past, most experts sound almost contemptuous (a way of talking that sounds more "liberal" than "conservative"):

> In the official debate . . . the remembered past is almost always considered a suspect, even unhealthy, guide for the present or the future . . . these memories harken back to what the official language is pleased to term the "mythical" or "nostalgic" family of the past – a sentimental fiction that blinds us to the real challenges of modern life.

But, she adds, this doesn't ring true to most people:

> [T]he mothers and fathers I met do not hesitate to look back at their own childhoods. And, in a majority of cases, they report that, compared to today, families were stronger, children better off, and neighborhood and community life more supportive of family well-being. In the official language, the family isn't getting weaker, it's just changing. Most parents I met believe otherwise.

Republicans have been far more effective than Democrats at addressing these anxieties and capturing the warm feelings people have for their families, whereas Democrats have been accused of having lost their moral compass. Ronald Reagan understood this, and in his speech at the 1980 GOP convention "family" came first in his "community of shared values." And most voters probably agreed that he reflected their values better than his Democratic rivals did. Democrats shouldn't echo Reaganite social conservatism. Instead, Democrats should offer a progressive pro-family policy that makes it easier for families to stay together. And Democrats can do that while respecting and supporting the heroic struggles of single parents, usually working mothers, to put food on the table and raise their children right.

Democrats need to address the economic realities of people's lives, the ethical imperatives on which they build their lives, and how these are intertwined. Political analysts Elaine Ciulla Kamarck and William Galston advise Democrats to advocate a "policy that recognizes that two-earner families are frequently necessary — and that two-parent families are usually best." If Democrats start with that premise, then they can offer American families the tangible assistance they need, and the moral support they deserve. And this support recognizes that the middle class upholds the social compact, and it puts the middle class at the center of the argument.

7
▬ Middle Class Mantras

In just about every stump speech in the fall of 1988, Michael Dukakis promised to do something for "the thirty-seven million people—two thirds of them from working families, ten million of them children—who don't have a dime's worth of health insurance."

That line was well received by most crowds. Most people think everyone is entitled to at least a minimal level of health coverage. And Dukakis talked about the uninsured in a way calculated to make them sympathetic figures. Working people and their families. Children, for God's sake. Who doesn't feel for kids who can't go to the doctor when they're sick just because their families don't have health insurance?

But by concentrating on the plight of the uninsured, Dukakis didn't make the case that universal health coverage would also help people who are covered but still have problems—such as rising costs, shrinking benefits, and the growing fear that their employers will cut back, or even eliminate, their health insurance. If he'd addressed these concerns as clearly and compellingly as he'd addressed the needs of those without any insurance, Dukakis would've been a much more attractive candidate. And even though most middle-class voters agreed on the need for a universal health plan, it was the way Dukakis talked about it, and what he left unsaid, that worked to confirm the stereotype that Democrats care mostly about the poor.

Unfortunately, just as most Republicans need pointers on how to talk to the poor, national Democrats need to think a bit before talking to the majority of Americans who are neither poor nor "worry-free." And in addressing this audience, Democrats would do well to remember these ten rules:

■ **RULE #1.** *Remember—America is a middle-class country. Most people identify themselves and others as middle class, and consider the middle class to be society's economic, social, and moral norm.*

Americans who aren't millionaires or mendicants appreciate being called "middle class." It doesn't matter where they work, talk about "the middle class," and most people think you mean them. If you talk about "working people," they think you mean blue-collar workers (who now comprise just 27 percent of the work force, and if you asked them, they'd probably call themselves middle class, too). Only older blue-collar workers are likely to call themselves "working people" or even "working class." For most, "middle class" is the label of choice.

At the start of the 1990s, median family income was around $30,000, but a fair guess is that most people think a middle-class income falls somewhere between $20,000 and $200,000. If you earn $200,000 or more, people think you're well-to-do. At the richly symbolic level of a million-dollar income, people think you're filthy rich. When a politician wants to increase taxes on families making $50,000 or so, most see this as soaking the middle class, and they won't appreciate it. Even tax increases for families making $100,000 won't meet with a lot of enthusiasm. But talk about raising taxes on millionaires, and most people will cheer.

Marge Laurino, a Democratic committeewoman, has an image of a family that might live in her ward: "They're a married couple. The husband and wife both work at white-collar jobs. Together, they make $50,000. They have two kids in parochial school, and that costs. And they want to send them to college, and that will cost a lot more. They figure a millionaire is wealthy, but $50,000 makes you middle class." (And maybe barely getting by.)

Back in 1984, Walter Mondale's proposal to increase federal income taxes started with a family of four earning more than $25,000 a year. At $30,000, that family's taxes would have gone up $95, and at $40,000, $305. By $100,000, taxes increased dramatically, and millionaires would be billed an additional $40,924. Mondale's staff may have thought they were soaking the rich but, in fact, they were scaring the hell out of the middle class, who only heard that tax increases would start in the $25,000 range.

I joined the campaign staff around the time this was proposed and, to put it gently, it seemed strange. I'd just come from seven years of working in union organizing campaigns, and when I thought about the households that would be affected, and whose votes Mondale so desperately needed, I'd see the union couples I'd met. While most commentators said Mondale was "pandering" to organized labor, "panicking" might have been a better word. The policy experts who formulated that tax plan may have suffered from any number of illusions, but one thing is clear: They didn't know the meaning of "middle class."

As pollster Geoff Garin told the Democratic state chairs in 1988: "If we're going to be the party of the middle class, we've got to go up [the economic scale] in who we think the middle class is. We can't stop at $12,000 or $25,000. The mainstream of America is making in the thirties. We've got to talk to these people."

Democrats should avoid programs that cut America in roughly even halves, with the fault line running right through the middle class. That was what George McGovern did in 1972, with his plan to raise taxes on the half of all American families that earned more than $12,000 in order to provide "demogrants" of $1,000 per person to the poor. And Mondale's deficit reduction plan began at $25,000 because that was what the "upper half" of American households earned in 1984. Whatever the merits of such plans as policy, they were terrible politics not only because they cost money for half the electorate, the half most likely to vote, but because they also divided America evenly into "the rich" and "the poor," implicitly denying the existence of a middle class.

■ **RULE #2.** *Talk to the middle class, in ways that don't make the poor feel left out.*

To its credit, the Democratic party represents not only people at the center of the economic spectrum, but those who work but can't afford even the bare necessities of life, the "poor," and those who suffer from racial and ethnic stereotyping and scapegoating. So Democrats do need to be concerned with how an emphasis on the "middle class" sounds. A Polish-American miner in Pennsylvania likely believes you're talking about him. But those who labor at low wages may not think that "middle class" accurately describes their social or economic situation. And even the substantial number of blacks and Hispanics who do earn middle-class salaries may still wonder if political rhetoric about the "middle class" really means to include them.

So the phrases and symbols of Democratic rhetoric need to show that Democrats certainly are embracing the black, Hispanic, and Asian middle class, as well as the white middle class, and that they will not abandon those of all races who work for low wages or who are unable to find work. Therefore, Democrats should leaven their discourse with references to "middle-class working people" and "people who work for a living," which include people with low-paying jobs as well as the middle class. And unlike Michael Dukakis, who campaigned almost exclusively in settings that seemed not only middle class but "white-bread," Democrats should seek audiences that symbolize the diversity of those who "work for a living."

Linda Williams, a leading analyst of black politics, suggests that Democrats "seeking to appeal to the middle class and the working class . . . might drop using the term, 'the poor,' " which, she warns, "has come to be a euphemism for blacks." So instead of the traditional formula of "the middle class and the poor," she advises Democrats to "use language like 'the average working person,' which would not cut them off from black America."

"The overwhelming majority of blacks see themselves as workers—even those who are unemployed or on welfare desperately want to work," notes Williams, who was associate research director at the Joint Center for Political Studies. Indeed, much of Jesse Jackson's appeal in his two presidential campaigns, particularly in 1988, was his "very strong economic populist message and his advocacy for working people, black and white."

Democrats need to define the common values that unite the middle class and those who are working hard to join it. Maryland senator Barbara Mikulski claims that this is the heart of the Democratic party's tradition:

> I believe the Democratic party came into existence to fight for economic advancement. We have stood for—and come to fight for—the preservation and extension of the middle class. I believe the Democratic party should help all of the people who are middle class stay there—and all of the people who are not middle class have the opportunity to get there.

One helpful phrase is "people who live from paycheck to paycheck." By emphasizing their shared virtue and vulnerability, it bonds people who too often have been pitted against each other. For instance, a hospital worker on Chicago's predominantly black South Side might be evicted from her apartment soon after she lost her job and missed a rent payment. A travel agent from a predominantly white suburb might be in danger of losing her home if she lost her job and missed a mortgage payment. Both live in different circumstances, but both are living from paycheck to paycheck and share the sense of insecurity that sets them apart from the most affluent.

■ **RULE #3.** *Never forget that the middle class is ambivalent about government.*

Actually, ambivalent may be too weak a word for the skepticism, hostility, even contempt that middle-class people feel for government. And for all the pretentious punditry about the differences between the generations, the greatest gap may lie in their attitudes towards government.

For the generation that came of age during the Depression, World War II, or the beginning of the postwar era, government did its job—and did it well. But for succeeding generations—particularly those of the late sixties and beyond—government has very different connotations: the Vietnam War, the Watergate scandal, Carter's "malaise," the Defense Department's $600 toilet seats, and the savings-and-loan scandal. And if the political climate and popular culture of recent years had any message, it was that the public sector was less efficient than the marketplace, and less moral—and less secure—than personal and familial space.

Taking some public services for granted, holding many public institutions in contempt, and never forgetting the bite taxes take out of their paychecks, middle-class people see government as a cost, not a benefit and are likely to complain that it "does nothing for me." While their parents believed that government was on their side, these folks feel that government has its hand in their pockets and its nose in their business.

In a campaign dominated by anger at Gov. Florio's tax increases, Sen. Bill Bradley of New Jersey almost lost his 1990 reelection bid. Afterwards, Bradley said, "What middle-class people want and need is more money in their pockets. What's more, they feel that government is no longer accountable." So Democrats are learning that calling for new bureaucracies to solve social ills won't work, and instead, they're offering proposals to raise taxes on the very wealthiest people, to put more money in the hands of the middle class and the working poor.

Tennessee senator Albert Gore and New York congressman Tom Downey have recently come up with such a plan. Downey is worth watching. He represents a suburban district on Long Island that voted Republican in the last three presidential elections, and he's one of the Democrats' most sophisticated students of middle-class attitudes. Downey first made his mark on national policy by reshaping child-care legislation that had originally emphasized government-operated day-care centers. Instead, Downey's approach was to give tax credits so parents could choose their own child-care providers. The bill was passed by Congress and signed by President Bush.

■ **RULE #4.** *Avoid the stereotype that Democrats support means-tested programs that exclude the middle class and reward dependency.*

Democrats built a national majority with the universal programs they developed from the 1930s to the 1960s, which benefitted everyone, or excluded only the wealthiest, or rewarded those who'd served their country. But they lost that support when they became identified with "means-tested" programs, which exclude the middle class. Although these meet real, sometimes desperate needs, programs exclusively for the poor and near-poor seem doomed to unpopularity because middle-class taxpayers, rightly or wrongly, see these as rewards for behavior that the government should discourage, not encourage, and they resent the recipients.

Republicans have been able to paint Democrats as "out of the mainstream," and oblivious to middle-class concerns. Now most people associate Democrats with the Great Society rather than the New Deal, expect them to reward dependency, and assume that any new program offered is a variant of means-tested welfare-liberalism. (Indeed, during the Dukakis campaign, polling discovered that the very word "program" got an unfavorable response from voters when mentioned in the context of government, Democrats, liberals, or Michael Dukakis.)

So Democrats need to consciously avoid—and play against—this stereotype. They should develop ideas (forget "programs") that will help the middle class as well as the poor, emphasizing how these will encourage self-reliance, rather than dependency, and how eligibility will be based on good behavior rather than bad. Some examples are proposals that require welfare recipients to work or enroll in job training, or that link student loans to participation in service programs.

Meanwhile, Democrats should be on the alert for the emergence of a new phenomenon: Republican means-testing. Early in 1991, the Bush administration's budget director, Richard Darman, floated a number of ideas that would exclude some or all of the middle class from social benefits. Democrats should've jumped on Darman's proposal to eliminate college aid for children of families earning more than $40,000, and for tightening standards for Medicare, school lunches, and farm aid. That's "the heart of the middle class"—the same territory where Walter Mondale committed hari-kiri. In the name of "increasing fairness in the distribution of benefits," federal support would be restricted to the poor. Ironically, Darman's words recalls the Democratic rhetoric that's so offended middle-class voters.

In fact, it looked like Darman was doing his best to reverse *that* political stereotype. Now instead of the "limousine liberal," we've got Darman, the "Cadillac conservative," the affluent budget-cutter who wants to slash services for the middle class while supposedly sparing the poor.

Of course, government does need to save money, especially now. But rather than plans like Darman's, Democrats should propose progressive taxation on the cash value of government benefits. Rather than drawing the line on eligibility in the middle of the middle class, progressive taxation of benefits would ensure that the wealthy would pay more and the middle class would lose less.

■■ **RULE #5.** *Concentrate on the points in people's lives where they may need a helping hand.*

Middle-class people are likely to insist that they earn everything they get, that government never does anything for them, and can't do anything right, anyway. Even so, there are points in the life cycle where people have specific needs and would accept a helping hand—even from government: day care for small children, college tuition, loans for a first home, health insurance for workers and their growing families, job retraining, long-term care for elderly relatives, and retirement benefits. In fact, surveys show that most people think government should take a larger role in these areas. What must be reckoned with is people's reluctance to pay higher taxes and their understandable concern that the services be provided in an effective, efficient, and unbureaucratic way.

"What's a government child-care center?" one woman reportedly asked in a discussion group. "I can't imagine what it would be like. It sounds like something in China."

To make the case that government can help people meet their needs, Democrats should discuss it from the views of those who need these services, not the institutions that provide them. It'd be far more appropriate and meaningful to frame these issues in the story of one family's life—and show the points where government can aid, not supplant, a family's support system.

■ **RULE #6.** *Explain the value of social programs from the viewpoint of the anxious middle class, not just the poor.*

The debate over universal health insurance offers a classic example of how *not* to make the case for social programs.

During 1987, advocates of "health care for all" stressed the plight of the uninsured—a substantial constituency but nowhere near a majority. According to most surveys, the issue was a winner—but not as big a winner as it could have been.

What should have been stressed was the "all": the tens of millions more people who have some coverage but have good reason to worry if it's adequate. And Democrats are finally learning the importance of addressing this audience. If people are made aware that universal coverage will allay their real fears about their insurance—that employers might cut back or eliminate it, that premiums might rise, that it won't cover a real emergency, or that if they need to get a new job, it might not have health benefits—

then they'll agree that government should guarantee a basic level of health insurance for everyone. And the case for insuring the uninsured can be made as well by appealing to enlightened self-interest. Consider a family that doesn't have health coverage, and doesn't get regular medical checkups. Eventually someone in that family becomes seriously ill and ends up in a hospital emergency room as a charity case. Who pays the bill? We all do — in higher taxes, insurance premiums, and hospital costs.

This strategy puts the middle class at the center of the argument, and it can work for other social programs, too. For instance, Democrats who talk about "decent housing" sound like they're talking about housing projects, but those who advocate "helping every family afford a home of their own," are talking about benefitting everyone.

■ **RULE #7.** *Present programs not only in terms of middle-class interests but middle-class values.*

Democrats do better when they can show voters that their proposals will promote values like family, work, and self-reliance. Avoid abstract terms like "compassion," which sound bureaucratic, or controversial ideas like redistributing wealth.

For example, when Sen. Albert Gore and Rep. Tom Downey proposed funding tax cuts for thirty-five million middle- and low-income families by raising taxes on the richest six million, they didn't talk about redistribution of wealth, or even about taking money from the filthy rich. Instead, they made it clear that theirs was a "pro-family" tax cut which would help hard-pressed families stay together, make ends meet, and raise their children right.

Just as the Gore-Downey tax cut would reward families by providing an additional $800 tax credit per child, other progressive programs can be promoted as rewards for work. (And in fact, the most popular and most successful always have been.) The best goal for activist government is not to keep people in a permanent state of dependency, but to provide them with the opportunity for self-sufficiency. Americans are most favorable to calls for compassion if these recall the parable about teaching someone how to fish, rather than merely feeding him a fish.

In the 1984 campaign, of all the arguments Mondale made against Reagan's budget cuts, the most persuasive came from an unlikely source: the surgeon who saved Reagan's life after he was shot by John Hinckley.

Always eager to hail American heroes, the grateful Reagan told an Italian-American audience about this successful surgeon, the son of immigrants who had struggled to send their boy to college and medical school. But the surgeon, Dr. Joseph Giordano, later explained that he and his family hadn't made it entirely on their own. His father had benefitted from membership in a strong union. While his family had sacrificed much, Dr. Giordano was able to attend medical school because he got low-interest student loans. And, his parents, who had worked hard all their lives, needed social security and Medicare for their retirement. Even the medical technology that helped save Reagan's life was developed with federal research funds.

During his final weeks on the stump, Mondale told Dr. Giordano's story as living proof that government programs could promote, rather than discourage, self-reliance. And with this approach, Mondale got a better response than with his litany of misfortune: "If you're poor, they give you cheese. . . . "

Self-reliance was also the theme of one of the most famous — or notorious — Democratic stump speeches of the 1988 primaries. During the early laps of the race, Sen. Joseph Biden quoted a speech by British Labor party leader Neil Kinnock, which told how government programs gave his family the "platform" to climb from poverty into the middle class:

> Why am I the first Kinnock in generations to be able to get to university? Was it because our predecessors were thick? Was it because they were weak, these people who could work eight hours underground? It was because they had no platform on which to stand and reach for their dreams.

Of course, Biden had to leave the race for using this speech (at least once) without attribution, thus implying that it was the story of his own family. Yet, the point is that the use of Kinnock's story was remarkably effective because of how "American" it is. Far from assuming that class divisions are permanent and that the primary obligation of the party of the Left is to protect those at the bottom, Kinnock's speech suggests that society is fluid and progressive policies can help people move up in the world.

As Biden understood, there is much here for American liberals. Kinnock's words acknowledge that worthy people can find themselves trapped in poverty, and by admitting this possibility, a middle-class audience is forced to face two uncomfortable truths. First, unless they would dishonor their own ancestors, they must realize that they owe their own relative comfort and security not only to their own efforts but to the advantages that the larger human community has provided them. And second, they must also acknowledge that many of those who have not been able to "reach for their dreams" are people who have had no "platform" on which to stand.

And as the 1992 presidential campaign got underway, Iowa senator Tom Harkin used a similar metaphor when he praised those who have climbed "the ladder of opportunity," saying that Americans are too decent to knock the ladder down while others are working their way up.

Intriguingly, the Democrats' new metaphors for social programs—the "platform" and the "ladder"—show more respect for the middle-class value of self-reliance than the favorite metaphor of the Reagan administration: "the safety net" that provides a minimal amount of security for those who have fallen down on hard times. While the "safety net" can entangle those in it, the platform and the ladder give people the boost they need to "reach for their dreams." Indeed, Democrats should exploit these differences. While Republicans offer a dwindling dole, Democrats should offer a helping hand, so that the poor can become middle class and the middle class can remain secure.

■ **RULE #8.** *Speak the language of the social contract—the linkage between rights and responsibilities.*

At the heart of the American experiment is the concept of the social contract: the web of rights and responsibilities that link people with each other and connect individuals to the larger community. While Americans don't use abstract terms, when they talk about "playing by the rules," "doing the right thing," or "I've worked all my life for that company, and I expected more," they are speaking the language of the social contract. Political language and political programs are most appealing when they recognize the value Americans place on the social contract.

Much has been said about linking benefits with behavior for ordinary citizens, whether that means job training for welfare recipients or college aid in return for community service. But Democrats should insist that similar requirements be set for those who enjoy even bigger benefits from our society: corporations and the wealthy. For example, corporations should participate in progressive programs such as universal health coverage and guaranteed parental leave as their part of the social contract with working Americans and the country. If they don't hold up their end of the deal they should be attacked, not as "big business and the rich," but for failing to "play by the rules."

■ **RULE #9.** *The middle class will respond to challenge, not chastisement.*

The best example of a Democrat addressing an affluent, but anxious, nation remains John F. Kennedy's appeal in 1960: "America is a good country, but we can do better."

The last thing the middle class wants to hear is a rhetoric that crosses the line between challenging them to do better and accusing them of being sinful. And there has been a strain in liberal rhetoric—although it survives more in conservative caricatures of liberalism than in anything most Democrats are actually saying—

that condemns the middle class as racist, narrow-minded and, in general, too fat and complacent for its own good. Since Republicans are ever eager to re-fight the battles of the sixties, when angry young people were condemning America's faults, they'll try to attack Democrats on that basis. So Democrats have to be careful not to say anything that can be misunderstood, or made to sound, as an attack on Middle Americans.

Thus, in calling the eighties "a decade of greed," Democrats need to make clear whose greed they're talking about. Not the struggling middle-class family, the ordinary businessperson, or the entrepreneur. The term "greed" is appropriate only for those who got rich by breaking the rules and providing nothing of value—inside-traders in the stock market, the savings-and-loan looters, or the financial wizards whose "contribution" was the intricate take-over mechanisms that left companies tottering on towers of debt. And if Democrats extend the metaphor and talk about the eighties as a party that left America with a grim morning after, they should also say that most Americans didn't go to the party, but merely got stuck with the bill.

■ **RULE #10:** *Don't address the middle class as one more interest group. It's the majority—and the mainstream—of America.*

All this advice will be worthless if Democrats address middle-class Americans as one more interest group, somewhere in the litany between family farmers and elementary school teachers.

The middle class sees itself as the majority and the main-stream, with its fate and fortunes uniquely linked to America's success. Ultimately, any appeal to the middle class depends upon inspiring hope in a successful American future.

8
■ Glory Days

★ **"THE BEST YEARS"**

At the GOP Convention in 1984, right after Ronald Reagan accepted his party's nomination for re-election, the band struck up Franklin Roosevelt's campaign tune, "Happy Days Are Here Again." Many of the delegates couldn't believe their ears. This was a song that had soothed Americans' spirits during the Great Depression; it was the traditional Democratic anthem. And up until August 1984, it had never been heard at a Republican convention.

In fact, that year, it hadn't even been heard at the *Democratic* convention. Forgetting that voters liked FDR (it was more recent Democrats like George McGovern and Jimmy Carter they couldn't stand), the Mondale campaign, not wanting to seem like traditional Democratic liberals, took "Happy Days" off its hit parade. So the song was just waiting for someone to play it, and Reagan put his quarter in the jukebox.

Reagan understood what the Democrats didn't: The traditional symbolism of the Democratic party—embodied in the presidencies of FDR, Truman, and John F. Kennedy—retains positive connotations for most voters. It's still the most powerful symbolism in American politics, which is why Republicans, wisely, keep trying to steal these Democratic heroes.

Roosevelt and Truman were the founding fathers of post-World War II America, an era of "firsts"—families' first homes,

1 6 5

166 ★ SPEAKING AMERICAN

the first son or daughter to attend college, and first place in the world economy. *The Best Years of Our Lives* was the title of a Hollywood movie about veterans returning home to this newly prosperous America and for most people, even today, the era from 1945 through 1965 has a kind of mythic resonance, not only for the generation that fought World War II, but for their children—the product of the famous "baby boom." Indeed, a cultural phenomenon of the tag-end of the 1980s was a fifties nostalgia craze. (Perhaps the most extreme example is the popularity of the cable TV channel Nickelodeon's "Nick at Nite" programming, which is devoted to showing reruns of fifties sit-coms.) And from a diverse assortment of politically minded baby-boomers— Reagan-Bush speechwriter Peggy Noonan, angry Vietnam veteran Ron Kovic, and populist filmmaker Michael Moore—came a slew of books and movies that presented the America of their childhoods as a golden age for middle-class working people (sometimes glossing over the less attractive features of that period, from racial discrimination to sexual stereotyping).

Even Peggy Noonan, the lone Republican in the trio, writes respectfully of the Democrats of this era. Democrats told a simple story about the economy and made it work. While Republicans said (as one Eisenhower cabinet secretary put it) what's good for General Motors is good for America, Democrats said what's good for working people is good for America. Put money in people's pockets and they'll be able to afford houses, cars, washing machines, and TV sets. Companies will make money and the economy will keep humming along. And it did.

That was why, for the three-and-a-half decades after the end of World War II, Democrats consistently led public opinion surveys that asked the question, "Which party best manages the economy?" But, by the campaign of 1980, when Democrat Jimmy Carter presided over an America plagued by rising unemployment and soaring inflation, the parties' traditional roles had been reversed. A joyless Carter seemed to be saying that things weren't likely to ever get much better, so Americans had better get used to "an era of limits." His Republican rival Ronald Reagan, a former Democrat, borrowed heavily from Roosevelt's rhetoric and symbolism, and promised a new era of economic growth. But this would be achieved not by expanding government but by limiting it, thus liberating private industry from excessive taxation and regulation—classically Republican principles.

★ SUPPLY-SIDE SOUNDED LIKE COMMON SENSE

Reagan's advisers had a new way of talking about economics. Traditional Democratic economics, they said, was "demand-side" because it emphasized promoting people's purchasing power, while Reagan's economics was "supply-side" because it emphasized incentives for investment, savings, and productivity. The Reaganites found new ways to justify traditional Republican goals: Cut taxes across-the-board, especially for the wealthy, because that encourages people to invest more, deregulate business because companies are more productive if they're not hampered by federal red tape and meddlesome bureaucrats, and cut government poverty programs because the ready availability of welfare discourages work.

The biggest mistake Democrats ever made was in underestimating Ronald Reagan, or dismissing him as a former movie actor whose only aptitude was for reading other people's lines. In fact, as a former union president and, later, as a kind of corporate morale officer touring General Electric factories, Reagan had years of experience talking to working people about bread-and-butter issues and he used something almost unheard-of in discussions of economics: simple declarative sentences. Supply-side may have been bad economics, but its principles sounded like common sense, particularly to people building businesses of their own or dreaming of doing that—and that's a lot of Americans.

By the 1988 elections, even the patrician George Bush had learned to make classically Republican economics sound like the hard-earned wisdom of a self-made man. Addressing a Detroit audience consisting mostly of businesswomen, Bush said:

> Our policies work because they play to the best in human nature. Low tax rates give people an incentive to work—for the simple reason that they want to keep more of what they earn. It's common sense: If you want less of something, you tax it.

Democrats need to sound just as down-to-earth. One reason why they've been losing economic policy debates is because too often they sound like graduate school professors while Republicans sound like grocery store owners. So Democrats need to develop their own form of supply-side populism, one that emphasizes purchasing power and productivity. While Republicans, particularly in the Bush era, have seemed fixated on giving incentives solely to wealthy investors, Democrats should focus on incentives for the entire society: working people, whether new, white, or blue collar; small-business owners; poor people striving to become productive workers. Meanwhile, Democrats should also point out that any new incentives require safeguards to prevent the excesses of the rich and big business. They already have an inordinate share of wealth and power, and many have been using these in selfish and shortsighted ways.

Democrats can make a credible case for new economic ideas in the 1992 campaign—when President Bush may sound a lot more like Herbert Hoover than Franklin Roosevelt. Well into the third year of his administration, Bush has presided over the lowest average annual growth rate in almost thirty years: 1.6 percent a year, compared to 3.5 percent for Reagan, 3.1 percent for Carter, 2.1 percent for Ford, 2.4 percent for Nixon, and 4.6 percent for Johnson. Bush promised to create 35 million jobs in eight years, but, before the recession deepened, the number of jobs in America increased by only 200,000, which is less than under any president in recent memory. Worse yet, a year before Election Day 1992, the nation has been in a recession for more than a year. As *Business Week* noted in a cover story entitled "The New Face of Recession," this slump has hurt white collars, professionals, and managers, as well as blue-collar workers.

Bush's behavior during the "downturn" has reawakened traditional perceptions that Republicans are the kind of people who would veto an extension of unemployment benefits in the middle of a recession. And his complacency has strengthened the sense that our national leaders are unwilling to cope with the threats to America's long-term economic future, from both international competitors and our own failings.

★ PRAGMATIC POPULISM

The time is right for a Democratic populism, one that seeks to make the economy both fair for working Americans and successful in the world marketplace. There's a story waiting to be told, one that's filled with moral indignation and the peculiarly American sense that some highfalutin' theories have been tried but just aren't working.

For instance, the liberal advocacy group Citizens for Tax Justice estimates that the richest one percent of the population will get an $84-billion tax break in 1992 alone, a result of the supply-side tax cuts of the 1980s. Democrats need to show voters how these tax breaks, instead of being used for productive investment, have been spent on just about everything else imaginable: a wave of mergers and acquisitions, bigger dividends for stockholders, higher pay for corporate executives, and mega-consumption by the super-rich. None of this is what Reagan said supply-side would produce. But that's what happened.

Americans might not be outraged by any of this if they thought it was serving a useful purpose. But, as Citizens for Tax Justice points out, supply-side failed to bring about the promised private investment. From 1981 through 1986—the years immediately following the Reagan tax cuts—investment increased by the relatively low annual rate of 2.1 percent. But from 1986 through

1989 — following a bipartisan tax reform that eliminated many tax breaks for the wealthy — investment actually increased to 4.9 percent a year. Indeed, as J. Gregory Ballentine, a former Reagan Treasury official, told *Business Week*, "It's very difficult to find much relationship between tax rates and investment. In 1981, manufacturing had its largest tax cut ever and immediately went down the tubes. In 1986, they had their largest tax increase and went gangbusters [on investment]."

Democrats can present the squandering of these windfalls in terms of classically American symbolism: the default on a solemn covenant between the wealthy and the rest of society.

Americans don't begrudge successful people rewards for their accomplishments. We don't mind if an inventor like Apple Computer founder Steven Jobs or a beloved entertainer like Bill Cosby makes millions of dollars a year (although we want them to spend it responsibly). But if there are two types Americans despise, it's the unproductive speculator and the undisciplined wastrel. In recent years news weeklies and supermarket tabloids have been filled with stories about the likes of Donald Trump and Leona Helmsley, who seemed to produce little of value but consumed — extravagantly. (Helmsley even declared that only the little people pay taxes.) Jeff Faux, president of the Economic Policy Institute, a think tank funded largely by labor unions, puts it this way: "The social contract was supposed to be that the rich were allowed to get rich, but they would re-invest in their country. Now, they get rich, they have obscene ostentation and invest all over the world, but not here."

Democrats should show their populist anger about such excess. Mario Cuomo has talked about money "that might be used for falling bridges and the drug war" ending up "in minks and Jaguars when the top rate drops to 28 percent." Ticking off a checklist of culturally elitist tastes, Sen. Howell Heflin of Alabama has attacked the "Gucci-clothed, Mercedes-driving, jacuzzi-soaking, Perrier-drinking, Aspen-skiing Republicans." These images support the increasingly accepted idea that the

eighties were a party that most Americans didn't attend. As Jeff
Faux says, "We should send the bill to the people who went." In
other words, those who benefitted the most should pay the most
for the bail-outs and the clean-ups.

There are important moral and pragmatic dimensions to the
economic problems that are the legacy of the eighties, but
Democrats tend to discuss these in technocratic rather than
populist terms. (Democrats often sound like Republicans when
talking about the federal budget deficit. Much worse, they seem to
suggest that we've *all* been living too well and need the bitter medicine of increased taxes and reduced services.) Ironically, it's the
professorial Democrat from New York, Sen. Daniel Patrick Moynihan, who's found appropriate populist language. He points out
that the interest payments alone – $179 billion in 1990 – amount to
a massive transfer of wealth from hardworking taxpayers to the
wealthy bondholders. Ninety-five percent of these bonds, sold in
$10,000 denominations, are owned by the wealthiest 10 percent of
Americans. Money that goes to pay interest on the debt performs
no public purpose at all – it just lines people's pockets.

Another example of massive waste is the estimated $500-
billion cost of bailing out the savings-and-loans. This scandal
highlights the failings of the Republican philosophy of deregula-
tion; it happened because of Reagan-Bush administration policies. Republicans will counterpunch, claiming that Democratic
senators are among those implicated in the S&L debacle (although
its most famous figure is President Bush's son Neil). But
Democrats need only shift the debate to the larger issue: While
some Democrats can be induced into favoring the fat cats, Republicans do it as a matter of principle.

Yet another result of Republican policies has been the wave of
corporate mergers and acquisitions. Companies are sinking in a
sea of debt and many employees are being thrown overboard –
along with health benefits, pension plans, and investment in research and development. People see this happening, which is why
Jesse Jackson always roused the crowd in 1988 when he talked

172 ★ SPEAKING AMERICAN

about "merger maniacs" who *merge* corporations, *purge* workers, and *submerge* the American economy.

At a time when people are concerned about holding on to their jobs and realize that their security depends upon the success of American corporations, does this kind of populism run the risk of being self-defeating and "antibusiness"?

Paul Tsongas, former senator from Massachusetts and a 1992 Democratic presidential contender, gave that warning in an impressive eighty-six-page paper, entitled "A Call to Economic Arms." He also urges greater government activism to help American business compete in the world market:

> Democrats are going to have to go back to the original act—the creation of national wealth. They are going to have to sit down with the business community and jointly establish policies of wealth creation. It means giving up comfortable political nuclear weapons—such as the marvelous boost gained from routinely attacking corporate America and big business. Some robust Democratic rhetoric presents itself as traditional populism, an "us-them" view of the world where the "them" is anyone in the manufacturing, service, or banking industries. Wake up, Democrats. Without viable manufacturing, service, and banking sectors, there is no country.

Tsongas is right when he says that Democrats shouldn't present themselves as antibusiness. Yet, they need not forfeit the "marvelous boost" that comes from attacking the excesses of big corporations that flout the social contract, gut each other, or move jobs overseas. A solution might be for Democrats to model their rhetoric about business on how Republicans talk about education. Nobody wants to be "anti-education," yet Republicans have managed to present themselves as friendly critics of the education establishment. And the education system has actually benefitted from many of the points raised by Republican education secretaries and reformist governors of both parties.

So when Democrats criticize the problems of big business—they should not do it merely to flail at the fat cats, but to help whip those cats into shape for the competitive world marketplace. An obvious place to start is with the pay and benefits received by chief executive officers (CEOs), a scandal that was a staple in the business press long before even the most populist Democrats caught on. According to *Business Week*, CEO pay rose by *212 percent* during the 1980s. U.S. executives' salaries are fifty to one hundred times the pay of the average worker.

While Americans believe in rewards for success, they resent rewards for failure. In 1990, United Airlines president Stephen Wolf earned $18.3 million, although profits fell 71 percent; ITT's CEO Rand Araskog doubled his salary, to nearly $9.7 million, although ITT stock plunged 18 percent. People's jaws dropped. Even Wall Street wondered what was going on.

Bashing CEOs' excessive salaries is a sure-fire applause line with blue-collar workers. As United Mine Workers president Richard Trumka says, "Ask the average American worker if the head of LTV should have gotten the largest bonus in history the year he took the company into bankruptcy."

Many at the management level (many of whom are rock-ribbed Republicans) are just as resentful. Social commentator Ralph Whitehead interviewed a group of these corporate managers in Orange County, California, one of the most conservative parts of the country:

These were middle-level executives making $50,000 to $75,000 themselves. They are critically concerned with the fortunes of their companies. They're willing to believe the contribution made by a CEO is ten times greater than their own, but they're hardpressed to understand how the hell it could possibly be one hundred times greater. There just aren't enough hours in the day for anyone to be worth that kind of money.

These people in Orange County saw a disturbing similarity between the buddy system in corporate boardrooms, where directors vote on salary increases for CEOs, and insider politics in Washington, where Congress votes itself a pay increase. Whitehead summarizes their feelings: "There are two kinds of people in America—people who set their own salaries and people who don't. For the privileged few, there's the, 'Hey I'll give you a raise if you give me a raise,' principle. [It is seen] not so much as unfair but stupid."

So for Democrats, criticizing exorbitant CEO salaries offers an opportunity to get nods of agreement from those on the factory floors and from those whose offices aren't on the top floor. And it's something worth saying, for practical and moral reasons.

The issue of swollen CEO salaries is just one of the most visible ways that corporations have let the American economy down. When companies are more interested in new mergers than new markets, when research and development is the first budget line cut, and when executives can't think beyond the next quarterly profit statement, our entire society suffers. Democratic pollster Stanley Greenberg writes:

> The corporations, many voters believe, have walked away from the competitive battlefield without even putting up a good fight. Japanese workers and management, it is believed, do a better job than their counterparts—especially management—in the United States. In the factories, 69 percent believe that American workers are doing a better job than five years ago, but only 42 percent think management is (General Media/Associated Press, 1987). Across the country, voters expressed frustration with management's failure to invest in corporate productivity and growth. In Pennsylvania, even outside the steel-producing areas, workers could not understand why management was investing in "fancy golf courses" and why it preferred to "take care of the stockholders," while leaving the worker with a machine that was "built in 1920."

Of course, the danger in this kind of talk is in being tagged "antibusiness." To escape that, and also to clarify their point, Democrats should not only criticize corporate bad guys, they should praise corporate good guys—those who do invest in research and development, make quality products that are competitive in world markets, respect job safety and environmental standards, and treat their employees like indispensable partners, not disposable parts. Indeed, when Democratic candidates soliciting campaign contributions work a room of business people, they should think of which one has a personal story that is a positive example for the nation. And they should tell it.

★ INVESTMENT ECONOMICS

Investment is an idea that appeals to Americans because it embodies one of our strongest values: We put aside some of the fruits of our labor to provide for the future. It's the opposite of the short-term thinking that seemed to dominate decision-making in both business and government during the 1980s. Democrats have always stood for an economy of investment: one that educates young people, trains workers, retools factories, develops new technologies, and rebuilds highways and mass transit. They should encourage an investment economics from business and individuals as well as government, on the principle that long-term benefits outlive short-term gains.

So far, much of the Republican side of the argument has centered on President Bush's plan to stimulate investment by cutting the tax rate on capital gains—a proposal he introduced during the 1988 campaign and has revived every year since. That idea has never been popular with the voters. Democratic pollster Tom Kiley recalls that during the 1988 campaign voters opposed cutting the capital gains tax, by a margin of 57 percent to 40 percent. During the federal budget debates in the fall of 1990, an NBC News/*Wall Street Journal* poll found that voters hadn't changed their minds and, in fact, favored increasing the capital gains tax rate, by 51 to 43 percent.

Democrats can make that case by citing the statistics compiled by Congress's Joint Committee on Taxation. As interpreted on the editorial page of the *Washington Post*, the Committee's figures reveal that 80 percent of the benefits from a capital gains tax cut would go to the fewer than 5 percent of all families with incomes of more than $100,000 a year; 60 percent would go to those with incomes over $200,000. The 375,000 richest families in America would gain, on average, $25,000 a year.

Michael Dukakis's "On Your Side" stump speech centered on Bush's proposal to cut capital gains taxes. "This tax bonanza for the wealthiest one percent of our society" was proof that Republicans cared about "Wall Street, not Main Street." Part of the reason why his audiences cheered was their sense that the rich would spend the money on themselves, rather than re-invest it. "He [Bush] says it's a jobs program," Dukakis would say. "Who's he kidding? What are they going to do with that extra money? Hire a second butler? Hire a lifeguard for the pool?"

Americans are deeply concerned about the recession, the sluggish recovery, and the need to rebuild the country's competitiveness. Democrats should propose tax cuts for investment. The difference between their tax cuts and the Republicans' can be described simply, succinctly, and with a populist spin.

Since Democrats favor tax cuts for middle-class families as well as wealthy investors, populist rhetoric is plausible. Thus: Republicans believe in giving tax breaks to wealthy investors; Democrats believe in giving help to small business investors, inventors, and innovators. And: Republicans favor the existing rich; Democrats favor people who are sweating and striving to make it.

While Republican tax cuts come with no strings attached, the Democrats target theirs to specific purposes like research and development. So Democrats should use the rhetoric of public purpose: Republicans encourage speculation; Democrats favor productive investment. Or: We encourage *venture* capitalists, not *vulture* capitalists.

Any Democratic tax-cut proposals that include breaks for the wealthy should be premised on the social contract: *Do something good for society, and get something back in return.* For example, Mario Cuomo favors a cut in the capital gains tax rate, but only for assets held more than five years — to encourage "long-term investment," rather than "speculation." In addition, Cuomo proposes a "net investment tax credit" limited to "productive" investment in "things like pollution-control equipment." Similarly, Paul

Tsongas favors a "research-and-development tax credit." Since voters want to see results from those who receive government help (assistance that is, after all, paid for with taxpayers' money), the Democrats' tying tax cuts to investment would win the debate. The alternatives could be presented in symbolic terms: Republicans' across-the-board tax cuts for the rich yield second (or third) luxury homes and empty office buildings, while Democrats' investment-oriented tax cuts result in state-of-the-art factories.

This concept has been described as "producerism," and it could be a winner for Democrats. "Producerist" tax reforms would raise the rates of the wealthiest individuals but would lower them for corporations, thereby encouraging the rich to put their money into the company that builds a Chevy, rather than into a Mercedes for themselves. Economist Jeff Faux suggests that this include a combination of carrots and sticks. Along with targeted subsidies, the carrots would be eased government regulations and foreign-import protections for companies that invest in new equipment and technology. The sticks would include additional taxes on short-term financial turnover and restrictions on speculative bank lending.

★ "PUBLIC ENTERPRISE"

Investment is needed in the public sector as well. People expect government to provide basic services, but now there's a sense that things are breaking down, figuratively *and* literally. We live with dangerous bridges, water-main bursts, transmission-rattling roadways, and unreliable mass transit. Our schools seem mired in mediocrity and too many of the high-value items we cherish—from video cassette recorders to personal computers to compact disk players—are no longer, or never were, made in America. All of this contributes to the feeling that we need to "rebuild America."

"Rebuilding America" is a potentially powerful political message for Democrats. The bipartisan "Battleground 1992" survey revealed that voters are more afraid of Republicans not investing in America than they are of Democrats raising taxes. Indeed, 327 economists signed their names to a statement released by the Economic Policy Institute that called lack of public investment "America's third major deficit" (after the federal budget deficit and the trade deficit). As Jeff Faux puts it: "Each year of not repairing a bridge or not teaching a child represents an additional unfunded liability for our budgets in future years. Because, one way or another, we're going to pay the cost some day."

Too often, though, Democrats with good ideas on this issue have talked about rebuilding America in a rhetoric likely to put voters to sleep. Few words are less inspiring — or intelligible — than "infrastructure," the term frequently used to mean roads, highways, bridges, railroads, and airports. Democrats would do better to banish that word and call these things by their proper names. Even more deadening is "human capital," a bureaucrat's catch-all phrase for children, students, and workers — or, in other words, "people." The Democrats have won national elections not as the party that wants to "invest in human capital," but as the party that helps people get a good education, learn new skills, and get good jobs.

It is more important than ever that Democrats address the pervasive anxiety that our kids aren't being prepared for the high-tech, post-industrial future. A powerful symbol of the "low skills/low wages" future of many of our children is in the pictures printed on the cash register keys in fast-food restaurants. The teenagers working behind the serving counter punch pictures of hamburgers, shakes, or fries to ring up the sale, because fast-food companies aren't confident that they could ring up the prices on their own. And the people on the other side of the counter must be wondering: What kind of jobs are those kids are going to get when they get out of school? As House Majority Leader Richard Gephardt explains:

> With our living standards at stake, we face a fundamental choice. We can either compete with dollar-an-hour, unskilled Third World

labor—and lower our families' earning capacity in the process. Or
we can compete with the high-skill, well-trained work forces of the
other Western democracies.

Americans want their kids to be ready to compete, so "a computer in every classroom" could be a powerful populist slogan for
the post-industrial age. There's also populist appeal in making college education more affordable and, because so many young people won't go on to college, in making job training more effective
and more available.

As for investing in the bricks-and-mortar side of our future,
most people do support what used to be called "public-works programs." Sure, some in the media and policy elites call these pork-
barrel projects but, for most voters, the practical necessities are
obvious and the emotional and cultural resonances are positive.
Too often though, what government does seems abstract or even
adversarial. Many remain skeptical of the Great Society because
it calls to mind social workers whose work doesn't have an easily
determinable value, but the same people look back fondly on the
New Deal. It calls to mind construction workers—who built
things people could see and touch and use. And, most people believe it's just plain common sense that the road to a prosperous
economy isn't one that's pockmarked with potholes.

In fact, there's an American tradition of government aid that
helps build prosperity. Early in the nineteenth century, the federal
government built highways and canals. Later, it helped build the
railroads that helped build the West. And, in the middle of this
century, the government created the interstate highway system,
which made the middle-class suburbs—and the booming postwar
economy—possible.

The Democratic party has always promoted an active role for
government, so it should champion the renewal of "public enterprise" (a phrase frequently used by James Blanchard when he was
governor of Michigan). Government can and should build things
people need, things that can make us more productive, things that
can make our country more prosperous. A new "public enter-

prise" also means government giving a helping hand to the industries that are as crucial to our success in the global economy of the twenty-first century as the auto industry was in the twentieth.

While most Americans are understandably disturbed that the United States is losing its lead in making such conspicuous consumer goods as cars and TV sets, we have also fallen behind in the production of important high-tech items like sophisticated machine tools, semiconductors, and computer chips. People have prided themselves on the American know-how that won the Persian Gulf War, but the M-1 Abrams tank was built with Japanese machine tools, and the F-16 fighter jet required Japanese parts for its radar. Indeed, as a "60 Minutes" segment pointed out, in 1985 the Japanese parliament seriously debated whether to sell the United States the computer chips that were key components of Tomahawk missiles.

In the past, the Pentagon provided funds for research in computer science, data transmission, high-speed aircraft, and high-definition television. This research had civilian as well as military uses, so private industry was able to create and market "spinoff" products from defense projects. With the winding down of the Cold War and the arms race comes the possibility that technological research and development will also wind down, leaving America vulnerable, not to a Soviet military threat but to global economic challenges.

Rep. Mel Levine of California (a candidate in the 1992 Senate race) is among Democrats who have criticized the Bush administration for firing Craig Fields, head of the Pentagon's research arm. Bush's reason? He didn't want to use federal funds to subsidize research in advanced technologies that didn't have immediate military applications. But Levine disagrees. He says that government needs to be much more active in promoting American leadership in cutting-edge technologies. Without some government role in research and development, America's prospects for the future will be at the mercies of recession, debt-ridden corporations cutting back on R&D, and a shortage of the "patient" capital needed for long-term growth.

For Democrats advocating a more active government role, there's no ready-made rhetoric. Echoing John F. Kennedy's cadences of challenge and commitment, they can decry a "technology gap," or say that government "shouldn't stand on the sidelines" while America's destiny is being determined. People may not want government on the sidelines, but it's also unclear what exactly they want government to do out on the playing field.

The idea of a national "industrial policy" has been proposed, but its opponents have argued, with some plausibility, that government would inevitably favor the "sunset" industries, which have large, well-organized constituencies, over the "sunrise" industries, which don't. Their most devastating argument was that an industrial policy would amount to government "picking winners and losers," an image that suggests a group of corrupt or incompetent bureaucrats who decide which companies would, and which wouldn't, get federal help. By 1984, industrial policy was so unpopular among media and policy elites that, although Walter Mondale and Gary Hart had spoken favorably about it in the past, neither included it in his campaign platform. Nor did any Democrat in 1988. (And, at the start of the 1992 presidential campaign, it was noticeably absent.)

Thus, in the late 1980s, when "Rebuild America," a think tank associated with Rep. Levine, began arguing for a helping hand for high technology, it avoided the label "industrial policy." Instead, it argued for an "industry-led policy"—a subtle change of emphasis, which implied that business would take the lead. The federal government's role would be to aid consortia of companies in high-tech industries by making research more available, relaxing antitrust laws to encourage cooperation, and helping them gain access to long-term capital. Support for ideas like this one offers Democrats the opportunity to be pro-growth, even pro-business, while keeping the emphasis on productive, rather than speculative, investment.

When many Americans think of government's domestic activities, they think of welfare, the S&Ls, or congressmen bouncing

182 ★ SPEAKING AMERICAN

checks in a private bank. But Democrats, by championing non-military projects that promote new technologies, can echo economist Robert Reich and remind people that "those American industries that are now among the most productive and competitive—aerospace, aircraft, telecommunications, agriculture, pharmaceuticals, and biotechnology—are also the industries in which the government has been most actively involved through public procurement, publicly funded research and development, and regulation."

What's needed is *visionary* leadership—leadership that can paint a positive picture of the future. This new world will pose new challenges, requiring new technologies and new skills to meet those challenges. Voters still have fond memories of Roosevelt, Truman, and Kennedy because, from the New Deal to the New Frontier, these leaders had visions for America—and made them happen. At the edge of the twenty-first century, today's Democrats can, and should, offer Americans a more inspiring future than punching picture-coded keys on Japanese-made equipment.

9
■ "Special Interests"

Michael Dukakis has been a supporter of the labor movement almost all his public career. But when he addressed the AFL-CIO in August 1988, he didn't even mention the word "union."

And Dukakis doesn't have a speck of prejudice in his system. But in his entire general election campaign, he appeared before black audiences only five times — usually at night, when there was no danger he'd end up on the evening news. Partly because of his failure to fire up the black community, Dukakis actually got fewer votes in most major cities in the East and the Midwest than Mondale had gotten four years earlier. Low voter turnout in Chicago and Philadelphia contributed to his narrow defeats in Illinois and Pennsylvania.

Dukakis wasn't the only Democrat who seemed to be acting out of character during his presidential campaign. Walter Mondale had been one of the most creative and courageous liberals ever to serve in the U.S. Senate but, when he campaigned for president, he didn't offer a single new program for health, education, jobs, housing, child care, or any of the social problems he'd devoted his career to solving.

What was psyching out Dukakis and Mondale, and many other Democrats in the eighties and nineties, can be summed up in two words: special interests.

In 1948, while Harry Truman proudly sought the support of labor, blacks, Jews, and other Democratic voting blocs, he blasted the Republicans as beholden to the special interests of

1 8 3

bankers and Wall Streeters. And people believed him. But now Republicans are setting the terms of debate and their campaign oratory labels as "special interests" the organized groups that support Democrats. (And not only Republicans say this, but the news media and, often, even Democrats themselves.)

However, the voters are beginning to see through this rhetoric. In fact, the bipartisan public opinion survey "Battleground 1992," shows Democrats outscoring Republicans, 48 to 21 percent, on who's best at "resisting [the] influence of big special interests." Voters do understand that the Fortune 500 has more clout than the AFL-CIO Executive Council—and that when big money talks the GOP listens even more attentively than the Democratic party. Even so, many Democrats remain frightened of the special interests charge, but the last thing they should do is run away from their base of support. What they need to do is redefine their relationship to the constituencies and institutions that many voters equate with the Democratic party.

These groups run the alphabetical gamut, from abortion-rights advocates to Zionists (and include environmentalists, feminists, gays, and Hispanics—to name just four more). Nothing, however, makes Democrats more nervous than their relationship with three groups that they've championed for at least the past fifty years: organized labor, black Americans, and government itself. But, undeniably and proudly, Democrats do have a "special interest" in labor, blacks, and government (just as they should have a special interest in women's rights, environmentalism, and other worthy causes).

Democrats created the modern labor movement, and labor helped build the modern Democratic party. So close were Franklin D. Roosevelt's ties to labor that organizers stationed at factory gates would hand out leaflets bearing the slogan: "The President wants you to join the union." Even in recent years, unions have been the Democrats' last line of defense. Mondale lost the election 59 to 41 percent, but he carried 54 percent of voters in "union households." And, while Dukakis lost by eight points, he carried 65 percent of union families' votes.

Republicans first branded organized labor as being a special interest during Roosevelt's time, when they called the CIO (the Congress of Industrial Organizations) the tail that wagged the Democratic dog. For instance, in 1944, Republicans said that whenever FDR made an important decision, he first had to "clear it with Sidney"—a reference to Sidney Hillman, who was president of the Amalgamated Clothing Workers Union. (Hillman was a Jewish immigrant from Lithuania, and the charge that all major decisions had to be cleared with him was one of the earliest examples of the use of ethnic stereotyping in attacks on special interests.)

For the past quarter-century, blacks, even more than labor, have been closely identified with the Democratic party. Democrats forfeited their historic base in what was once "the Solid South" to push through civil rights, voting rights, and fair housing laws during the 1960s, and blacks have returned that loyalty, casting 85 percent or more of their vote for every Democratic presidential candidate since 1964.

But some analysts contend the link with black America has cost Democrats white support in the North as well as in the South, particularly once civil rights became associated with unpopular policies like school busing and racial quotas in hiring. These policies were vulnerable to attack because they seemed to defy the American principle of treating people as individuals, not as members of groups (a principle that has been preached more often than it's been practiced). And, as the journalists Thomas and Mary Edsall point out in their book *Chain Reaction*, Republicans have seized on the potency of racially tinged rhetoric and have extended the phrase "the special interests" to include all groups they have stereotyped as outside of society's mainstream: blacks, militant feminists, gays, and other racial, ethnic, religious, or lifestyle minorities. By the 1984 campaign, "clear it with Sidney" had become "clear it with Jesse [Jackson]."

Then there is government itself—which may be the ultimate special interest group. Ever since the New Deal, government, as a means of providing a better life for people of less-than-lavish incomes, has been a central concern of Democrats. And people who depend on government for their livelihoods—from public employees to recipients of every form of government assistance— have been reliable Democratic supporters.

As my old boss, the public-employee union leader Jerry Wurf, understood, Americans like America a hell of a lot more than Americans like government. Most people connect government not with services, but with public employee unions, welfare recipients, and ivory-tower elitists who dream up policies like school busing and job quotas. So when they read in their newspapers, as they did in 1980 (and '84 and '88), that the largest delegate bloc at the Democratic National Convention consisted of people who work for government, they started thinking of the Democratic party as the party of tax-eaters, not taxpayers.

Democrats face a difficult balancing act. If they turn away from the causes and constituencies that have defined the party, they risk losing not only their most reliable voters but any rationale for their candidacies. In fact, 1990 Democratic gubernatorial candidates Neil Hartigan in Illinois, John Silber in Massachusetts, and Anthony Celebrezze in Ohio were all defeated because, in different ways, they were perceived as insufficiently devoted to Democratic voters and values. Indeed, Silber's Republican opponent, William Weld, got 42 percent of the black vote. Yet, if Democrats allow their party to be perceived as the sum total of its special interests, they end up playing into Republican stereotypes.

Therefore, the challenge for Democrats is to redefine their core commitments by emphasizing what's most likely to appeal to the common concerns of the majority of voters. And once the Democratic party offers a convincing—and contemporary— definition of its commitment to the labor movement, black America, and activist government, it will have gone a long way toward offering a compelling definition of its own identity.

★ WHY BORIS YELTSIN WENT TO THE GARMENT
  DISTRICT

Some time late in October 1988, I was at a meeting in
Dukakis's Boston headquarters discussing where Dukakis should
hold his final rallies in New York City.

To my surprise, the campaign did *not* intend to hold a rally in
Manhattan's Garment District. Every Democratic presidential
candidate since FDR had held a rally there; even losers like Adlai
Stevenson and Hubert Humphrey had drawn large, enthusiastic
crowds. I had been there with the Mondale campaign less than
two weeks before Election Day, and more than one hundred thousand people had jammed the ten city blocks stretching south of
34th Street. It was a sea of humanity: older Jews and Italians,
younger blacks, Hispanics, and Chinese-Americans—many
wearing paper hats identifying them as members of the ILGWU
(International Ladies Garment Workers Union), or the unions
representing men's clothing workers, furriers, hatters, and
department store workers. They cheered Mondale, his running
mate, Geraldine Ferraro, and most of all, they cheered Ferraro's
mother, who (like almost everyone's parents or grandparents in
New York) was a retired garment worker.

At the very moment when Dukakis was finally trying to rouse
the Democratic faithful with his "On Your Side" appeal, his staff
was skeptical about a Garment District rally. I was shocked. If he
wasn't on the side of these workers—many of them immigrants
like his own parents—whose side was he on?

Someone at that meeting said the rally would make Dukakis
look like a captive of special interests. I got mad. "Give me a
break," I said. "This isn't 1936 when Republicans scared people
by talking about union bosses with foreign names like Dubinsky
and Hillman. Now the ILGWU is those nice ladies on TV who
sing 'Look for the union label.' For New Yorkers, the Garment

District is a positive symbol that brings together groups often at each other's throats, like the Jews and Italians, whose families got their start there, and the blacks, Puerto Ricans, and Chinese-Americans, who work there now. The Garment District means working your way up. Someone working at a sewing machine isn't what scares people about New York; it's everything else about New York that scares them."

In spite of my uncharacteristic vehemence, the campaign did not hold a Garment District rally. However, I felt vindicated when Russian Federation president Boris Yeltsin visited New York in 1991. A true populist, his homing instinct took him to the Garment District, where he talked about wages, hours, and working conditions with people who included recent immigrants from the Soviet Union. The next day, photographs on front pages all across America showed a crowd of workers wearing ILGWU caps surrounding Boris Yeltsin who was sitting behind a sewing machine, looking like an old-time Democratic presidential candidate. At least Yeltsin understood that the union label is still a positive symbol that stands for hardworking people trying to get by.

The workplace is the most integrated institution in American life, reflecting what Gov. Douglas Wilder of Virginia calls America's "new mainstream"—whites, blacks, Hispanics, and Asians, women and men, young and old. Union-sponsored events are more likely to feature that diversity than any other event a candidate might attend. Realizing this fact and emphasizing its symbolism is important, especially in racially polarized communities. Unions are among the few institutions where diverse people join together to pursue a common purpose. That's one reason why Boris Yeltsin went to the Garment District; Michael Dukakis should have gone there too.

The wrenching economic changes of the 1980s have created new job-related issues that need to be addressed. Although the labor movement has been weakened, the best way for workers to meet these problems head on and get results is with an organized voice. Therefore, unions are more important than ever. There's a compelling message that must be offered, and a challenge that must be met, by the union movement and the Democratic party: Business, government, and the entire society must invest in workers' technical and self-managerial skills, so they can take on more responsibility, earn a living wage, and keep America competitive in the world marketplace.

So Democrats need to revitalize their alliance with the unions, rather than hide from or apologize for it. By doing so, they will win working people's votes in the era of the microchip just as they did in the age of the assembly-line. By keeping a few points in mind, Democrats can present their support for working people and their unions not as a special interest but as the public interest.

■ **POINT #1.** *There's a motherlode of issues where most Americans already stand with unions and Democrats against employers and Republicans.*

For instance, polls by both CBS News and Louis Harris found that from 74 percent to 83 percent of voters support the family medical leave bill, which was passed twice by the Democratic majorities in Congress. A top priority of the unions, the bill has been opposed by business interests and was vetoed by President Bush. And, supporting another priority of the unions and the women's movement, the *Washington Post*/ABC News poll found the 57 percent of the people favor increased federal funding for "daycare programs for the children of working parents who can't afford to pay."

Similarly, a *Wall Street Journal*/NBC News poll found that 69 percent of all voters (including 60 percent of conservatives and 62 percent of people with household incomes of more than $50,000), support a Canadian-style, government-paid health system. And, by that same margin, voters supported health insurance for every American—even if it means a tax increase. Indeed, a growing number of the corporations that do provide insurance coverage favor a national health plan, reasoning that, in the end, they get stuck with the health costs of people who aren't covered through higher premiums, higher hospital fees and higher taxes. The potency of national health insurance as a political issue was underscored by the upset victory of Democratic candidate Harris Wofford in Pennsylvania's 1991 Senate race. Wofford made health care the centerpiece of his campaign and overcame the more than forty-point lead held by the Republican candidate, Dick Thornburgh (President Bush's attorney general and a popular former governor), to win the special election by ten points.

■ **POINT #2.** *Unions are built on all-American ideas.*

Freedom of association, guaranteed in the Bill of Rights, is the basis of unionism—working people joining together to pursue common goals. That principle is so basic and should be so uncontroversial that you'd think that workers who exercise that right wouldn't have to pay with their jobs but, even today, they do. In fact, a small industry has grown around this: There are more than 1,500 consultants earning $500 million a year advising companies on how to defeat union organizing campaigns. Harvard Law School professor Paul Weiler estimates that each year ten thousand people are illegally fired for attempting to bring unions into their workplaces.

Of course, the principle of unionism is to provide representation (as in "no taxation without representation"), to protect individual workers, and to give the entire work force a voice in determining wages, hours, and working conditions.

Sometimes, Republican leaders and the business community inadvertently admit that union representation is, after all, necessary. For example, in 1988 Congress passed a law requiring that a company about to shut down a plant give sixty days notice to its workers. The Reagan administration argued against the bill, saying that government shouldn't get involved, and businesses and unions should work it out between themselves. Two years later, when Congress (first) passed the Family and Medical Leave Act, the Bush administration made the same excuse when vetoing the bill. These statements let the cat out of the bag: Workers need unions or they have no voice at all. If taxation without representation is tyranny, then employment without representation can be slavery.

In FDR's day, the Democratic party understood that simple but powerful truth; and today's Democrats should follow that example by championing workers' rights and setting tough penalties for employers who fire workers for exercising those rights.

If anyone calls this "special interest legislation," Democrats should say yes, they *do* have a special interest in making sure that American workers enjoy their constitutional rights. And they should remind those who applauded the Polish workers' struggle against communist tyranny that "solidarity" isn't only a beautiful word in the Polish language, it's a beautiful word in the English language as well.

■ **POINT #3.** *Unions are culturally mainstream.*
Unionism is still as American as apple pie. Just read this excerpt from a newspaper report on the Fourth of July celebrations in Lincoln, Nebraska:

> His [flag shop owner Don Johnson's] customers are the people who look for the union label, buy American cars no matter what the consumer guides say, and get a chill when they hear the first strains of "The Star-Spangled Banner."

In 1984, Democratic presidential aspirants John Glenn and Gary Hart tried to score points against Mondale by attacking his supporters in the unions as "special interests." And in 1988, Michael Dukakis seemed sheepish about accepting union support. While Republicans oppose unions on substantive issues, they have understood that unions still are positive symbols, and shrewdly, Republican presidents have posed as friends of working men and women by emphasizing their own tenuous union ties. Thus, Ronald Reagan's television spots in 1980 stressed that he had been president of the Screen Actors Guild. And even George

Bush boasted that, during his days in the Texas oil fields, he was a member of the United Steelworkers Union. (The spectacle of Bush brandishing a union card is enlightening when you think how unlikely it is that he would brag about having been a "card-carrying member" of any other liberal group.)

Alone among the special interests in the traditional Democratic coalition, labor still has a mainstream image that can appeal to the swing voters Republicans have wooed away from the Democrats. Steelworkers, autoworkers, and garment workers have long exemplified the American work ethic; the "hardhats" symbolized the "silent majority" that elected Richard Nixon. While Republicans have dissociated themselves from unions as institutions (particularly public employee unions, which they've called tax-eaters), George Bush flew to Boston during the 1988 campaign to accept the endorsement of Boston's police union. And, in his rare visits to American cities during his globe-trotting presidency, Bush frequently sought photo opportunities with other public workers like teachers and drug treatment counselors.

■ **POINT #4.** *Unions are becoming more popular.*

Ironically, while unions lost jobs, wages, benefits, and political clout during the eighties, they seem to have gained in public esteem. According to the Roper poll, the number of Americans who have fair to great confidence in labor leaders has risen from 48 percent in 1977 to 62 percent in 1991. Meanwhile, those with a negative image of labor declined from 42 percent to 27 percent during those same years. After more than a decade of layoffs and cutbacks, organized labor is looking less like a featherbedded fat cat and more like a lean and hungry underdog. Indeed, when negative sentiments are expressed in polls and focus groups, unions are faulted for being ineffective, not for wielding too much clout.

This shift in the public's image of labor can be charted in the difference between the two well-publicized "air wars" bracketing the decade. In 1981, newly elected president Ronald Reagan won public support and built his reputation for decisiveness by breaking the strike by PATCO (the Professional Air Traffic Controllers Organization). Despite the extraordinary demands of their job, Reagan succeeded in portraying PATCO members as do-nothings who had violated the public trust—and the no-strike pledge they had taken when they accepted their jobs.

But at the end of the eighties, when Eastern Airlines employees went on strike they enjoyed solid public support—46 percent as opposed to the 27 percent who favored management, according to a *Washington Post* poll. Frank Lorenzo, the airline's owner, was in Barbara Walters's words, "the most hated man in America," because he symbolized the new breed of corporate managers who took on enormous debt and then tried to slash-and-burn their way to profitability. Eastern's striking unions, on the other hand, were seen as defenders of the human community that constitutes a corporation.

Public sentiment for the Eastern strike was so strong that House Republican Whip Newt Gingrich came within 974 votes of losing his 1990 re-election bid in a district he'd always carried comfortably. The Atlanta suburbs Gingrich represents are home to many Eastern employees but, nonetheless, he had opposed a bill before Congress to create a federal panel to resolve the dispute. Even in that solidly Republican area, the strike had support not only among airline employees but throughout the entire community.

That same year in southwestern Virginia, a twenty-two-year Democratic incumbent in the state House of Delegates was defeated for failing to support the Pittston coal strike. In that race, Jackie Stump, a leader of the Mineworkers Union, was elected by a two-to-one margin as a write-in candidate.

While strikes like those at Eastern and Pittston had public support, few nationally prominent Democrats rallied 'round the workers. To their credit, congressional Democrats did push for the federal board to settle the Eastern dispute, but they didn't make Bush's veto a high-visibility, national, workers' issue. Among the handful of Democrats who marched with Eastern workers on their picket lines or addressed their rallies were Jesse Jackson, Mario Cuomo, and Michael Dukakis.

Democrats would have done better to overcome their sheepishness and stand shoulder to shoulder with the strikers. It's high time for the Democratic party to re-examine its relationship with unions, since it's no accident that the Democrats' glory years and the unions' glory years were the same years. And the unions have always been the most effective preachers of the Democratic gospel: Government *can* help working people. Indeed, in the politics of the nineties, the union remains the only institution in America through which Democrats can reach white, male, blue-collar workers who might otherwise be tempted to vote for candidates like Reagan, Bush—or even Patrick Buchanan or David Duke. That last Saturday morning of the Mondale campaign, when we went to suburban Mount Clemens, Michigan, if it hadn't been for the United Auto Workers, we might have faced the ultimate existential question for post–New Deal Democrats: What if we gave a rally and nobody came?

■ **POINT #5.** *Emphasize the worker, not the union.*

In national labor battles such as the Eastern and Pittston strikes, most people sided with the airline mechanics and the miners, understanding that the corporate kingpins were the real special interests.

There are fifteen million union members all across America, and chances are they're your father or mother, husband or wife, son or daughter, friend or neighbor. And, for all the griping about American-made products and government-provided services, most people believe that union members are hardworking and earn their money.

The union movement's most attractive face is its own membership. The smartest labor leaders know this—and capitalize on it.

That's why during the strike against Pittston Coal, the United Mine Workers Union aired TV spots that showed miners' faces while the narrator intoned, "They believe in God," and added that miners are churchgoers and veterans who believe in the American dream, and deserve a better deal than they're getting.

Because Americans prefer individuals to institutions, a union's support needs to be presented as a *workers'* endorsement. Democratic candidates who come under attack for accepting union endorsements would do well to emphasize the human side of the unions, as did David Dinkins. During his successful 1989 campaign for mayor of New York City, Dinkins said that he refused to apologize for having the support of those who teach our kids, make our clothes, and care for our sick.

The worst way to announce a union endorsement is at a news conference in a hotel meeting room, where several middle-aged men in business suits pledge their support to another middle-aged man in a business suit. The best ways are those that involve both candidates and the union membership. Have the rival candidates debate at membership meetings, conduct a vote, and announce the endorsement at a later meeting, at a rally, or a media event near a work site. Open up the process. And make clear that support is being given because of the candidate's record on issues that all working people, union and non-union, care about.

■ **POINT #6.** *Working people are America's team and the labor issues of the 1990s are those centered on making that team a success.*

When Democrats champion the cause of American workers, they must present the issue as one of economic patriotism.

American workers, unlike CEOs, stockbrokers, and investment bankers, can't move their jobs, their money, and their loyalties overseas. Their personal prosperity depends on the prosperity of the American economy. And, as the Harvard political economist Robert Reich has written, the success of the American economy depends upon the skills of its work force.

Unfortunately, what has been happening instead is the de-skilling of American workers. The bipartisan Commission on the Skills of the American Work Force, co-chaired by former Labor secretaries Bill Brock and Ray Marshall, surveyed employers and found that fewer than 10 percent are creating jobs that require broad-based skills or the training and the ability to adapt to fast-changing technology and markets. As *Business Week* columnist John Hoerr warns, we are "on a de-skilling binge . . . that could prove disastrous for business and the economy in the long run."

Instead, Democrats should champion the re-skilling of American workers by calling on corporations to develop new strategies premised on the fact that high skills and high quality go hand-in-hand, and offer incentives—like federal contract requirements, and funding for apprenticeship programs, and ongoing job training—to encourage them to do so.

Success in today's and tomorrow's marketplace depends on the re-skilling of American workers. Consumers are demanding high-quality, customized products and services—the days of low-quality, standard issue, "one size fits all" are long gone. To achieve this, workers will need to exercise more discretion on the job and assume more responsibility for the quality of their company's products and services.

So the changing marketplace has created new, practical reasons for greater democracy in the workplace. If workers are going to be asked to show more discretion, then companies will no longer be able to treat them as brainless bodies. If workers are shouldering more responsibility, they deserve more money and increased opportunity. And, if American workers are truly to help improve quality and service, they will need to speak the truth about how they could do their jobs better, without fear of reprisals from insecure managers. Workers will need a mechanism for making their voice heard, and unions will be more important than ever.

Some companies are getting that message and are cooperating with workers and their unions. Ford's most successful new model in the 1980s—the Taurus/Sable nameplate of the Mercury line—

was designed by a team that included assembly-line workers as well as engineers. The most far-reaching experiment is being conducted by General Motors for their Saturn model, which was designed to compete with the small Japanese and Korean cars. GM worked closely with the UAW in putting together a team of ninety-nine people, from managers to engineers to frontline workers, which devised a new way to build cars and designed and built a new auto plant from scratch to do it. At the Saturn factory in Spring Hill, Tennessee, workers in self-managing teams decide such issues as job assignment, scheduling, inspection, maintenance, absenteeism, and health and safety.

Shrewdly, companies like these have used the newly dignified, responsible worker in their advertising. Ford's TV spots feature assembly-line workers, some wearing UAW caps, pledging to uphold Ford's slogan: "Quality is Job 1." Ads for Saturn, produced by Hal Riney, who wrote Ronald Reagan's 1984 "It's morning again in America" spots, show individual workers telling why they take pride in their jobs. One woman says: "You can stop the production line if that's what it takes to get something right."

Democrats should learn from the automakers and their admen and pick up on this theme for their campaigns: It's time for a new day in the American workplace, where workers are dignified, not demeaned.

★ "THE EARLY BUS"

Of all the oratory at both parties' national conventions in 1988, few moments were as moving as Jesse Jackson's tribute to people like his mother, who had worked as a maid: "Most poor people are not on welfare, they work hard every day that they can. They sweep the streets. They catch the early bus. They pick up garbage. They feed our children in school. . . . They take care of other people's children. No job is beneath them. They work every day."

While Jackson's rhetoric spoke to an audience that needed to be reminded that most poor people aren't on welfare, it must also have been enormously satisfying for those who do some of society's most dirty, difficult, and low-paying jobs and who are infuriated at being stereotyped as welfare cheats or worse. With his speech Jackson underscored the importance of answering negative stereotypes with positive symbols.

But, from Ronald Reagan's "welfare queen" to George Bush's use of Willie Horton to Jesse Helms's ad showing white hands tearing up a rejection slip for a job reserved for "a minority," Republicans have successfully used racially charged symbols to win the votes of resentful whites.

This form of racial politics has continued potency because Democrats have failed to respond. First, they haven't emphasized the issues that bring together moderate-income people of all races. Second, they've failed to address racially charged issues, from street crime to welfare dependency, that voters have good reason to care about and that Republicans exploit. And third, they haven't offered positive images of the overwhelming majority of blacks who play by society's rules but who, like most Americans who aren't wealthy, may still need a helping hand from government and, unlike their white counterparts, still face the sting of discrimination.

The first two issues have received most of the attention, but emphasizing positive symbolism is just as, perhaps even more, important. The fight for racial equality was symbolized by the plight of the black seamstress who refused to ride in the back of the bus, and white Americans responded sympathetically. But, when civil-rights enforcement evolved into social engineering, symbolized by the school bus that transported children far away from their homes, the civil-rights consensus started to evaporate. To begin again to bridge racial gaps, the symbol for liberal social policy should not be white children taking long rides in the school bus but black men and women taking "the early bus" and commuter trains and carpools to work—like everyone else.

That imagery suggests that less divides people than they think, and it opens up the possibility that people can meet on a common ground of shared interests and values, not a battleground of rage and resentment. The black electorate is not merely a separate voting bloc; it's part of the larger constituency of Americans who work hard but have a hard time making ends meet. So for Democrats grappling with racial issues, the best strategy isn't changing the subject but enlarging it—from race to class. As the sociologist William Julius Wilson writes:

> Many white Americans have turned, not against blacks, but against a strategy that emphasizes programs perceived to benefit only racial minorities. In the 1990s, the party needs to promote new policies to fight inequality. . . . By stressing coalition politics and race-neutral programs . . . the Democrats can significantly strengthen their position.

Wilson belongs to a tradition in African-American political thinking, which includes the legendary union leader A. Philip Randolph and the civil-rights strategist Bayard Rustin, which says that upon reaching the goal of full equality under the law, blacks should emphasize building majority support for programs that lift poor people of all races into the working middle class. That tradition has much to teach today's Democrats.

With the enactment of the civil-rights legislation of 1991, Democrats can now shift the debate from race-based to race-neutral programs. The bill had originated in 1989, when Democrats responded to a series of Supreme Court decisions that made it more difficult for victims of job discrimination to sue and collect damages. Inevitably, debate focused on technical issues few people understand: whether employers or employees should have the burden of proof at different stages of legal proceedings, how much importance statistics should have in proving a pattern of discrimination, and whether employers have the right to set hiring standards that may have the effect of screening out large numbers of minorities and women.

Yet for all the technicalities of the issues involved, the civil-rights debate reflected real fears that resonated throughout society: For blacks, there was the fear of a return to the days before there were laws against job discrimination. For many whites, there was the fear of "quotas" that would deny them job opportunities at a time when the economy was stagnating.

President Bush set the terms of the debate early on by saying that he would sign a civil-rights bill but not a quota bill—a formulation that sums up how most people feel. The civil-rights legislation of the 1960s remains a powerful symbol of what's right with America and, even more than in the heyday of the civil-rights movement, Americans overwhelmingly favor the idea of equal rights for individuals. (In fact, those who opposed the legislation in the sixties, like Robert Bork, suffer when their past positions are known.) On the other hand, programs that seem to distribute benefits or burdens on the basis of race—for instance, strict numerical goals in hiring—tend to be unpopular. Indeed, Democratic candidate Dianne Feinstein lost support in the 1990 governor's race in California when her Republican rival, Pete Wilson, attacked her promise to make appointments that reflected the numbers of minorities and women in the state.

Now that the two-year debate over the job discrimination bill is finished, Democrats may have learned some important lessons about how the case for civil rights can (once again) be put in terms of mainstream values. Public opinion held that a civil-rights bill was desirable but a quota bill wasn't; for all the disagreement about details, both sides in the debate accepted that principle (although there was some early hesitation before President Bush agreed there was a need to revise the Supreme Court decisions and before Democrats declared their opposition to quotas and the adjustment of employment-test scores along racial lines). Similarly, Democrats learned that most people do believe that employers often treat women and minorities unfairly and agree that strong protections against discrimination are needed.

The compromise on civil-rights legislation between Congress and the White House has brought new opportunities. To be sure, there will continue to be skirmishes over what the new law means, and the Bush administration may stake out positions on issues like affirmative action that will provoke conflicts with civil rights advocates. Meanwhile, more extreme leaders within the Republican party, from the old right's Patrick Buchanan to the racist right's David Duke, can be expected to do something Bush no longer can do: noisily and wholeheartedly attack the new civil rights law.

For Democrats, the enactment of the new law offers the opportunity to move the debate from issues that set economically vulnerable people against each other to issues that bring them together. Health insurance, job training, college assistance—all have special appeal to people near the bottom of the economic ladder, whatever their color, and enjoy solid support from members of the middle class, whatever their color.

In pursuing this strategy, Democrats should challenge the new conventional wisdom that multiracial politics has become a "zero-sum game," where candidates who enjoy solid black backing inevitably lose white support, and candidates who cultivate the white middle class run the risk of alienating their black base. Indeed, the Dukakis campaign demonstrated how Democrats can get the worst of both worlds—low black voter turnout and loss of white support. The campaign shunned black audiences and also displayed the classic elitist liberal disdain for middle-class social anxieties. Far from being reassured by the fact that Dukakis rarely appeared in public with ordinary black voters, many whites remembered the national convention and assumed that Dukakis had simply cut a deal with Jesse Jackson to deliver the black vote. Meanwhile, there was little evidence that blacks, who care even more about crime than other voters, appreciated Dukakis's soft-peddling of social issues.

In today's television age, candidates can't say anything in one place that they don't want voters to hear somewhere else. On the other hand, if they practice the politics of avoidance, as Dukakis did, they'll end up not having much of anything to say to anybody. Democrats need a more high-risk strategy. To bridge racial gaps,

202 ★ SPEAKING AMERICAN

they should frame a populist message that allows them to woo white swing voters and campaign visibly and vigorously among black voters. Campaigning across this cultural divide, Democrats should keep these rules in mind:

■ **RULE #1.** *When the subject is race remember, the sixties are over.*

Steeped in the traditions of the black church and forged in the crucible of a nonviolent revolution, traditional civil rights rhetoric is a language of sin, sacrifice, and redemption. National leaders have repented for society's injustices, past and present, and pledged that America will finally uphold its egalitarian creed. In turn, civil-rights advocates have offered the inspiring vision of an America redeemed from its original sin of racism. Not surprisingly, the presidents who have spoken most movingly about civil rights were white Southerners: Lyndon Johnson, who apologized for the region's wrongs, and Jimmy Carter, who bore witness that desegregation had redeemed it.

Decades later, Democrats still reach for that rhetoric when they discuss race. Yet the rhetoric that once moved millions no longer persuades, much less inspires, now that the starkest moral issues have been resolved and complex social and economic problems remain. The old white/black dialogue of repentance and forgiveness has less resonance at a time when there's frustration on one side of the divide and resentment on the other.

What's needed is a fresh political language that addresses the compelling questions of the nineties, not the sixties. What will happen to a person born in the inner city in 1992? What obstacles will that child face? How will society help that child achieve his or her God-given potential? What should society expect in return from that young person — or any person? And what will happen to our society if too many people grow up without opportunity and responsibility? Political leaders should talk to voters about these issues, directly and unsentimentally.

■ **RULE #2.** *The rhetoric of victimization should be used sparingly.*
There are victims of injustice in George Bush's America. For instance, the twenty-five workers killed in a poultry factory fire in Hamlet, North Carolina, were trapped by doors locked from the outside by employers more concerned about theft than employee safety. These workers, many of whom were black women, were victims of injustice. And Democrats should sound like Old Testament prophets in condemning such injustices.

But it's demeaning to address an entire segment of society— whether it's black Americans, or any poor person—as victims. In 1965, it made moral and political sense for President Johnson to say, when introducing the concept of affirmative action: "You do not take a person who had been hobbled by chains, liberate him, bring him up to the starting gate of a race, and then say, 'You are free to compete with all the others' and still justly believe you have been completely fair."

It's a generation later, and commentators, both black and white, have pointed out that this metaphor strips black people of dignity and autonomy as individuals. A more accurate metaphor for today is of a runner who is already weary from sprinting to the same starting line where the other contestants, fresh, hopeful, and unexhausted, begin the race. Indeed, in the debate over the nomination of Clarence Thomas to the Supreme Court, his Republican advocates shrewdly and legitimately presented him as a man who deserved respect, not pity, for having overcome an impoverished childhood.

■ **RULE #3.** *Defy—and disprove—stereotypes.*
Democrats can use the media spotlight of presidential campaigns to present images and ideas that can change how Americans think about each other.

For decades, Republican campaigning has capitalized on

stereotypes that present black Americans as outside the main-stream. Democrats can provide a real service to this country by calling attention to the ways in which blacks are not only prototyp-ically American but are perhaps even *more* American than the rest of society, in ways most people admire. After all, blacks are more religious, more likely to serve in the military and, in general, more socially conservative than most Americans.

Democratic campaigns can help overcome stereotypes: Talk to audiences in black churches about crime, the immorality of popular culture, or the need for more respect for religion in public school curricula. Appear in the inner cities in front of businesses where job openings have been announced, and introduce to the media all the people who have stood on line since midnight to make sure they'd be among the first to apply. Meet with black veterans to talk about the need for lifelong job training and retraining programs.

Similarly, Democrats should appear in "white" settings to dis-cuss stereotypically "black" problems. Talk to young people in white suburbs about saying no to drugs. Go to a dying factory town, to Chicago's predominantly white "Uptown," or to Ap-palachia to talk about the problems of poverty. Emphasize that none of these are problems of race; they are American problems.

The point is to talk about issues that concern all citizens. Au-diences of all colors want new ideas and some passionate interest in national health insurance, job training for kids who don't go to college, and community environmental concerns. Joseph Gard-ner, an official of the Metropolitan Water Reclamation District in Chicago, talks about how the working-class black and white fami-lies in his area have been affected not only by the loss of factory jobs, but by the fact that those plants "left behind toxic wastes that could seep into the soil, then up into people's yards and houses, and poison them."

In some areas there will be problems that specifically affect whites or blacks. The point is to discuss problems that don't divide people along racial lines. For example, Patrick Quinn, the populist state treasurer of Illinois, dealt with an issue that mostly affects blacks but would not divide them from the white electorate when he attacked commercial banks that redline inner city neighborhoods and the abuses of the "money exchanges" that cash checks for people who don't have bank accounts.

■ **RULE #4. *Affirmative action may not be popular, but it need not be political suicide.***
To too many whites, affirmative action means quotas. But there is still support for affirmative action in its original sense: special efforts by employers to seek a more diverse pool of applicants for job openings. These efforts are needed more than ever as demographic changes leave employers little choice but to rely more heavily on women, minorities, and others who have suffered discrimination.

What Democrats need to do is distinguish between affirmative action and quotas. Harvey Gantt, the black North Carolina Democrat who lost a close race to Sen. Jesse Helms in 1990, has a great deal of insight on the issue:

> The most vocal opponents of affirmative action are often those who actually hire by the numbers to "keep the government off our backs." Companies with the sorriest records are most likely to have lazy recruiting and personnel departments. Their unwillingness to do the necessary outreach helps to make their negative perceptions a self-fulfilling prophecy.

■ **RULE #5. *Identify with individual aspiration.***
Democrats should present civil rights as the way to tear down barriers to individual achievement. They should say, with feeling, that merit must be rewarded and that the ultimate responsibility for success rests with the person, not society. The black middle class is an American success story. It exists because of individual achievement, often against great odds. And Democrats should embrace that constituency by campaigning actively in black middle-class communities such as the Chicago suburb of May-

wood and Prince Georges County in Maryland, as well as in the impoverished inner cities.

Democrats should also embrace the working poor, who have middle-class values but threadbare family budgets. To back up their rhetoric, Democrats should align themselves with union organizing efforts among low-wage workers, such as the Service Employees International Union's Justice for Janitors Campaign. Without a union, the people who clean office buildings in the major cities often earn no more than the minimum wage, and have no health benefits. With a union, they earn much more, plus health benefits. And when poor people can earn a living wage, it sends a powerful message of encouragement to others.

■ **RULE #6.** *Realize that America is still an emerging nation, and it can't be portrayed in black and white.*

For all the criticisms of Michael Dukakis's presidential bid, he performed a real service by campaigning actively among Latinos, offering them more respect and recognition than any previous contender in either party.

The sad truth is that race in America has been seen almost exclusively through the prism of the relationship between blacks and whites. But the 1990 census paints a picture of an America that is 3 percent Asian, 9 percent Latino, 12 percent black, and 75 percent white. Democrats would do well to see and portray the real "rainbow" that is America. By emphasizing America's diversity and its tradition of inclusion, Democrats can turn down the emotional volume of the conflict between whites and blacks.

★ **"ALL THE GOVERNMENT WE NEED"**

At a time when Democrats have been attacked as spendthrift supporters of "big government," Mario Cuomo has perfectly set the terms of debate: "Of course, we should have only the government we need. But we must insist on *all* the government we need."

Democrats should advocate all the government services that our society needs and can afford—no more, and no less. To convince people that what Democrats advocate is the government people need, Democrats need to find new ways to define government's purpose, its relationship to the people, and its own size and structure. *Reinventing Government,* the title of a forthcoming book by the journalist David Osborne, sums up a mood that's sweeping our society—from angry taxpayers to innovative public officials: Government needs to be more efficient, effective, and accountable. These rules should help Democrats re-invent their rhetoric about government:

■ **RULE #1.** *Concentrate on what government does best.*

While people are suspicious about government, they do support programs that serve everyone, have a minimum of bureaucracy, and provide basic services—like education, health care, and help with home ownership. For example, national health insurance has recently become a popular issue (propelled by Sen. Harris Wofford's upset victory in Pennsylvania) not only because it serves an urgent—and unmet—need but because it sounds like social security and Medicare, government programs that people know and like.

Bob Creamer, the director of Citizen Action's Illinois affiliate, has come up with an excellent metaphor to make the case that Americans need to pool their resources, through government, to get health care for all:

> There are some things in America we've decided to do for each other because it's right and it's cheaper. One example is the fire department. When someone's house catches fire, the fireman doesn't ask you if you have Blue Cross. They just put it out, because that's your right as a citizen, and, if your house catches fire, we're all in trouble. It should be the same way with health care. It's your right as a citizen. And, if you get seriously ill, ultimately we all pay for it anyway.

While policy experts disagree about the best means of financing and structuring national health insurance, public opinion agrees that the ideal plan would replace the costly private bureaucracies of insurance companies, provide universal coverage, and preserve people's right to choose their own doctors. And all this talk about national health insurance is a good model for talking about other social programs. Political leaders should define a universal need, offer a universal benefit and, as much as possible, find a non-bureaucratic way to provide the service.

■ **RULE #2.** *Government should treat people as citizens, not clients or consumers.*

Young visionaries are a rarity in the Bush administration, but that's the best way to describe James Pinkerton, a White House staffer who has called for a "new paradigm" for government. Rather than merely do things for Americans, it would create programs to "empower" them, like tenant-managed public housing, tax credits for child care, and education vouchers, which could be used for private or public schools.

These ideas are appealing to people because the middle class and poor alike want to be treated as dignified and intelligent individuals, not as childlike clients of government bureaucracies. Yet, if public services are handed over to the private marketplace, the Republican model might change the "client" into the "consumer." Then those who start out with the most money would use government tax credits to subsidize their purchasing the best services, while the less affluent would have to settle for cut-rate providers and the public sector would be abandoned by all but the poor.

Democrats should treat people as citizens, not clients or consumers. That concept justifies tenant management of public housing, parents' right to choose from among different public schools, and child-care tax credits for moderate-income families. That idea repudiates paternalistic government, and it would not justify handing over public institutions like schools to a private marketplace where the rich buy the best, the middle class settles for less, and the poor are left out yet again.

■ **RULE #3.** *Government should have less fat, more muscle, and more heart and soul.*

Trimming fat from government is and will continue to be a hot political issue, and Democrats won't be able to guarantee that there will be as many government jobs and services. But they can offer new social contracts for recipients and providers of public services. Two timely ideas have been offered by House Democratic Leader Richard Gephardt and Mayor Sharon Pratt Kelly of Washington, D.C.

Gephardt proposes "rewards for results" under which federal programs like Head Start or the Job Corps would receive additional funding for proven success—for instance, rises in test scores of children enrolled in Head Start pre-schools.

Despite her difficulties in implementing and winning support for her efforts, Kelly has strived to reduce the fat—the number of middle managers in city government—and spare the muscle (garbage collectors, teachers, firefighters, hospital workers, and police). (As she entered her second year as mayor, Kelly's administration threatened to eliminate the jobs of some union members as well—a move she might not have made had she succeeded in eliminating more than two thousand middle managers, as she had tried to do during her first year.)

Middle managers aren't union members, so this kind of government reform should be attractive to the public employee unions whose members would otherwise be facing the threat of massive layoffs. Perhaps more important, it points the way to creating a new social contract for public employees that would save money and make government more efficient. Government workers would be given a greater degree of autonomy on the job, managing themselves rather than being directed by middle managers.

There have been successful experiments in worker self-management, proving that it can improve quality and cut costs.

In New York City's sanitation department, the division that repairs garbage trucks allows its employees an unusual amount of autonomy. Not only do workers decide what supplies and equipment to order, but they have designed robots that perform repetitive tasks like painting, and have even developed a model refuse wagon to set the standard for the outside companies that build the department's vehicles. Once considered a high-cost, low-quality trouble spot, the motor-equipment division now does such good work that other city agencies ask it to repair their vehicles.

In trimming fat it's inevitable that some government agencies will be cut back or closed down. But, rather than lose their livelihoods, workers should be offered the opportunity to prepare for new jobs. Manhattan Borough president Ruth Messinger suggests that workers whose positions are eliminated by restructuring be given not job security, but *employment security,* "provided by extensive job retraining and placement" during which workers would maintain their wages and benefits." This is a new social contract that makes workers partners in change, not casualties of change.

When it comes to advocating—and administering—government, a little guts and imagination go a long way.

Afterword:
■ The Fighting Underdog

For Democrats who still have photographs of John F. Kennedy and Martin Luther King, Jr., on their walls, Sen. Harris Wofford of Pennsylvania represents the best in American politics.

A World War II veteran and an intellectual who became a student of the Gandhian techniques of nonviolence, Wofford was an adviser to King during the civil-rights struggles of the 1950s. As a staffer on John F. Kennedy's 1960 presidential campaign, Wofford convinced him to make a historic telephone call of support to Coretta Scott King when her husband, Dr. King, was being held in a Georgia state prison—a dangerous place for a black leader. That gesture called national attention to King's predicament and may have saved his life. Later, as an aide in the Kennedy White House, Wofford was a strong voice for civil rights, and he also helped found the Peace Corps.

During the decades after Camelot, Wofford shuttled between government and academia, serving as president of Bryn Mawr College and state labor secretary in Pennsylvania. In July 1991, when Gov. Robert Casey named the sixty-five-year-old Wofford to fill the U.S. Senate seat left vacant by the death of John Heinz, most observers predicted that, distinguished as he was, Wofford was doomed to defeat in the special election that November. After all, his Republican opponent was Richard Thornburgh, the popular former governor and former U.S. attorney general, who started out with a nearly forty-five-point lead in the polls. While Thornburgh was an experienced campaigner, Wofford had never

run for public office. Even his campaign coordinator in Philadelphia thought he was "very nice, but . . . a little cerebral."
Yet Wofford had the intelligence and the discipline to become what the times required: a fighting populist. Campaigning in a state where blue-collar workers hadn't fully recovered from the last recession, where there was severe urban poverty, and where the white-collar middle class and even the affluent suburbanites felt anxious about the future, Wofford hammered away at bread-and-butter issues that appealed to most Pennsylvanians. He called for tax relief for the middle class. He attacked the Bush administration for putting American workers' jobs "on the fast track to Mexico" because of its trade agreement with that country. But most important, he spoke directly to voters' concerns about the cost and availability of health care, and made the call for national health insurance the centerpiece of his campaign. "If criminals have the right to a lawyer," he said, "I think working Americans should have the right to a doctor."

This was the most memorable line of Wofford's campaign. It always got applause because it recognized people's gut-level belief that society does too little for those who play by the rules and too much for those who break them.

A liberal with an unshakable commitment to the poor, Wofford nonetheless put the middle class at the center of his argument. As he later explained:

I want[ed] to build a fire under my own party on a point that I presented to Democrats in Pennsylvania—that it's time for us to recognize that we do best and are strongest when the programs we advance help all the people and are not just targeted programs for the very poor. It's best for the very poor and it's best in getting a consensus . . . [for] programs that help everybody.

Wofford defined the issues of the campaign—taxes, trade, and health care—rather than letting the Republicans define him as a liberal egghead. Understanding that people hate the arrogance of career politicians, Wofford's campaign jumped on Thornburgh's boast that he knew "the corridors of power" and the foolish statement by one of his staffers that Thornburgh was "the salvation of this sorry-assed state." On Election Day, Wofford won, 55 to 45 percent.

Democrats across the country were inspired by Wofford's victory, not only because he proved that a quality candidate can win in the nineties, but because Thornburgh, a moderate Republican who'd lurched to the right when he went to Washington, seemed so similar to his ex-boss, President Bush. Democrats asked themselves: If Wofford can beat the odds, why can't we take the White House?

A year before the 1992 elections, people were anxious and angry, with 57 percent telling pollsters that the country was "on the wrong track." Yet much of what made people angry were things they connected with Democrats, from check-bouncing and free lunches in Congress to social disintegration and fiscal crises in the big cities. Surveys found that fewer than half of all voters definitely planned to vote for Bush in '92 and that a generic "Democratic nominee" could beat him, although that unknown Democrat ran much stronger than any of the real-life contenders. However, a *Washington Post*/ABC News survey found that Bush still outpolled the Democrats among voters who worry "a great deal" about problems ranging from crime and drugs to education, welfare dependency, and the decline in spiritual values.

Meanwhile, much more alarmingly, Harris Wofford's polar opposite, the "former" Ku Klux Klansman David Duke, tapped into some of the same social and economic discontents and won 39 percent of the vote for governor of Louisiana, another state hit hard by the recession. As the man who defeated him, Edwin Edwards, wisely observed on election night, Duke's thinly veiled racism may appeal to frustrated voters all over America, particularly if a similar message is offered by a messenger with a less bizarre background. Duke's candidacy shows that populism can take many forms—reactionary as well as progressive, mean spirited as well as hopeful, resentful of those at the bottom as well as those at the top.

Thus, at the onset of the 1992 presidential campaign, Democrats found themselves in a familiar position: the underdogs. But that needn't be cause for despair. Americans root for underdogs—and they love to see the arrogant overdog in top hat and tails trip on a banana peel and land on his rear end (Thornburgh's role in '91 and the part Bush may play in '92). At a time when people are angry at the establishment and anxious about their futures, Democrats should welcome the role of "challenger" in every sense of that word. Indeed, it's the best strategy for Democrats: *challenge* Republican smugness, *challenge* liberal shibboleths, *challenge* stereotypes and, ultimately, *challenge* every sector of society to uphold its end of the social contract.

Challenging the president and the Republicans is actually the easy part. When it comes time for Bush to boast about what he's done to create new jobs and protect existing ones, to keep the economy growing, to help our children learn better, to defend our communities from crime and drugs, and to make sure every family can find health care, well, even Peggy Noonan might not be able to make him persuasive.

In fact, in the fall of 1991, there were encouraging signs for Democrats that even Bush's supposed foreign policy prowess was vulnerable in light of his domestic failures. In a perceptive address to the Economic Policy Institute, Wisconsin Democrat Rep. David Obey called for activist leadership at home *and* abroad:

> [Bush] says it's important for us to be engaged internationally and points to Harry Truman as an example, and I agree with that; I'm a committed internationalist. But the American people allowed Harry Truman to be engaged abroad because they understood he was already engaged at home. . . . Truman presented the Marshall Plan . . . in the context of expanding economic opportunity for all American families . . . in the context of a politics of his time which understood that government was clearly on the side of average people.

In the end, it's challenging the party's own shibboleths that may be more difficult for Democrats. So, in reaffirming their commitments, Democrats must do so in mainstream and contem-

porary ways that challenge popular stereotypes. With the extraordinary amount of media coverage that any major party nominee
receives during the general election campaign, there will be a real
opportunity for Democrats to begin to change how Americans
think about the party's traditional constituencies by changing the
way Americans think about each other: Remind middle-class
voters that union members want greater responsibility for the
quality of their products and services, that inner city blacks fear
crime more than anyone, that most poor people work or want to
work, and that government programs can be "public enterprises"
that make the economy more successful.

Even though they don't have the bully pulpit of the White
House, it may be up to the Democrats to persuade Americans that
we're a better people than we think we are, capable of doing better
than we've done in the recent past. In 1960, John F. Kennedy's
theme was "We can do better." Thirty years later, this message
is still effective because it's so profoundly optimistic. It doesn't
just say we *should* do better; it says we *can* do better. And, for
all the allegations about his personal life, that summons to social
responsibility and achievement explains why Americans still rank
JFK as one of our greatest presidents.

As Kennedy did, today's Democrats, in challenging Americans to "do better," should do so with the understanding that
government can set goals, offer opportunities, and provide
resources but, ultimately, people must do the job themselves.

Democrats should challenge every sector of society, starting
at the top. When the wealthy don't pay their share of taxes, when
they spend their tax breaks on luxury consumption, and when corporate CEOs take care of themselves and not their companies,
then neither business nor government can provide for the future.
From reductions in corporate R&D to cutbacks in funding for the
schools, America suffers from an "investment gap." That should
be as potent a political issue as Kennedy's "missile gap" was in
1960.

Challenging the rest of society will be more difficult. When

Kennedy urged Americans to "ask what you can do for your country," he addressed a people who remembered the national effort that had brought America out of the Depression and won World War II and who had seen their standard of living rise steadily during the postwar era. But today's America has suffered more than a decade-and-a-half of stagnant economic growth and has fewer positive memories of collective action—national or local. As Walter Mondale and Jim Florio discovered, when people are asked to sacrifice for their communities and their country, they must see themselves as being challenged to act, not merely pay higher taxes. As Maryland senator Barbara Mikulski has put it, most folks feel that when it comes to money they have "nothing left to give." But, for all the pressures on their time, people do appreciate being asked to contribute their ideas and energy, being made to feel like participants in America.

So, when Democrats challenge everyone—the middle class and the poor, as well as the rich—part of that challenge should concentrate on things that will help people work smarter and keep families together, because when individuals and their families succeed, the entire society succeeds. Putting the challenge in the language of the social contract, Democrats should champion social policies that reward people who shoulder the responsibility to improve their own condition: High school students who study hard and graduate, college students who perform community service, communities that organize block patrols, and unemployed workers willing to be trained for new jobs will have earned the right to a helping hand from government.

Such policies appeal to people's common values as well as their common interests. And the Bush administration can be faulted not only for doing so little for most Americans, but for asking so little of us, particularly the most privileged among us.

This Democratic message is populist in the best sense of that tradition. It serves people's interests and affirms their values, shows special concern for people in the middle and at the bottom of the economic spectrum, and challenges arrogant, irresponsible, and shortsighted behavior by those at the top. And this message is most compelling when it is offered by political leaders who speak directly to the people, as candidates as diverse as Wofford, Florida's governor Lawton Chiles, senators Bob Graham of Florida, Barbara Mikulski of Maryland, and Paul Wellstone of Minnesota, and Boston's mayor Ray Flynn have all done. They've answered questions at community meetings; visited people in schools, health clinics, unemployment offices, and job training centers; and some have even held "work days" where they've done regular jobs, like waiting tables or working at construction sites, and talked to people in their workplaces.

After Wofford's upset landslide, his staffers fondly recalled that, early in the campaign, he could discourse learnedly about Gandhiism but didn't know that the Kroc family had founded the McDonald's fast-food chain. Just as Wofford tutored his staff on political philosophy, they tutored him on what they called "McDonald's thinking"—addressing the realities of people's daily lives.

The professorial Wofford earned an A-plus in speaking American. And he won. By challenging the voters and themselves, other Democrats can win, in the nineties and beyond.

NOTES
■

INTRODUCTION

Page 3
For the story of Dukakis's reluctance to criticize "country club Republicans" see Sidney Blumenthal, *Pledging Allegiance: The Last Campaign of the Cold War* (New York: Harper Collins, 1990), p. 314. Kevin Phillips also mentions this in *The Politics of Rich and Poor: Wealth and the American Electorate in the Reagan Aftermath* (New York: Random House, 1990), p. 30.

Page 5
For George Orwell's essay on political language, see "Politics and the English Language," *The Orwell Reader* (New York: Harcourt, Brace, and Co., 1956), p. 355.

Page 6
The concept that political parties have two wings, the "presidential" and the "congressional," is explored in James McGregor Burns, *The Deadlock of Democracy: Four-Party Politics in America* (Englewood Cliffs, NJ: Prentice Hall, 1967).

Page 11
Jerry Wurf on older union staff addressing younger workers, see Haynes Johnson and Nick Kotz, "For Young Workers, Old Leaders," *Washington Post* (Apr. 11, 1972), p. A8.

Page 12
For liberal critiques of the ACLU, see Jim Sleeper, *The Closest of Strangers* (New York: W. W. Norton and Co., 1990), pp. 170 and 187; and Fred Siegel, "What Liberals Haven't Learned and Why," *Commonweal* (Jan. 13, 1989), pp. 16–20.

Pages 12–13
For Falwell's, Robertson's, and Schlafly's efforts to censor public school textbooks and curricula see David Bollier, *Liberty and Justice for Some*, People for

2 1 9

220 ★ SPEAKING AMERICAN

the American Way (New York: Frederick Ungar Publishing Co., 1982) pp. 143, 153.

Page 13
On the ACLU against metal detectors in high schools, see John B. Judis, "How the ACLU Left Itself Open to Right Wing Attacks," *In These Times* (Nov. 9–15, 1988), pp. 7, 22.

Pages 13–15
For an account of the making of the Gregory Peck spot and Fitzwater's comments on it, see Michael Pertschuk and Wendy Schaetzel, *The People Rising: The Campaign Against the Bork Nomination* (New York: Thunder's Mouth Press, 1989), pp. 171–176.
For Bork's positions on the 1964 Civil Rights Act, the Supreme Court's poll tax decision, and his "intellectual feast" comment, see Ethan Bronner, *Battle for Justice: How the Bork Nomination Shook America* (New York: W. W. Norton and Co., 1989), pp. 67, 275–276.

Pages 17–18
For "traditionalists" vs. "revisionists," see Ronald Brownstein, "Democrats Search for an Identity," *Los Angeles Times* (July 2, 1991), p. A1.

CHAPTER 1

Page 19
For Mondale in Michigan, see Patricia Mountemurri, "Mondale Woos Voters in Mount Clemens," *Detroit Free Press* (Nov. 4, 1984), p. 1.

Page 21
On the growth of Macomb County, see Michael Barone and Grant Ujifusa, *The Almanac of American Politics, 1992* (Washington, D.C.: National Journal, 1991), p. 635.
On suburban voters in Macomb and Warren counties, see Stanley Greenberg, "Report on Democratic Defection." Paper prepared for the Michigan House Democratic Campaign Committee, April 15, 1985.

Page 22
On percentages for Mondale and Reagan among different income groups, see "Portrait of the Electorate," *New York Times*/CBS News poll, published in the *New York Times* (Nov. 8, 1984), p. A19.

Page 23
For Mondale at Labor Day rally in Merrill, Wisconsin and at George Washington University, see Elizabeth Drew, *Campaign Journal* (New York: Macmillan Publishing Co., 1985), pp. 632, 670.

Pages 23-24
For Springsteen on America in the eighties, see Dave Marsh, *Glory Days: Bruce Springsteen in the 1980s* (New York: Pantheon Books, 1987), pp. 263-264.

Pages 24-25
For Mondale in Los Angeles, see Bernard Weintraub, "Grinning, Fist Clenched, Mondale Ends Campaign," *New York Times* (Nov. 6, 1984), p. A23.

Page 25
Joe Morgenstern, "Why All Those People Were Smiling—Music, Marigolds, and Mondale," *Los Angeles Herald Examiner* (Nov. 5, 1984), p. 1.

Page 26
Mondale, "yuppie and lunchpail" quote, see 1984 Democratic convention acceptance speech published in the *New York Times* (July 20, 1984), p. A12.

Page 27
On Dukakis in Philadelphia, Mississippi, see "Southern Strategy," editorial, *New York Times* (Aug. 11, 1988), p. A24.

Page 29-30
For Dukakis's and Bush's police rallies in Boston, see Thomas Oliphant and Christine Chinlund, "Rivals Wage Police Battle in Boston," *Boston Globe* (Sept. 23, 1988), p. 1.
On Bush's "mugging," see Oliphant (sidebar to "Rivals Wage") *Boston Globe* (Sept. 23, 1988), p. 18.

Page 31
Dukakis-Shaw exchange, see Jack W. Germond and Jules Witcover, *Whose Broad Stripes and Bright Stars? The Trivial Pursuit of the Presidency 1988* (New York: Warner Books, 1989), p. 5.

CHAPTER 2

Page 35
On the Kelly endorsement, see "The Mayoralty: Summing Up," *Washington Post* (Sept. 6, 1990), p. D4.

Page 40
Ralph Whitehead talked to me about "American exceptionalism." See also John Aloysius Farrell, "George Bush, War, and the Spirit of American Exceptionalism," *Boston Globe Magazine* (March 31, 1991), p. 21.

Page 41
For Reagan's acceptance speech at 1980 GOP convention, see *New York Times* (July 18, 1980), p. A8.
For Bush's acceptance speech at 1988 GOP convention, see *Washington Post* (Aug. 19, 1988), p. A28.

Page 42

For "city on a hill," see John Winthrop, "A Model of Christian Charity" (sermon given on board the Arbella, en route from England to America, 1630), in Robert N. Bellah, Richard Madsen, William M. Sullivan, Ann Swidler, and Steven M. Tipton, eds., *Individualism and Commitment in American Life* (New York: Harper & Row, 1987), pp. 22–27.

Page 43

For Bill Clinton announcing his presidential candidacy and calling for a "new covenant" between citizens and their government, see David Shribman, "Clinton, Joining the Presidential Race, Hitches Wagon to 'Middle Class' Star," *Wall Street Journal* (Oct. 4, 1991), p. A16.

For Bob Kerrey on the social contract see Thomas B. Edsall, "New Hampshire May Test New Democratic Message," *Washington Post* (Oct. 13, 1991), p. A8.

Page 44

Tony Podesta told me the story of "Big Green."

Pages 44–45

Robert S. McElvaine, *The Great Depression* (New York: Times Books, 1984), pp. 95–120.

Roosevelt's "log cabin," see Henry Fairlie, *The Parties: Republicans and Democrats in this Century*, (New York: St. Martin's Press, 1978), p. 138.

Page 45

Carter at Warm Springs, Georgia, see David E. Rosenbaum, "Carter Opens Drive by Denouncing Ford as Timid President," *New York Times* (Sept. 7, 1976), p. A1.

Page 46

Bush's 1988 GOP convention speech, see Peggy Noonan, *What I Saw at the Revolution* (New York: Random House, 1990), p. 11.

Page 47

For public opinion on Reagan and Supreme Court in 1987, see Marttila & Kiley, Inc., "A National Survey of Attitudes Toward the Supreme Court and the Bork Nomination." Compilation of polling data, published August 24, 1987.

Page 49

Peggy Noonan, "A Bum Ride," *New York Times* (Oct. 15, 1991), p. A25.

Page 50

For Cuomo on San Francisco, see his "Two Cities" keynote address to the 1984 Democratic National Convention, San Francisco, Calif., July 17, 1984, published in Bellah, et al., *Individualism and Commitment,* p. 419.

For Kirkpatrick on "San Francisco Democrats," see Elizabeth Drew, *Campaign Journal* (New York: Macmillan Publishing Co., 1985), p. 595.

Page 51
For excerpts from Jackson's speech at 1988 Democratic convention, see *New York Times* (July 20, 1988), p. A18.

Page 52
On Reagan-Bush trade officials who lobbied for foreign interests after leaving government, see Pat Choate, *Agents of Influence* (New York: Alfred A. Knopf, 1990), pp. 52–57, 225, 226, 227, 231, 232, 236, 234.

CHAPTER 3

Page 55
For portions of Dukakis's final stump speech, see Sidney Blumenthal, *Pledging Allegiance* (New York: Harper Collins, 1990), p. 313.

Page 56
For polling figures on final weeks of 1988 campaign, see Peter Goldman, Tom Matthews, and the Newsweek Special Election Team, *The Quest for the Presidency: The 1988 Campaign* (New York: Simon and Schuster, 1989), pp. 421–422.
Kevin Phillips, *The Politics of Rich and Poor* (New York: Random House, 1990).

Page 57
For the definition of "populism," see Robert Kuttner, "Cashing in on Pocketbook Populism," *Boston Globe* (July 19, 1991), p. 13.

Pages 59–60
For Truman on Republicans and working people, see *Public Papers of the Presidents of the United States, Harry S. Truman* (Washington, D.C.: U.S. Government Printing Office), January 1 through December 31, 1948, pp. 406, 470.

Page 61
On Stevenson's campaign, see "Stevenson and the Intellectuals" in Irving Howe, *Steady Work: Essays in the Politics of Democratic Radicalism, 1953–1966* (New York: Harvest Books, 1966), p. 212.
Polling on sources of Stevenson's and Kennedy's support: Victor Fingerhut, "Two Weeks to a Humphrey Victory . . . What Must Be Done." Memo to Vice President Humphrey, Lawrence O'Brien, Ted Van Dyck, Joe Napolitan, John Stewart, Secretary Freeman, William Connell, and Gerry Harsh (Oct. 15, 1968), p. 9.

Page 62
For Johnson's remarks in 1964 campaign, see Theodore H. White, *The Making of the President 1964* (New York: Atheneum, 1965), p. 375.
On advice to Humphrey campaign, see Fingerhut, "Two Weeks to a Humphrey Victory."

For Humphrey's 1968 stump speech, see Theodore H. White, *The Making of the President 1968* (New York: Atheneum, 1969), p. 358.

Pages 62-63
On Humphrey's final surge in 1968, see Victor Fingerhut, "Populism as an Enduring Feature of American Politics." Data, memos, and articles collated and made available to attendees of the Conference on Progressive Federalism of the Center for Policy Alternatives, December 14-16, 1990.

Page 63
For McGovern rejection of Humphrey's advice and his record loss, see Theodore H. White, *The Making of the President 1972* (New York: Bantam Books, 1973), pp. 409, 454-455.
Carter's acceptance speech at 1976 Democratic convention: *The Presidential Campaign 1976, Volume One, Part One, Jimmy Carter* (Washington, D.C.: U.S. Government Printing Office, 1978), p. 349.

Page 64
On Carter at Seattle rally in 1980, see Jack W. Germond and Jules Witcover, *Blue Smoke and Mirrors* (New York: Viking Press, 1981), pp. 301-302.

Page 66
For Mondale's acceptance speech at 1984 Democratic convention, see *New York Times* (July 20, 1984), p. A12.

Page 67
For details of Mondale's tax plan, see Fay S. Joyce, "Mondale Program Would Raise Taxes $85 Billion by '89," *New York Times* (Sept. 11, 1984), p. A1; Jonathan Feurbanger, "Mondale's Plan, the Middle Class Is Not Exempt," *New York Times* (Sept. 11, 1984), p. A25; and David E. Rosenbaum, "Taxpayers' Idea of Wealth May Not Be the Same as Mondale's," *New York Times* (Sept. 12, 1984), p. B8.
Typical of the response by union leaders to Mondale's tax plan was this statement made after the election by John Sweeney, president of the Service Employees: "I've yet to meet the union leader who successfully ran for office on the promise that, if elected, he'll raise the members' dues to pay off a deficit no one's foreclosing on." Quoted in *John Herling's Labor Letter,* (June 15, 1985), p. 2.

Page 68
On Mondale's gain toward the end of the 1984 campaign, see Peter Goldman and Tony Fuller, *The Quest for the Presidency 1984,* A Newsweek Book (New York: Bantam Books, 1985), p. 454.
On Dukakis's gain in the last three weeks of the 1988 campaign, see Goldman, et al., *Quest for the Presidency . . . 1988,* pp. 421-422.

Pages 68-69
"Forty-five percent" strategy, see Victor Fingerhut, "Misunderstanding the 1984 Presidential Election: Myths About the Democrats," *Campaigns and Elections*

(Winter 1985), pp. 21–28, and Victor and Dan Fingerhut, "Labor and the Democrats: Who's Out of Touch?" *Commonwealth Report* (July/August 1989), p.1. I also talked to Victor Fingerhut about this issue.

On populism as "self-defeating," see Peter Brown, *Minority Party: Why Democrats Face Defeat in 1992 and Beyond* (Washington, D.C.: Regnery-Gateway, 1991), p. 30 and throughout.

Page 70
On Dukakis's uptick in key demographic group, see Richard Morin, "Largest Urban Downtowns Eluded Bush's Grasp," *Washington Post* (Nov. 25, 1988), p. A29.

Pages 70–71
On Dukakis's gains, losses among income groups, see E. J. Dionne, Jr., "Bush Still Ahead as End Nears, But Dukakis Gains in Surge," *New York Times* (Nov. 6, 1988), p. A1.

Page 71
For the Hart/Divall analysis, see Linda Divall "Re: Assessment of National Survey Findings," American Viewpoint, Inc., memorandum to Robert Harman, Director of Public Affairs, AFSCME; and Peter D. Hart Research Associates, "A Post-Election Survey Among Voters Conducted for AFSCME," December 1988, p. T4 (Hart's survey includes support for Bush, Dukakis on different issues).

Page 72
For polling after 1990 budget controversy, see Harold Meyerson, "A Politics in America," *Dissent* (Winter, 1991), p. 37.

Page 75
On Atwater, "two establishments," see Thomas Byrne Edsall and Mary D. Edsall, *Chain Reaction* (New York: Norton, 1991), pp. 144–145.

Page 76
For findings on Reagan Democrats, see Victor Fingerhut, Item #6, "Political Hotline" (Oct. 31, 1988); Fingerhut, memo to Susan Estrich, John Sasso, Tom Kiley, Rico Petrillo, Paul Jensen, and George Tyler, November 1, 1988; Fingerhut, "Misunderstanding the 1984 . . . Election," pp. 21–28; Victor and Dan Fingerhut, "Labor and the Democrats," p. 1.

Pages 76–77
For Garin/Hart poll on "Duke Democrats," see Garin/Hart Strategic Research, "How It Can't Happen Here Almost Happened in Louisiana: A Study of the David Duke Phenomenon in the 1990 Senate Race." Paper prepared for the Center for National Policy, March 1991, p. 4.

CHAPTER 4

Page 79
For "Get tough on the radiator?" see Peter Goldman, Tom Matthews and the

Newsweek Special Election Team, *The Quest for the Presidency: The 1988 Campaign* (New York: Simon and Schuster, 1989), p. 406.

On "tough liberals," see William Schneider, "Tough Liberals Win, Weak Liberals Lose," *The New Republic* (Dec. 5, 1988), pp. 11–15.

Patrick H. Caddell, "An Analysis of the Presidential General Election Circumstances Confronting the Democratic Party in 1988," p. 41. Paper prepared for IMPAC '88, January 1, 1987.

Page 80
On "testosterone level," see Elaine Ciulla Kamarck, "Getting Tough With the GOP, and the Faithful," *Newsday* (March 31, 1991), p. 25.

Republican lead on national defense, see Ed Goeas, president, Tarrance and Associates, and Celinda Lake, partner, Greenberg-Lake: The Analysis Group, "Battleground 1992," July, 1991, p. 29.

Page 82
On Dinkins, "draw the line," see Josh Barbanel, "New Slogan Says Dinkins Is Strong (Not Too Strong)," *New York Times* (June 8, 1989), p. B1.

Pages 84–85
On "community's shared moral commitments," see E.J. Dionne, Jr., *Why Americans Hate Politics* (New York: Simon and Schuster, 1991), p. 314.

Pages 86–87
For Lieberman on religious values, see " 'Scoop Jackson Democrat,' Senator Joseph Lieberman's Case for Economic and Military Strength, An Interview by Adam Meyerson," *Policy Review* (Summer 1990), p. 29.

Page 88
For "If you are in a fistfight," see Willie A. Richardson and Gwenevere Daye, "The Thomas Hearings Demolished Many Myths About Blacks," *Philadelphia Inquirer* (Oct. 23, 1991), p. 15A.

Page 90
For the "five-minute fix," see Paul Taylor, *See How They Run: Electing the President in an Age of Mediaocracy* (New York: Alfred A. Knopf, 1990), p. 268.

Page 91
E.J. Dionne, Jr., *Why Americans Hate Politics*, p. 332.

Page 92
For polling on voters' views of campaign tactics, see Victor Fingerhut, memo to Susan Estrich, John Sasso, Tom Kiley, Rico Petrillo, Paul Jensen, and George Tyler, November 1, 1988, p. 2.

For Bentsen's politics as a "contact sport," see Jack W. Germond and Jules Witcover, *Whose Broad Stripes and Bright Stars?* (New York: Warner Books, 1989), p. 409.

Page 93
For Florio's "tough" anecdote, see Peter Kerr, "Read His Lips: More Taxes," *New York Times Magazine* (May 20, 1990), p. 56.
For Harkin's "tough" anecdote, see David Nyhan, "Here's a Guy Who'd Give Bush Hell," *Boston Sunday Globe* (June 2, 1991), p. 73.

Page 94
For Truman's welcome of opposition by "Wallace and the Communists," see Michael Barone, *Our Country: The Shaping of America from Roosevelt to Reagan* (New York: Free Press, 1990), p. 220.

Page 95
On Stevenson's campaign, see "Stevenson and the Intellectuals" in Irving Howe, *Steady Work* (New York: Harvest Books, 1966), p. 212.
On Kennedy's vote for Eisenhower, see Arthur M. Schlesinger, Jr., *Robert Kennedy and His Times* (New York: Ballantine Books, 1978), p. 146.
Johnson's rhetorical style: Richard N. Goodwin, *Remembering America: A Voice from the Sixties* (Boston: Little, Brown, and Co., 1988), p. 253.

Page 96
McCarthy and McGovern rhetorical style: Clifford Adelman, *No Loaves, No Parables: Liberal Politics and the American Language* (New York: Harper's Magazine Press, 1974), p. 189 and throughout.

Pages 96–97
The "age of toughness" and David Garth: Sidney Blumenthal, *The Permanent Campaign: Inside the World of Political Operatives* (Boston: Beacon Press, 1980), p. 87.

Page 98
Feinstein slogan: Roberto Suro, "An Old Refrain, Crime, Sounded in New Contests," *New York Times* (Oct. 16, 1990), p. A22.

Page 99
Shrum, Mondale's "stigmata": Ben Wattenberg's interviews of Ervin Duggan, William F. Gavin, and Robert Shrum in "Word Perfect," *Public Opinion* (May/June 1987), p. 9.

Pages 99–100
On Babbitt the "stand up" guy, see Goldman, et al., *Quest for the Presidency . . . 1988*, pp. 104–105.

Page 100
On Florio the "tough liberal," see John B. Judis, "A Taxing Governor," *The New Republic* (Oct. 15, 1990), pp. 22–31.

Page 101
Jonathan Rieder, *Canarsie: The Jews and Italians of Brooklyn Against Liberalism* (Cambridge: Harvard University Press, 1985), p. 107.

Page 102
For Moynihan on Hell's Kitchen, see Peter Steinfels, *The Neoconservatives* (New York: Simon and Schuster, 1979), pp. 112–114.

Pages 102–103
On popularity of a Democrat "like Truman," see Victor Fingerhut, Item #6, "Political Hotline"; and Fingerhut, memo to Susan Estrich, et al., p. 3.

Page 103
For Goldwater on atom bomb, social security, TVA, see Theodore H. White, *The Making of the President 1964* (New York: Atheneum, 1965), pp. 317–319, 352, 362.

Pages 103–104
For a "tough guy with a big heart," see Hugh Morrow, "A Change in the Weather (Reagan Era Draws to a Close)," *Time* (March 30, 1987), pp. 28–34.

Page 104
For Reagan's public manner, see Garry Wills, *Lead Time: A Journalist's Education* (New York: Doubleday and Co., 1983), p. 258. See also Wills's biography of the president, *Reagan's America: Innocents at Home* (Garden City, N.Y.: Doubleday, 1987).

Pages 104–105
On Bush's "strength," see Peggy Noonan, *What I Saw at the Revolution* (New York: Random House, 1990), p. 314.

Page 106
On the "ruthless Bobby," see William F. Gavin, *Street Corner Conservative* (New Rochelle, N.Y.: Arlington House Publishers, 1975), pp. 68–69.
For a general overview of Robert Kennedy's message, see Jack Newfield, *Robert Kennedy: A Memoir* (New York: Dutton, 1969).

Pages 106–107
For middle-class voters in Detroit suburbs on Robert Kennedy, see Stanley Greenberg, "Report on Democratic Defection." Paper prepared for the Michigan House Democratic Campaign Committee, April 15, 1985.

CHAPTER 5

Page 110
For Kennedy's "law and order with justice," see Arthur M. Schlesinger, Jr., *Robert Kennedy and His Times* (New York: Ballantine Books, 1978), pp. 946–947; and Theodore H. White, *The Making of the President 1968* (New York: Atheneum, 1969), p. 170.
For Humphrey's "civil order," see Albert Eisele, *Almost to the Presidency* (Blue Earth, Minn.: The Piper Co., 1972), p. 432.

For Clark's, "poverty, injustice," see Robert L. Turner, "Victims of a Crime," *Boston Globe* (Nov. 15, 1988), p. 13.

Page 111
For Mellman's "crime is about values," see Robert Guskind, "Hitting the Hot Button," *National Journal* (Aug. 4, 1990), p. 1890.

Page 112
For Feinstein as "tough but caring," see Roberto Suro, "An Old Refrain, Crime, Sounded in New Contests," *New York Times* (Oct. 16, 1990), p. A22.
For poll on the death penalty, see Frank Phillips, "Poll: Mass. Voters Support Death Penalty Law," *Boston Sunday Globe* (Sept. 23, 1990), p. 33.

Page 113
For Atwater on Willie Horton, see Thomas Byrne Edsall and Mary D. Edsall, *Chain Reaction* (New York: Norton, 1991), pp. 223–224.

Page 114
For New York City crime figures, see Jonathan Greenberg, "All About Crime," *New York* (Sept. 3, 1990), p. 27.
For U.S. crime figures, see William J. Eaton, "Blacks Found More Likely to Be Major Crime Victims," *Los Angeles Times* (Apr. 23, 1990), p. A19.
For Rivera's comments on crime, see Constance L. Hays, "Dinkins Urges New Yorkers to 'Take Back' Streets," *New York Times* (Sept. 10, 1990), pp. A1, B2.

Page 115
For Richards's, "take a woman to get tough," see James Ridgeway, "Of Honey Hunts and Bustin' Rocks," *Village Voice* (Oct. 30, 1990), p. 19.
For Wilder TV spot, see Dwayne Yancey, *When Hell Froze Over: The Story of Doug Wilder* (Dallas: Taylor Publishing Co., 1990), pp. 252–255.

Page 116
For Biden on crime, see David Lauter, "Biden Says Bush Fights Wrong Drug War," *Los Angeles Times* (Jan. 25, 1990), p. A15.
Mario M. Cuomo, "President Declares War But Can't Pay for Troops," *Los Angeles Times* (Sept. 10, 1989), sec. V, p. 1.

Page 117
On LAPD chief Daryl Gates's tenure, see Harold Meyerson, "Gatesgate," *The New Republic* (June 10, 1991), pp. 20, 22.
For police corps bill and Lewis's comments, see Robert W. Stewart, "Dornan, Liberals Back Police Corps Bill," *Los Angeles Times* (July 13, 1989), p. A7.

Pages 118–119
For controversy over Arkansas education reform, see David Osborne, *Laboratories of Democracy: A New Breed of Governor Creates Models of Economic Growth* (Boston: Harvard Business School Press, 1988), pp. 94–96.

Page 119
For survey on priorities for schools, see Ed Goeas, president, Tarrance and Associates and Celinda Lake, partner, Greenberg-Lake: The Analysis Group, "Battleground 1992," July, 1991, p. 15.

Page 120
On Bush education plan, see Richard N. Ostling, "A Revolution Hoping for a Miracle," *Time* (Apr. 20, 1991), pp. 52–53.
For Gephardt's "rewards for results," see Kenneth J. Cooper, "Gephardt Bill Offers Rewards for Education," *Washington Post* (July 24, 1991), p. A17.

Pages 120–121
For Shanker and the AFT on schools see Thomas Toch, *In the Name of Excellence: The Struggle to Reform Our Nation's Schools* (New York: Oxford University Press, 1991), pp. 141–145; and Albert Shanker, "The Making of a Profession," *American Educator* (Fall 1985), pp. 10–17 and 46–48.

Page 122
For survey on Bush's travels abroad, see David S. Broder and Richard Morin, "Economic Worries Eroding Support for Reelection of Bush, Poll Finds," *Washington Post* (Oct. 23, 1991), p. A1.
For Republican's lead on foreign policy and defense, see Goeas and Lake, "Battleground 1992."

Page 125
For Mitchell on China and human rights, see Peter Truell, "Broad Coalition Opposes Bush on China Trade, But He Could Prevail with a Few Key Concessions," *Wall Street Journal* (June 3, 1991), p. A12.
On Tsongas, Cold War and Japan, see Howard Fineman, "Bush: The Churchill Scenario," *Newsweek* (Sept. 16, 1991), p. 41.

Pages 125–126
For Kerrey on the Cold War, see Charles Krauthammer, "A Democrat Who Bears Watching," *Washington Post* (Nov. 5, 1991), p. A23.

CHAPTER 6

Pages 127–128
For Cuomo's "Two Cities" keynote address to the Democratic National Convention, San Francisco, Calif., July 17, 1984, see Robert N. Bellah, Richard Madsen, William M. Sullivan, Ann Swidler, and Steven M. Tipton, eds., *Individualism and Commitment in American Life* (New York: Harper & Row, 1987), p. 412.

Page 129
On Cuomo and Forest Hills, see Robert S. McElvaine, *Mario Cuomo, A Biography* (New York: Charles Scribner's Sons, 1988), pp. 180–189.

On Cuomo embarrassed by keynote, see Elizabeth Kolbert, "The State of the Governor," *New York Times Magazine* (Feb. 10, 1991), p. 32.

Pages 129–130
For Kennedy's 1980 Democratic convention speech, see *New York Times* (Aug. 13, 1980), p. B1.

Page 130
For Mondale's stump speech, see Elizabeth Drew, *Campaign Journal* (New York: Macmillan Publishing Co., 1985), p. 478.
For Jackson's "economic common ground" theme in his 1988 Democratic convention speech, see Frank Clemente, ed., *Keep Hope Alive: Jesse Jackson's 1988 Presidential Campaign* (Boston: South End Press, 1989) p. 28; for his address to the 1984 convention see Bellah, et al., *Individualism and Commitment*, pp. 363–365.
On Democratic rhetoric and middle-class voters, see Stanley Greenberg, "Report on Democratic Defection." Paper prepared for the Michigan House Democratic Campaign Committee, April 15, 1985.

Page 131–132
For statistics on the middle class and taxes see Lawrence Mishel and David M. Frankel, "The State of Working America 1990–1991." Paper published by the Economic Policy Institute, M. E. Sharpe, Inc., 1991, p. 69.

Page 132
Sen. Al Gore and Rep. Tom Downey have proposal on cutting taxes, see "Soak the Rich? No. Help the Poor," editorial, *New York Times* (May 10, 1991), p. A30.

Page 134
For Trumka biographical material, see *Current Biography Yearbook 1986* (New York: H.W. Wilson Co., 1987), pp. 565–567.
For Hightower's comments, see R.W. Apple, Jr., "Where Humor Is Still Alive," *New York Times* (Oct. 19, 1988), p. B7.
The term "overclass" has been used by social commentators Ralph Whitehead and Barbara Ehrenreich. See Ehrenreich's *Fear of Falling: The Inner Life of the Middle Class* (New York: Pantheon Books, 1989).

Page 135
For "America is still wide open," see Peggy Noonan, *What I Saw at the Revolution* (New York: Random House, 1990), p. 346.
For "Such folk owe no man anything," see Alexis de Tocqueville, "On Individualism in Democracies," in Bellah, et al., *Individualism and Commitment*, pp. 12–13.

Page 136
For census results, see Felicity Barringer, "The Clustering of America, Part II," *New York Times* (Jan. 27, 1991), p. E7.

On Detroit population loss, see Isabel Wilkerson, "Detroit Desperately Searches for Its Lifeblood: People," *New York Times* (Sept. 6, 1991) p. A1; and "Census Bureau Cries a Million After a Furious Push by Detroit," Associated Press, *New York Times* (Oct. 22, 1990) p. B16.

Pages 136–137
On California cities, see Felicity Barringer, "State Capitals Show Population Gains," *New York Times* (Jan. 27, 1991), p. A10.

Page 137
William A. Galston, "Rebuilding a Presidential Majority." Background paper prepared for DLC Conference, Philadelphia, Penn., March 9–11, 1989. For Reagan's remarks in debate, see *New York Times* (Oct. 29, 1980), p. A26.

Page 138
For public opinion on economy, see Ed Goeas, president, Tarrance and Associates and Celinda Lake, partner, Greenberg-Lake: The Analysis Group, "Battleground 1992," July, 1991, p. 6.

Pages 139–140
For EPI statistics on wages, tax burden, see Mishel and Frankel, "Working America," pp. 55, 69.

Page 140
For Downey on taxes, see Alan Murray and Jeffrey H. Birnbaum, "Suburban Populism," *Wall Street Journal* (Oct. 24, 1991), p. A1.

Page 141
For Whitehead on couple in Parma, see "Declining American Incomes and Living Standards." Transcript of forum conducted by the Economic Policy Institute in May 1986.

Page 143
Democrats hold 31 percent advantage on health care: Goeas and Lake, "Battleground 1992," p. 29.

Page 144
"I don't know how I'm going to make it," Remark made at a focus group conducted by political scientist Dr. Ethel Klein.

Page 145
For EPI on housing costs, see Mishel and Frankel, "Working America," p. 225.

Page 146
On "you're creating an elite," see Stanley Greenberg, "Democratic Defection," p. 10.
"The middle class today . . . " see Stanley Greenberg, "Reconstructing the Democratic Vision," *The American Prospect* (Spring 1990), p. 87.

"The average person . . . " see Stanley Greenberg, "Democratic Defection," p. 11.

Page 147
For a "conservative Democrat," see Jonathan Rieder, *Canarsie* (Cambridge: Harvard University Press, 1985), p. 98.
For children, parents, and the "cultural squeeze," see Barbara Dafoe Whitehead, "Parents' 'Paranoia' Masks a Deeper Dread," *Chicago Tribune* (Nov. 30, 1990), p. C27.

Page 148
Barbara Dafoe Whitehead, "The Family in an Unfriendly Culture," *Family Affairs*, Institute for American Values (Spring-Summer, 1990), volume 3, p. 3.
For Reagan's 1980 GOP convention acceptance speech, see *New York Times* (July 18, 1980), p. A8.

Page 149
Elaine Ciulla Kamarck and William A. Galston, "Putting Children First: A Progressive Family Policy for the 1990s." Paper prepared for the Progressive Policy Institute, September 27, 1990.

CHAPTER 7

Page 153
For details of Mondale's tax plan, see Fay S. Joyce, "Mondale Program Would Raise Taxes $85 Billion by '89," *New York Times* (Sept. 11, 1984), p. A1; Jonathan Feurbanger, "Mondale's Plan, the Middle Class Is Not Exempt," *New York Times* (Sept. 11, 1984), p. A25; David E. Rosenbaum, "Taxpayers' Idea of Wealth May Not Be the Same as Mondale's," *New York Times* (Sept. 12, 1984), p. B8.
For Geoff Garin's comments see Peter Brown, "The Democratic Dilemma," *Campaigns and Elections* (May/June 1989), p. 39.
For McGovern's "demogrant" plan, see Theodore H. White, *The Making of the President 1972* (New York: Bantam Books, 1973), pp. 137, 154, 156, 166, 169.

Page 155
Senator Barbara A. Mikulski, quoted from a transcript of her remarks to the New Hampshire Democratic Party 1990 Roundtable and "100 Club," March 23, 1990, p. 7.
The phrase "paycheck to paycheck" was frequently used by Patrick Quinn in his successful 1990 campaign for Illinois State Treasurer.

Page 156
For Bradley on the middle class, see Andrew Glass, "Bradley's Middle Class Conversion," *Baltimore Evening Sun* (June 24, 1991), p. A6.

Pages 156–157
For Downey on day care, see Michael Barone and Grant Ujifusa, *The Almanac of American Politics, 1992* (Washington, D.C.: National Journal, 1991), p. 841.

Page 158
On Darman urging cutting aid to middle class, see Kevin Phillips, "Bush Domestic Policy? It's Soaking the Middle Class," *Los Angeles Times* (Feb. 24, 1991). p. M1; and David S. Broder, "Who's the Fairest of Them All?" *Washington Post* (Feb. 13, 1991), p. A19.

Page 160
On Gore-Downey tax cut, see "Soak the Rich? No. Help the Poor," editorial, *New York Times* (May 10, 1991), p. A30.

Page 161
For Mondale on Dr. Giordano, see Elizabeth Drew, *Campaign Journal* (New York: Macmillan Publishing Co., 1985), p. 672.

Pages 161–162
On the Biden/Kinnock speech, see Jack W. Germond and Jules Witcover, *Whose Broad Stripes and Bright Stars?* (New York: Warner Books, 1989), pp. 230–242.

Page 164
Jeff Faux originated the line "Let's send the bill to the people who went to the party."

CHAPTER 8

Page 165
On "Happy Days Are Here Again," see Elizabeth Drew, *Campaign Journal* (New York: Macmillan Publishing Co., 1985), p. 594.

Page 166
"The Best Years" is also the title of a history of the post-war era. See Joseph Goulden, *The Best Years, 1945–1950* (New York: Atheneum, 1976).

Pages 167–168
Vice President George Bush, Remarks to the Economic Club of Detroit and Women's Economic Club, Detroit, Michigan, Wednesday, October 26, 1988. Source: The Vice President, Office of the Press Secretary.

Page 168
For Bush's economic record, see Charles Stein, "Bush's Economic Growth Record: Poor," *Boston Sunday Globe* (Sept. 29, 1991), p. 35.

Pages 168–169
Paul Magnusson with Patrick Oster, "The New Face of Recession," *Business Week* (Dec. 24, 1990), pp. 58–65.

Pages 169–170
For tax statistics and Ballentine quote, see "Inequality and the Federal Budget Deficit," report published by Citizens for Tax Justice, September, 1991, pp. 7,13.

Page 170
For "minks and Jaguars," see Mario M. Cuomo, "President Declares War But Can't Pay for Troops, *Los Angeles Times* (Sept. 10, 1989) sec. V, p. 1.
For Heflin on "Gucci-clothed . . . Republicans," see Robin Toner, "Stakes High in Contest for Alabama Governor," *New York Times* (Sept. 26, 1990), p. A12.

Page 172
Paul E. Tsongas, "A Call to Economic Arms." Campaign position paper, 1991, p. 11.

Page 173
For CEO pay, see statistics from *Business Week* as quoted in Rich Thomas and Larry Reibstein, "The Pay Police," *Newsweek* (June 17, 1991), p. 44.
For "fifty to one hundred times the pay of average worker," see Robert J. Samuelson, "The Boss as Welfare Cheat," *Washington Post* (Nov. 6, 1991), p. A25.
On ITT executive's salary, see Joan S. Lublin, "Highly Paid Corporate Chiefs Earn Criticism, Too," *Wall Street Journal* (June 4, 1991), p. B1.

Page 174
"The corporations . . . have walked away," see Stanley Greenberg, "Looking Toward '88: The Politics of American Identity," *World Policy Journal* (Fall 1987), p. 703.

Page 175
For polling on capital gains, see Kevin Phillips, "Capital Gains Cut – A Worse Idea than Ever," *Wall Street Journal* (Feb. 7, 1991), p. A15; and David Shribman, "Skirmish Over Capital Gains Is Likely to Set Terms for Political Battles of the Bush Years," *Wall Street Journal* (Sept. 28, 1989) p. A24.
For statistics on capital gains tax cuts, see "$25,000 Apiece for the Rich," editorial, *Washington Post* (Sept. 28, 1989) p. A30.

Page 176
For Cuomo's economic proposals, see Hobart Rowen, "Cuomonomics," *Washington Post* (Sept. 19, 1991), p. A21; and Lee Walczak, "Cuomo's Voice Is Getting Louder and Louder," *Business Week* (Aug. 26, 1991), pp. 50–51.

Page 177
On R&D tax credit, see Tsongas, "A Call to Economic Arms," p. 22.
For the term "producerism" as used by Jonathan Rauch, see his article "Now It's Producerism," *National Journal* (July 27, 1991), p. 1851.

On "carrots and sticks," see Jeff Faux, "Beyond the Budget Deal: A Program for Fairness and Growth," *Economic Policy Institute Journal* (Feb. 1991).

Pages 177–178
For investment anxieties, see Ed Goeas, president, Tarrance and Associates, and Celinda Lake, partner, Greenberg-Lake: The Analysis Group, "Battleground 1992," July 1991, p. 8.

Page 178
"A Warning About America's Third Deficit from 327 Prominent Economists." Statement released by the Economic Policy Institute, Washington, D.C., 1991.

Pages 178–179
Support for public works, see Victor Fingerhut, "The American Electorate and the Goals of the American Labor Movement." Paper based on polling conducted in November 1990 and sponsored by the Aluminum, Brick, and Glass Workers International Union, the International Association of Machinists and Aerospace Workers, the Seafarers International Union of North America, the United Automobile, Aerospace and Agricultural Implement Workers of America International Union, the United Mine Workers of America, and the United Steelworkers of America.

Pages 179–180
On renewing "public enterprise," see Philip H. Power, chairman, Michigan Job Training Council, "Making Government Work: From Programs to Public Enterprise." Paper prepared for Progressive Policy Institute, September 5, 1990.

Page 181
On "industry-led policy," see "The 'Wake Up America!' Project." Paper prepared by the advocacy group Rebuild America, 1988, p. 1.

CHAPTER 9

Page 183
On Dukakis at AFL-CIO executive council, see E. J. Dionne, Jr., "Labor Federation Endorses Dukakis," *New York Times* (Aug. 25, 1988), p. B14.
On Dukakis's appearances before black audiences and low voter totals in cities, see James A. Barnes, "Creaky City Machinery," *National Journal* (Nov. 3, 1990), p. 2656.

Page 184
For poll findings on special interests, see Ed Goeas, president, Tarrance and Associates and Celinda Lake, partner, Greenberg-Lake: The Analysis Group, "Battleground 1992," July 1991, p. 33.

Pages 184–185
On Mondale's showing in union households, see Victor and Dan Fingerhut, "La-

bor and the Democrats: Who's Out of Touch?" *Commonwealth Report* (July/Aug. 1989), p. 6.

Page 185
For "clear it with Sidney," see Michael Barone, *Our Country* (New York: Free Press, 1990), p. 178.
For a discussion of racially tinged language, see Thomas Byrne Edsall and Mary D. Edsall, *Chain Reaction* (New York: Norton, 1991), pp. 198–215.

Page 186
On Weld's support from blacks, see Michael K. Frisby, "The New Face of Black Politics," *Boston Globe Magazine* (July 14, 1991), p. 37.

Pages 187–188
On the Dukakis campaign's decision against a Garment District rally, see Rowland Evans and Robert Novak, "A Game Plan to Lose New York," *Washington Post* (Oct. 26, 1988), p. A23.

Page 188
On Yeltsin in the Garment District, see Gary Lee, "Yeltsin Wears Well in the Garment District," *Washington Post* (June 22, 1991), p. A1.

Page 189
On support for family leave and day care, see Dr. Ethel Klein, "Public Opinion Polls, Family Policy; An Analysis." Data compiled and analyzed under a grant from the Ms. Foundation for Education and Communication, Inc., the Communications Consortium, publishers, June, 1989, pp. 4, 8, 9.

Pages 189–190
On support for national health insurance, see Michael McQueen, "Voters, Sick of the Current Health Care System, Want Federal Government to Prescribe Remedy," *Wall Street Journal* (June 28, 1991), p. A14.

Page 190
Wofford's "upset victory," see Robert Shogan, "Elections: Democrats Seen Gaining," *Los Angeles Times* (Nov. 7, 1991), p. A26.
On anti-union consultants, see David Kusnet, "A Dirty Business," *Commonweal* (Feb. 24, 1989), pp. 107–108.
For Weiler on firings, see Thomas Geoghegan, *Which Side Are You On? Trying to Be for Labor When It's Flat on Its Back* (New York: Farrar, Strauss and Giroux, 1991), p. 234.

Page 191
On Fourth of July in Lincoln, Nebraska, see Isabel Wilkerson, "After War, Patriotism Unfurls in a Nebraska City," *New York Times* (July 4, 1991), p. A8.
Glenn and Hart attack unions, see Elizabeth Drew, *Campaign Journal* (New York: Macmillan Publishing Co., 1985), pp. 191–193, 322, 326.

Pages 191–192
On Bush and Steelworkers card, see George Bush, *Looking Forward* (New York: Doubleday, 1987), p. 55.

Page 192
For findings on esteem for labor, see Paul Ruffins, "Why American Unions Believe Their Future Is Now," *Washington Post* (Sept. 1, 1991), p. C5.

Pages 192–193
For findings on support for strikers at Eastern, see Bruce D. Butterfield, "Who Owns Eastern Airlines?" *Boston Globe* (March 26, 1989), p. A18.

Page 193
For Walters on Lorenzo, see Aaron Bernstein, *Grounded: Frank Lorenzo and the Destruction of Eastern Airlines* (New York: Simon and Schuster, 1990), p. 125; and David Kusnet, "For Labor Day, a Tribute to Two Lousy Bosses," *Baltimore Evening Sun* (Aug. 31, 1990), p. A19.
On Gingrich being hurt by stand on Eastern strike, see Michael Barone and Grant Ujifusa, *The Almanac of American Politics, 1992* (Washington, D.C.: National Journal, 1991), p. 316.

Page 196
On Brock, Marshall commission, see John Hoerr, "Business Shares Blame for Workers' Low Skills," *Business Week* (June 25, 1990), p. 71.

Page 197
For Saturn experiment, see S.C. Gwynne, "The Right Stuff," *Time* (Oct. 29, 1990), pp. 74–84.
On Saturn ads, see David Kusnet, "Workers Esteemed in a New Ad Age," *Sacramento Bee* (Oct. 23, 1990), p. B7.
For Jackson's address at 1988 Democratic convention, see *New York Times* (July 20, 1988), p. A18.

Page 199
For "race-neutral programs," see William Julius Wilson, "Race-Neutral Programs and the Democratic Coalition," *American Prospect* (Spring 1990), p. 74.

Page 200
For polling on civil rights and quotas, see *New York Times*/CBS News poll cited in Steven A. Holmes, "Affirmative Action Plans Are Part of Business Life," *New York Times* (Nov. 22, 1991), p. A20.
For Feinstein being attacked on quotas, see Cathleen Decker, "California Elections/Governor: Feinstein Critical of Wilson for Actions in S&L Cases," *Los Angeles Times* (Aug. 13, 1990), p. A3.

Page 203
For Johnson's affirmative action speech at Howard University, see Richard N. Goodwin, *Remembering America: A Voice from the Sixties* (Boston: Little,

Brown, and Co., 1988), p. 345. For critique of speech, see Shelby Steele, *The Content of Our Character* (New York: Harper Perennial, 1990), p. 89.

Page 204
On black social conservatism, and being more religious, see Gerald David Jaynes and Robin M. Williams, Jr., eds., *A Common Destiny: Blacks and American Society,* Committee on the Status of Black Americans, Washington, D.C.: National Academy Press, 1987), p. 176. On being more likely to serve in military, see John J. Fialka and Andy Pasztor, "Shifting Sands: Older Army, with More Women and Blacks, Awaits Trial by Fire in the Desert," *Wall Street Journal* (Jan. 14, 1991), p. A14.

Page 205
For "opponents of affirmative action," see Harvey B. Gantt, "A Lose-Lose Strategy for '92," *New York Times* (March 17, 1991), sec. 4, p. 17.

Page 206
On *only* the government," see Mario M. Cuomo, *Diaries of Mario M. Cuomo* (New York: Random House, 1984), p. 457.

Page 207
For Osborne's ideas from his forthcoming book, see David Osborne, "Governing in the '90s: How Gov. William Weld Intends to 'Reinvent' State Government," *Boston Sunday Globe* (Feb. 13, 1991), p. 65.

Page 208
The "new paradigm" is discussed in Elaine Ciulla Kamarck, "This Time, 'New Ideas' Come from the Center," *Newsday* (Nov. 3, 1991), p. 49.

Page 209
For Gephardt on "rewards for results," see Congressman Richard A. Gephardt, "Policies that Work for People Who Work: Or, What I Learned in the Wal-Mart Parking Lot," Address to the Center for National Policy, Washington, D.C., December 6, 1990.

Pages 209–210
From author's interviews with workers at the Sanitation Department's Bureau of Motor Equipment in Queens, New York, May 1988, and David Kusnet, "New Ways of Working," *American Educator* (Fall 1988), pp. 18–24, 42–44.

Page 210
Ruth Messinger, "Taking the Pain Out of Pruning City Government," *New York Daily News* (Oct. 27, 1991), p. C23.

AFTERWORD

Page 211
For Wofford biographical material, see Taylor Branch, *Parting the Waters:*

America in the King Years 1954–1963 (New York: Simon and Schuster, 1988), pp. 207–208, 341–360.

Pages 211–212
On Wofford's gain, see Robert Shogan, "Elections: Democrats Seen Gaining," *Los Angeles Times* (Nov. 7, 1991), p. A26.

Page 212
On Wofford being "very nice . . . but a little cerebral," see Mary McGrory, "The Lessons of Pennsylvania," *Washington Post* (Nov. 7, 1991), p. A2.
For Wofford on the "fast track to Mexico," see Dale Russakoff, "The Bulldozer Behind Wofford's Landslide," *Washington Post* (Nov. 7, 1991), p. A33.
For Wofford's "if criminals" quote see Christopher Matthews, " '92 Testing Ground in Pennsylvania," *Washington Times* (Nov. 5, 1991), p. F3.
Wofford, "build a fire," see Shogan, "Elections."

Pages 212–213
On Thornburgh aide's "sorry-assed state" and Thornburgh's "corridors of power," see Russakoff, "The Bulldozer."

Page 213
For Wofford's election figures, see Shogan, "Elections."
Poll, 57 percent say country is on the "wrong track," see Rich Jaroslavsky, "Edgy Electorate: Voters Voice Dismay About Nation's Course a Year Before Elections," *Wall Street Journal* (Nov. 1, 1991), p. A1.
Bush runs ahead on crime and values, see "America's Biggest Worries," chart, *Washington Post* (Nov. 4, 1991), p. A13.

Page 214
Obey's remarks included in "Investing in America's Future." Transcript of conference held by Economic Policy Institute, Washington, D.C., October 21, 1991, p. 23.

Page 217
For Wofford's staff on Gandhi and McDonald's, see Russakoff, "The Bulldozer."

ABOUT THE AUTHOR

David Kusnet is a political consultant and speechwriter. For the past twenty years he has worked as a commentator, organizer, political activist, and journalist. Mr. Kusnet has been a speechwriter for Democratic presidential candidates Walter Mondale and Michael Dukakis and served as vice president of communications for People for the American Way. His articles have appeared in the *Washington Post,* the *Baltimore Sun,* and *The New Republic.*